ISLAMIC HIGHER EDUCATION IN INDONESIA

Also by Ronald A. Lukens-Bull

A Peaceful Jihad: Negotiating Identity and Modernity in Muslim Java, 2005.

Editor, *Sacred Places and Modern Landscapes: Sacred Geography and Social-Religious Transformations in South and Southeast Asia*, 2003.

Islamic Higher Education in Indonesia

Continuity and Conflict

Ronald A. Lukens-Bull

ISLAMIC HIGHER EDUCATION IN INDONESIA
Copyright © Ronald A. Lukens-Bull, 2013.

All rights reserved.

First published in 2013 by
PALGRAVE MACMILLAN®
in the United States—a division of St. Martin's Press LLC,
175 Fifth Avenue, New York, NY 10010.

Where this book is distributed in the UK, Europe and the rest of the world, this is by Palgrave Macmillan, a division of Macmillan Publishers Limited, registered in England, company number 785998, of Houndmills, Basingstoke, Hampshire RG21 6XS.

Palgrave Macmillan is the global academic imprint of the above companies and has companies and representatives throughout the world.

Palgrave® and Macmillan® are registered trademarks in the United States, the United Kingdom, Europe and other countries.

ISBN: 978–1–137–30857–3

Library of Congress Cataloging-in-Publication Data

Lukens-Bull, Ronald.
   Islamic higher education in Indonesia : continuity and conflict / Ronald A. Lukens-Bull.
      pages cm
   Includes bibliographical references and index.
   ISBN 978–1–137–30857–3 (hardback)
     1. Islamic education—Indonesia. 2. Education, Higher—Indonesia. 3. Educational change—Indonesia. I. Title.

LC910.I5L85 2013
378.59—dc23   2013020699

A catalogue record of the book is available from the British Library.

Design by Newgen Knowledge Works (P) Ltd., Chennai, India.

First edition: November 2013

10 9 8 7 6 5 4 3 2 1

For
Katryne, Emmy, and Ronan

Contents

List of Illustrations — ix

Foreword — xi

Preface — xv

List of Abbreviations — xix

A Note on Transliteration and Spelling — xxi

Dramatis Personae — xxiii

Chapter 1
The Politicization of the "Apolitical": Islamic Higher Education in Indonesia — 1

Chapter 2
Religious "Dialects," Variation, and Accusations of the Worst Kind — 21

Chapter 3
Becoming Universities: Old Traditions, New Directions — 43

Chapter 4
Splitting the *Kiblat*: Consequences of Alternative Strategies for Educating Faculty Members — 67

Chapter 5
Women Pushing the Limits: Gender Debates in Islamic Higher Education — 87

Chapter 6
Where Is the Islam, and What Kind? — 111

Theoretical Epilogue: Linguistic Modeling of
Variation in Islam   135

Notes   153
Glossary   157
Bibliography   161
Index   177

Illustrations

Figures

5.1	Examples of wrong and right female attire	107
5.2	Economic faculty examples of correct male and female attire	108
6.1	The UIN Malang campus mosque beduk	120
6.2	Sign in front of FPI HQ in Jakarta	127
7.1	Transformations of langue and the generative	145
7.2	Linguistic diagramming	146
7.3	Javanese variation in direction of prayer	147
7.4	Saints in different Muslim societies	148
7.5	Diagramming factors in different expressions	149
7.6	Linguistic rules modeling of apostasy accusations	151

Tables

2.1	What makes for an apostate	36
5.1	Dialect differences and women as imam	94
7.1	Reading rule diagrams	145
7.2	What makes for an apostate	150

Foreword

This is Ronald Lukens-Bull's second book about Islamic education in Indonesia, the world's most populous Muslim country. His first book examined Javanese *pesantren* (traditional Islamic boarding schools) at the end of the twentieth century. In this book he turns his attention to Indonesia's Islamic higher education system (*Perguruan Tinggi Agama Islam Negeri*—PTAIN) at the beginning of the twenty first century. Both of these books concern the interplay of and tension between the religious imperative to preserve and transmit religious knowledge deemed to be eternal and centuries old interpretive traditions and the equally important social imperative to prepare students for life in the present. Both books are, in this sense, located between time and eternity. While the reform of the *pesantren* system and the development of the PTAIN system are postcolonial Indonesian phenomena, the religious and intellectual debates about relationships between reason and revelation framed Muslim discourse for centuries, and indeed predate the beginnings of Islam.

In one sense, Indonesian Islamic higher education is located in Muslim intellectual and pedagogical traditions dating to the mid-nineteenth century when Muslim intellectuals, political and military leaders were confronted with the necessity of responding to what historian Marshall Hodgson (1974) called the "Great Western Transmutation." This was the wide-ranging set of scientific, technological, and institutional innovations that, over a period of two centuries (1600–1800), made the industrial revolution, what Wallerstein (1974) calls the capitalist world system and Western domination possible. Prior to this time there was something of a balance of power between "Christendom" and "Islamdom." Western European and Muslim nations and empires had been alternatively seen allies, rivals, enemies, trading partners and interlocutors in intellectual discourse. At the dawn of the twentieth century, most Muslims were subaltern colonial subjects. The few Muslim societies not subject to direct colonial rule were parts of "informal" European empires or capitulation regimes that were less than fully sovereign. The gap between Europe, and the rest of the world in scientific knowledge had expanded at an exponential rate that showed no signs of abating.

It is impossible to fix these developments precisely in time or space. They were gradual transformations of which participants on both sides of the divide were probably not fully conscious. Dates and events that have become iconic of this process include the failure of Ottoman siege of Vienna in 1683, Napoleon's 1789 invasion of Egypt, Diponegoro's failure to reestablish the sovereignty of the Javanese Sultanate of Yogyakarta in the Java War (1825–1830), and the failure of "mutinous" *sepoys* to drive the British from India in 1857. In Indonesia armed resistance to colonial rule continued into the 1940s, but after the Java war, never posed a serious threat to the colonial order. The final decades of colonialism were characterized by what the Dutch called "*rust en orde*" (tranquility and order), though Indonesians saw things differently.

The reform of education is among the strategies that Muslims in Indonesia and the world over adopted in response to what they correctly perceived to be an ever-increasing knowledge gap and in areas in which European control was formally established, and the futility of armed struggle. The first modern universities established in the Muslim world were in Ottoman Turkey in 1848. In British India Sir Syed Ahmed Khan founded the Mohammedan Anglo-Oriental College in 1875 with the dual purposes of raising the standard of modern education and training Muslim students for employment in the British Indian civil service. It became Aligarh Muslim University in 1920 and today is among India's most distinguished universities. The Egyptian educational reformer Muhammad Abduh (1849–1905) was more influential in Indonesia. Abduh was Grand Mufti of Egypt (1899–1905) and publisher of the modernist journal *al Manar* that exerted a profound influence on the development of Islamic modernism in Indonesia. His purpose was to transform Muslim education by emphasizing rational inquiry and modern science.

Schools with formalized curricula that taught "modern" as well as Islamic subjects emerged early in the twentieth century.

The most well known are those sponsored by the Yogyakarta-based modernist Muhammadiyah movement that was influenced by Abduh's educational philosophy. There were similar developments in other parts of what was then the Netherlands Indies, most notably in Sumatra. The Hadrami Arab al-Irshad movement also established a modern educational system. *Pesantren* began to teach subjects other than religion in the 1920s. Organizations rooted in Javanese culture, especially Budi Utomo and Taman Siswa also established modern educational systems in the early twentieth century.

The Dutch colonial government was less concerned with education than the British. Medical, technical, and law schools were not established until the 1920s. There were no universities in Indonesia at the time of independence in 1945, though a number of Indonesians had studied at universities in the Netherlands. Even basic education was limited. In 1945 the literacy rate among native Indonesians was less than 10 percent. The development of both Islamic and secular education systems is one of the greatest achievements of postcolonial Indonesia.

The Indonesian Islamic higher education system is also located in a much older theological and philosophical discourse about knowledge and authority. Attempts to define the relationship between revelation and reason have shaped the historical monotheisms (Judaism, Christianity, and Islam). These debates are the result of encounters between Hellenistic and Abrahamic traditions that predates the origins of Christianity and Islam by many centuries. The encounter between Hellenism and Judaism began at the time of Alexander the Great (356–323 BCE). Jewish, Christian, and Muslim thinkers have all wrestled with questions concerning reason and revelation, and especially how (or how not) to employ Aristotelian and Platonic thought in monotheistic revelation-based contexts. The Jewish philosopher Philo (20 BCE–50 CE) attempted to bring the revelations of the Hebrew Bible, Plato and Aristotle into a single philosophical system when Christianity was in its infancy and Islam had yet to appear. The Muslim Mu'tazilite 'Abd al-Jabbar (935–1025), Jewish philosopher Maimonides (1135–1204), and the Catholic scholastic theologian Thomas Aquinas (1225–1274) were all concerned with fundamental questions about reason and revelation and the place of Aristotelian logic in monotheistic theologies.

Debates about science and religion that date at least to the time of Copernicus (1473–1543) are derivatives of these earlier controversies, though they concern empirical as well as philosophical questions. These debates continue, especially in countries like the United States where revelation-based Christianity remains a potent political force.

These debates have always been politicized. Mu'tazilite rationalists persecuted their traditionalist opponents in the ninth century and were later subject to persecution. The Roman Catholic Church forced Galileo (1564–1642) to recant. Pope John Paul II referred to the Church's mistreatment of Galileo in a formal apology for errors committed over two millennia in 2000.

It should then come as no surprise that issues about reason and revelation, and science and religion are debated in the PTAIN system. It is both interesting and important that these debates are, as Lukens-Bull clearly demonstrates, about the social sciences rather than the physical sciences. The politics are also those of the twenty-first century, because social and religious conservatives now refer to Muslim social scientists as "Orientalists."

MARK WOODWARD

Preface

This book is based on research conducted in 2008–2009 as part of a Fulbright Senior Scholar Grant to Indonesia. My host institution was the State Islamic University of North Sumatra in Medan and there are a number of people to whom I am most grateful for their friendship and assistance, including Nur Fadhil Lubis, Zainal Fuad, and others. Moraluddin Harahap needs to be specifically recognized for his efforts. He helped with various problems from the mundane (shipping books), to the essential (visa issues), to helping me understand various aspects of the debates taking place on his campus and in the system more broadly. I am also thankful for my students in the graduate program for their good-natured interactions and for sharpening my thinking by asking me to think about things from a different angle, even as I asked them to do the same. While in Medan, the Foundation for the Development of Indonesian-American Friendship (PPIA) in Medan provided me a place to live for the cost of utilities. Various people at PPIA were helpful in various aspects of my stay in Medan and my research including Andan Tambunan, Trie Lubis, Nina Nasution, and many others. I am indebted to American-Indonesian Education Foundation (AMINEF) and its staff in Jakarta for expediting research approvals and other paperwork.

I returned to Indonesia in the summer of 2012 with a faculty development grant from the University of North Florida Office of Academic Affairs to examine the place of gender issues in the wider debates examined in my earlier research. The faculty and staff at the Women's Studies Center at UIN Yogyakarta were most welcoming and helpful in my learning about their operations. I am most grateful to my family for giving me the time away from them for both periods of research and for forgiving my distraction from more important matters while writing this book.

This project has benefited from presentations to various audiences and the feedback given by them. My first attempt to outline the basic argument was at a UNF Sociology-Anthropology Department brownbag presentation in 2009. A version of chapter 1 was presented as part of an Indonesia East Timor Studies Council–sponsored panel at the 2012 Association of Asian Studies meeting in Toronto. Parts of chapter 2 were presented at the 2011 American Anthropological Association Meeting in November 2011 and at a General Stadium at IAIN Sunan Ampel, Surabaya in June 2012. Particular thanks are due to Kristen Angelucci who through a year-long dialogue which included term papers helped in developing my theoretical approach. It has also benefited from the feedback of anonymous reviewers at the Journal of Religion and Society, the Journal of the American Academy of Religion, and Methods and Theory in the Study of Religion.

I must thank the following people for their feedback on various parts of the manuscript: Kristen Angelucci, James Hoesterey, Ronald Kephart, Katryne Lukens-Bull, Naima Lynch, Rick Phillips, Inayah Rohmaniyah, and Mark Woodward. The technology of social media has changed writing. When I needed to cross-check a fact or make what might seem like a hairsplitting decision to a nonspecialist, I was able to turn to my social media network. I want to specifically thank people who regularly responded to queries including: Kathleen Adams, Anthony Ciero, Julie Chernhov-Hwang, Sunarwoto Denar, Wahyuddin Halim, Lisa Marshall, Charley Sullivan, Mark Woodward, and Buni Yani.

Moving the book from manuscript to finished monograph has involved the work of many people including Burke Gerstenschlager, Sarah Nathan, and Scarlet Neath at Palgrave. I am also indebted to anonymous reviewers to whom the manuscript was sent. I would also like to thank the staff at Newgen Knowledge Works for their excellent work in the copy editing process. I thank Denise Doyle for her help with the page proofs.

The book is organized so that both specialists and nonspecialists can benefit from it. There are parts of the book that the specialist may never read, like the list of people involved in the debates discussed. And there are parts only meant for the specialist, like the last chapter, which I have called a theoretical epilogue. The first six chapters are the argument of the book in its totality. However, the theoretical frame I propose in the second chapter has limitations.

The theoretical epilogue is for those who see the limitations and wish to have certain theoretical problems addressed. Most readers will stop after chapter 6 and be none the poorer for it. However, I find the epilogue absolutely essential in order for the book to be complete in my mind and hope that at least some readers will agree.

Abbreviations

ACIS	Annual Conference of Islamic Studies
CRCS	Center for Religious and Cross-cultural Studies
DDII	Dewan Dakwah Islamiyah Indonesia (Indonesian Islamic Missions Council)
FPI	Fron Pembela Islam (Islamic Defenders Front)
HMI	Himpunan Mahasiswa Indonesia (Indonesian Students Association)
HTI	Hizbut Tahrir Indonesia
IAIN	Institut Agama Islam Negeri (State Islamic Institute)
ICG	International Crisis Group
ICMI	Ikatan Cendiakawan Muslim Indonesia (Indonesian Muslim Intellectuals Network)
ICRS	Indonesian Consortium for Religious Studies
IIUM	International Islamic University of Malaysia
INSIST	Institute for the Study of Islamic Thought and Civilization
ISTAC	International Institute of Islamic Thought and Civilization
JIL	Jaringan Islam Liberal (Liberal Islamic Network)
KAHMI	Kader Alumni Himpunan Mahasiswa Indonesia (Indonesian Students Association Alumni Group)
LIPIA	Institute of Islamic and Arabic Studies
MESA	Middle East Studies Association
MMI	Majelis Mujahiddin Indonesia (Indonesian Mujahiddin Council)
MORA	Ministry of Religious Affairs
MOU	Memorandum of Understanding
MUI	Majelis Ulama Indonesia
NU	Nahdlatul Ulama (Renaissance of Islamic Scholars)

PAN	Partai Amanat Nasional (National Mandate Party)
PKB	Partai Kebangkitan Bangsa (National Awakening Party)
PKS	Partai Keadilan Sejahtera (Prosperous Justice Party)
PPIA	Foundation for the Development of Indonesian-American Friendship
PPKI	Preparatory Committee for Indonesian Independence (*Panitia Persiapan Kemerdekaan Indonesia*)
PPP	United Development Party
PSG	Pusat Studi Gender (Gender Studies Center)
PSW	Pusat Studi Wanita (Women's Study Center)
PTAIN	Perguruan Tinggi Agama Islam Negeri (State Islamic Higher Education)
STAIN	Sekolah Tinggi Agama Islam (State Islamic Higher School)
UGM	Universitas Gadjah Mada
UIN	Universitas Islam Negeri
UNISMA	Universitas Islam Malang

A Note on Transliteration and Spelling

Indonesian and Javanese words are spelled according to the official conventions of the Republic of Indonesia set in 1972. The major changes were dj = j (as in John); j = y (as in yes); tj = c (as in choke); oe = u. The only exceptions to this are words within quotes, titles of books published before 1972, and the proper names of authors and major figures. Although Indonesian words are not pluralized by adding "s," I will do so for the benefit of the reader. Arabic words will be spelled as they are in Indonesian except when their words have become common in English, unless doing so would create confusion. For example, the word for Islamic law is commonly rendered in English as shariah. However, because I also write about academic units who teach about Islamic law, I follow the spelling used in the names of these units, *syari'ah*. It would be too confusing to read about a *syari'ah* faculty teaching about shariah.

Dramatis Personae

This book discusses debates and discourses that include a large number of people. To the specialist, most of them are already known by name if not personally. This short compendium of the biographical sketches of these key figures is not for the experts but for the more general reader who might need a list of the "cast of characters" to follow the debates discussed herein. A person who is only discussed in one chapter, will be described just in that chapter.

Person	Bio Sketch
Abdul Mukti Ali	Born in Central Java, August 23, 1923. Died on May 5, 2004. Pioneered comparative religion at IAIN and known for his willingness to respect pluralism, both within Islam and other religions. He served as minister of religious affairs (1971–1978); he developed a model of interreligious harmony that was based on Islamic principles of justice, absolute freedom of conscience, the perfect equality among humans, and powerful solidarity in social interaction. When Mukti Ali served as a lecturer at the State Islamic Institute Sunan Kalijaga Yogyakarta, he wrote many books in Indonesian, which include: *Comparative Religion: Its Method and System*, *Comparative Religion in Indonesia*, *The Spread of Islam in Indonesia*, *Modern Islamic Thought in Indonesia*, *Religion and Development in Indonesia*, *Various Religious Problems in Indonesia*, *The Muslim Muhajir and Muslim Bilali in the United States of America*, and *The Method of Understanding Islam*. Many of his books have been standard readings in comparative religion courses in Indonesia.

Abdurrahman Mas'ud	Abdurrahman Mas'ud was born on April 16, 1960 in Kudus. His first schooling was at his uncle's pesantren, memorizing the Quran. He earned a PhD from UCLA in 1997 on a Fulbright scholarship. He served at the Graduate Program of IAIN Walisongo as the deputy director from 1997 to 1999 and as the director of the Graduate Program in 2000. In 2006–2008, he served as the director of the Islamic Higher Education division of the Ministry of Religious Affairs. Since 2008, he has served as the director of one of several research arms of MORA.
Abdurrahman Wahid	Born on September 7, 1940 in East Java. Died on December 30, 2009. The son and grandson of two Indonesian national heroes, he was a *kyai (*Muslim cleric). Popularly known as Gus Dur, he was the general head of Nahdlatul Ulama from 1984 until he became president of Indonesia in 1999. He was impeached in 2001. During the Suharto Era, he was leader in the democracy movement and was widely respected by Indonesians of all religions for his positions on interfaith dialogue and harmony. Posthumously, he is called the tenth *wali (wali sepu,* see Walisongo)
Adian Husaini	Born on December 17, 1965, in East Java. He earned his undergraduate degree from the Saudi-funded Institute of Arabic Language Education, LIPIA Jakarta (1988). He also holds a degree in Veterinary Medicine, and a master's degree in International Relations from University Jayabaya Jakarta. He is currently pursuing a doctoral degree at the Institute of Islamic Thought and Civilization-International Islamic University Malaysia (ISTAC-IIUM) in the field of Islamic thought and civilization. He is the head of Dewan Dakwah Islamiyah Indonesia (DDII) and the secretary general of the Indonesian Committee for Solidarity with the Islamic World (Komite Indonesia untuk Solidaritas Dunia Islam, KISDI) among other positions within various Islamist organizations. He is the author of a number of books, articles, and blog entries criticizing IAIN and liberal Islam.

Amin Abdullah	Amin Abdullah was the Rector of the State Islamic University in Yogyakarta from 2001 to 2010. Born in Central Java on July 28, 1953. He served on the governing board of Muhammadiyyah from 2000 to 2005. He wrote several books, including *Religious Education in a Multi-Cultural and Multi-Religious Era*. He earned a PhD in Islamic philosophy from Middle East Technical University in Ankara, and did postdoctoral studies at McGill University.
Azyumardi Azra	Born on March 4, 1955, in West Sumatra. He earned his PhD in History from Columbia University in 1992. He was Rector of UIN Jakarta from 1998 to 2006 and the director of the Graduate Program starting in 2006. He is the author of more than 15 books. He is seen as an important Indonesian intellectual and has been honored by being named Commander of the Order of the British Empire.
Fazlur Rahman	Born on September 21, 1919. Died on July 26, 1988. He was a well-known scholar of Islam, born to a traditional Ulama family in what is now Pakistan. Rahman studied Arabic at Punjab University, and went on to Oxford University where he wrote a dissertation on Ibn Sina (Avicenna). He began his teaching career at Durham University in England and then taught at McGill University in Montreal, Canada until 1961. After a brief return to Pakistan, he taught at UCLA for a number of years before he took up a post at the University of Chicago in 1969. Here, Rahman taught many students from throughout the Muslim world including Nurcholish Madjid.
Hartono Ahmad Jaiz	Born on April 1, 1953, in Central Java. He earned his bachelor's degree in Arabic literature from IAIN (State Islamic Institute) Sunan Kalijaga Yogyakarta in 1981. He is strident critic of the IAIN system especially toward his alma mater, which chose not to recruit him as a young professor (*dosen muda*).

DRAMATIS PERSONAE

Harun Nasution	Born in 1919, died in 1998. He was an ethnic Mandeling from Sumatra and an Indonesian scholar who was instrumental in shaping Islamic studies in Indonesia. He was a self-described neo-Mutazilite, because he sought to champion rationalist and humanist principles in the study of Islam. He pursued education in Mecca, Cairo, and Montreal. In 1969, he earned a PhD in Islamic studies from McGill University in Montreal. Upon completing his doctorate, he returned to Indonesia and took up a position at IAIN in Jakarta. He is one of the framers of the modern IAIN system and his influence on the system is so pervasive that even those who did not agree with him, were influenced by him.
Hasyim Ashari	The Grand Master (Hadratus Syekh) of the Indonesian pesantren tradition. Founder of Pesantren Tebu Ireng (1899) and a co-founder of Nahdlatul Ulama (1926). Father of Wahid Hasyim and Abdurrahman Wahid.
Hasyim Muzadi	Born on August 8, 1944. Founded Pesantren Al-Hikam in 1991. Head of the East Java Regional Council for NU (1992–1999). Head of the National Council for NU (1999–2004).
Imam Suprayogo	Born on January 2, 1951, in East Java. He became Rector of the State Islamic University (UIN) Malang. He is an alumni of the Faculty of Tarbiyah (Islamic Education) at the campus where he eventually became Rector. He earned his doctorate in sociology from the University of Airlangga in 1998. Before becoming Rector of UIN Malang, he served as the vice rector of Muhammadiyah Malang University (UMM) from 1983 to 1996 and deputy director of Graduate Studies at UMM in 1996.
Inayah Rohmaniya	A faculty member in Tafsir-Hadith at UIN Yogya. Born to a pesantren family. Earned an MA in Religious Studies from Arizona State University. Completed PhD at ICRS at Universitas Gajah Mada.

Komaruddin Hidayat	He is a Muslim academic and intellectual who received a doctorate in Western Philosophy from Middle East Technical University in Ankara, Turkey in 1990. He also holds a doctorate in Islamic Education from IAIN Jakarta, which he earned in 1981. He has been the Rector of UIN Syarif Hidayatullah in Jakarta since 2006. He is a mass media columnist and has served on the editorial boards of the magazine, *Ulumul Qur'an* since 1991 and the Journal, *Studia Islamika* since 1994.
Muhammad Machasin	He is a professor of History of Islamic culture at the State Islamic University (UIN) Sunan Kalijaga in Yogyakarta. He served as the director of the Islamic Higher Education within MORA from April 2008 to October 2011. He has been actively promoting interfaith dialogue and is a member of the board of the Asian Council on Religion and Peace. He currently directs a number of research centers within the Ministry of Religious Affairs (MORA).
Muhammad Rasjidi	Born on May 20, 1915. Died on January 30, 2001. He earned a degree in philosophy from Cairo University in 1938 and a doctorate in Islamic studies from the Sorbonne in Paris in 1956. In 1959, he was a visiting professor at McGill's Institute of Islamic Studies. Rasjidi was Indonesia's first minister of religious affairs from November 14, 1945 until October 20, 1946.
Muhammad Sirozi	He earned his bachelor's degree in Tarbiya (Islamic Education) in 1987 from IAIN Palembang. In 1992, he received his MA in Social Anthropology from the School of Oriental and African Studies (SOAS), University of London. In 1998, He received his PhD in Educational Policy Studies from Monash University in Australia. He is a professor of Educational Studies and director of the Graduate Program at IAIN Palembang, Indonesia.

Munawir Sjadzali	Born on November 7, 1925 in Central Java. Died on July 23, 2004. He was a career diplomat who had served in the West and the Middle East. During the Suharto regime, he served two terms as the minister of religious affairs between 1983 and 1993 He was a postgraduate lecturer at the Syarif Hidayatullah State Islamic University (UIN), which awarded him with an honorary doctorate in 1994.
Nur Ahmad Fadhil Lubis	He earned a doctorate from UCLA in 1990 with funding from a Fulbright Fellowship. He is a professor of Islamic Law at IAIN North Sumatra and has served as the dean of the Sharia Faculty, he is the founding director of the Graduate School, and has been the Vice Rector of Finance. He is currently serving as the Rector (2009–2014). He has also served as director of the Foundation for the Development of Indonesia-America Friendship (PPIA) in Medan.
Nurcholish Madjid	Born on March 17, 1939, in Jombang, East Java. Died on August 29, 2005. A leading Islamic intellectual and a proponent for a modernized, moderate form of Islam. As a student, and throughout his career, Madjid advocated that the concepts of tolerance, democracy, and pluralism be embraced by Indonesian Muslims. His early education was in Islamic boarding schools (*pesantren*), particularly in the modern pesantren at Gontor, known for teaching students both Arabic and English. He earned a doctorate in Islamic studies from the University of Chicago, where Fazlur Rahman, the Pakistani-American scholar was his dissertation director.
Wahid Hasyim	A national hero. Served on the Preparatory Committee for Indonesian Independence and as minister of religious affairs during different periods (September 30–November 14, 1945; September 6, 1950–April 3, 1952). He innovated madrasah style education within his father's (Hasyim Asyari) pesantren.

Zamaksyari Dhofier	Born on July 25, 1941, in Salatiga, Central Java. Once a professor at IAIN Walisongo Semarang. He earned a PhD in Anthropology from Australia National University in 1980. His book *Tradisi Pesantren* launched the field of *pesantren* studies. He served as the director of Islamic Higher Education in MORA in the 1990s when the sending of faculty members to Western universities intensified. He is the founding rector of Universitas Sains al-Quran in Wonosobo, Central Java.

Chapter 1

The Politicization of the "Apolitical": Islamic Higher Education in Indonesia

Not for the first time, I was being told the tale of Harvard losing its religion.[1] However, instead of a cautionary tale pointing to the dangers of reforming religious education (cf. Lukens-Bull 2000: 27), it was being held up as a laudable goal. It was November 2007 and I was an invited plenary speaker at the Annual Conference of Islamic Studies (ACIS) in Pekanbaru, Sumatra. ACIS is the major conference for scholars at Islamic colleges and universities in Indonesia. In addition to presenters, invitees included the rectors of all the government institutes and universities of Islamic higher education and the rectors of select private institutions. One morning during breakfast, I spoke briefly with the rector (president) of one institution. Starting in 2005, it had been transformed from an exclusively religion-oriented institution into a full-fledged university by adding nonreligious divisions (*fakultas*[2]), including science and technology and health sciences. He told me that his goal was that his university become like Harvard and completely leave behind its religious character.[3] I had never heard this story told as pointing to a laudable goal. I was puzzled and disturbed by this; I remember thinking that more conservative elements of Indonesian society would be very upset by this idea and that it could fuel radicalization in Indonesia. Later, I would discover a substantial debate about whether the State Islamic institutes and universities had lost their way, or even fallen into apostasy. Much of the criticism came from what might be called the religious right or Islamic hard-liners. Further discussion of the variation in Islam including hard-line Islam is taken up in the second chapter.

Today, the State Islamic colleges and universities are playing a key role in the debates about the future of Islam in Indonesia. Even how to refer to it is part of the debate; to use the phrase "Indonesian Islam" implies Indonesian exceptionalism and isolation. However, the phrase "Islam in Indonesia" implies an essentialized, universal form of Islam that is not shaped by local context. Each term has proponents within Muslim discourse. The latter would be favored by the religious right, whereas others, who are more open to local wisdom, would favor the former. I will use the terms interchangeably because Islam in the Indonesian context is certainly connected to larger Muslim discourses, but it also has some distinctive elements.

State Islamic institutes and universities play an important role in current debates in part because they educate 18 percent of all public university students and in part because they attract students from diverse Islamic backgrounds (Kraince 2008: 348–349), across nearly the entire range of possible Islamic expressions which are discussed more fully in chapter 2. The central questions are what the State Islamic Higher Education, or Perguruan Tinggi Agama Islam Negeri (PTAIN), system should be and who speaks for Indonesian Islam (Azra 2011: 50).

In the official nomenclature, the system is called PTAIN (Perguruan Tinggi Agama Islam Negeri, State Islamic Higher Education). There are three types of institutions in this system. The smallest are the Sekolah Tinggi Agama Islam (STAIN), literally Islamic High School, but these are college-level institutions with only one or two fakultas, which are academic units comprised of multiple departments. Historically, many were branch campuses of larger institutions in a nearby larger town or city. The midsize campuses are what are formally called Institut Agama Islam Negeri (IAIN). They usually have at least four fakultas among the following possibilities: *Dakwah* (Missions), *Tarbiyah* (Islamic education), *Syari'ah* (Islamic Law), *Adab* (Islamic Civilization), and *Ushuluddin* (Theology). The largest are the *Universitas Islam Negeri* (UIN, State Islamic University), which have added nonreligious fakultas. Historically, all have been IAIN or branch campuses of IAIN. For example, what is now UIN Malang was a branch campus of IAIN Surabaya offering only Tarbiyah in the 1990s. Therefore most Indonesians will refer to them as IAIN even if a particular campus is not officially designated as such under the current official nomenclature. Further, even though UIN are becoming known by that label, everybody will still understand if someone calls them IAIN.

STAIN, IAIN, and UIN are organs of the Ministry of Religious Affairs (MORA); however nonreligious coursework must be reviewed and approved by the Ministry of Education (Meuleman 2000: 291). During the period covered by this book, there were two ministers of religious affairs: M. Maftuh Basyuni (2004–2009) and Suryadharma Ali (2009–present). Rectors at each campus report directly to the Directorate of Islamic Higher Education which, in addition to overseeing 35 IAINs, monitors and regulates approximately 500 private institutions. The oversight provided by the Directorate of Islamic Higher Education in MORA has become more of an accreditation process rather than the sort of top-down direct government design of curriculum and teaching method found in Saudi Arabia and Malaysia. Each campus and each instructor still has a degree of autonomy in the teaching and learning processes. MORA also accredits private Islamic colleges and universities as well as government-regulated day schools called *madrasah* that have both religious and general *(umum)* subjects. General subjects are by definition nonreligious and can include pretty much anything: math, science, history, sociology, language arts, among the myriad of possible academic disciplines. *Pesantren* (traditional Islamic boarding schools) often register with MORA but are not regulated by it, per se. The exception concerns the accreditation of government curriculum madrasah in pesantren. There are madrasah that do not follow the government curriculum, but their diplomas are not recognized for admission to a PTAIN school; students who wish to enter must take an equivalency exam.

IAIN are critical to understanding the Indonesian Islamic community both for the ways in which they define orthodoxy and act as culture brokers to the wider Islamic community, as well for their cultural brokerage with Western philosophy and scholarship. This system plays a central role in the critical reexamination of Islam as well as acts as a bridge between various strains of Islam because students come from diverse Muslim backgrounds (Kraince 2008: 349). Not only are the institutions and their faculty and staff important participants in the discourse about the future, they are subjects of it as well. There is no shortage of discussion from on and off campus about what Indonesian Islamic higher education should be and how best to achieve those goals. These discussions are a significant part of ongoing debates about the future of Indonesia. The State Islamic Universities, or UIN, have taken on some secular subjects. Some faculty members, particularly from the religious departments feel that these new fields will leach away their students and erode the Islamic character of the university. Further, historical and social scientific approaches to the study of religions have been integrated into the older religious fakultas. People outside of the State Islamic Higher Education system have gone as far as accusing faculty members of apostasy.

Because PTAINs are the official government form of Islamic higher education, PTAIN faculty members can be important opinion makers in the Indonesian Islamic community. Zamahksyari Dhofier, arguably the doyen of research on Indonesian Islamic education, averred in 1985,

> Graduates of these institutes (IAIN) at present tend to become the nucleus of the urban Islamic social structure. Combined with many Islamic social organizations based in cities and towns...they relate the Indonesian Muslim community to the wider Islamic world and define the nature of orthodoxy for it. (Zamahksyari Dhofier 1985)

Dhofier's observation applies as much today as it did more than 25 years ago, even if he glossed over the ways in which, even then, IAIN were controversial. In a very real way, debates about higher education in Indonesia are debates about the nature of society. This book explores efforts to define the future of Indonesian Islam by examining government-sponsored Islamic education.

In Indonesia, institutions of higher education and their faculty members play a much more public role than their counterparts in American society. They are players in both popular culture and national government. Professors regularly write newspaper columns, op-ed pieces, and best-selling books. As an example from within the PTAIN System, Komaruddin Hidayat, the rector of UIN Jakarta, is a best-selling author on various subjects including psychology, death and dying, and "knowing the will of God" (2003, 2005). Many are often recruited into leadership positions within the government bureaucracy. An Indonesian graduate student at Arizona State University in History at the same time I was in Anthropology entered the agency that regulates and approves all research projects conducted in Indonesia. Those within the PTAIN system may also be religious leaders preaching Friday sermons, running pesantren (Islamic boarding schools), or hosting religious lessons (*pengajian*) in their homes. Further some are known on the global stage, such as the late Nurcholish Madjid as well as Azyumardi Azra, whose work has been recognized and honored internationally, including being named an Honorary Commander of the British Empire for his service to interfaith understanding (Osman 2010).

This book is, in some ways, a continuation of my earlier work on traditional Islamic schools or pesantren (Lukens-Bull 2000, 2001, 2005). In that work, I was interested in the various debates and strategies concerning the negotiation of globalization and modernization through curricular modification. The focus of that work was pesantren that had added government-recognized curriculum mostly at the junior-high and high school levels. Central to that government curriculum was the teaching of both religious and nonreligious, or general subjects. While first conducting that research in 1994–1995, I was introduced to the PTAIN system. My research sponsor was Jabar Adlan, who was the acting rector of the IAIN Sunan Ampel in Surabaya. Because of a strong connection between IAIN and pesantren, I conducted some interviews and focus groups with IAIN Sunan Ampel faculty and students. Most of the practical contact was with the Tarbiyah Fakultas branch campus in Malang, which in time became an independent institution and one of six State Islamic Universities. The research done at both the Malang and the Surabaya campuses confirmed their close relationship with the pesantren community and that, at that time, they were institutions almost exclusively focused on religious issues. Although an imperfect analogy at best, the majority of IAIN in the 1990s most closely resembled the institution in the American academic landscape known as a Bible college—a place to study sacred texts, religious life, preaching, and ministry at the undergraduate level. In time, students and faculty wanted PTAIN to be more than such narrowly defined institutions.

When I returned to Indonesia in 2008 on a Fulbright grant, I was drawn to examining the PTAIN system. Some of the debates and processes facing pesantren in the mid-1990s had fed into the issues facing the Indonesian Islamic higher education system in the late 2000s. Therefore, I conducted six-month research on this system in 2008–2009. In addition to teaching in the doctoral program at IAIN North Sumatra, I presented guest lectures at other Islamic colleges and universities. I also conducted participant observation and interviews on five IAIN/UIN campuses. I returned in 2012 to revisit some of these issues. It is fair to say that there is considerable debate taking place on and between IAIN and UIN campuses. The debates are not only about the future of the colleges and universities, but about the future of Islam in the Indonesian context as well. In this regard, the campuses are deeply embedded in the culture wars between the forces of what others have called "Wahhabi Colonialism" (Woodward 2008) and the more moderate, accommodative forms of Islam historically more common in Indonesia (cf. Lukens-Bull 2008).

Islamic Education in Indonesia

Since the pesantren tradition is intricately linked with the PTAIN system, it is useful to briefly describe the pesantren milieu. Pesantren, by that name, are local Islamic institutions nearly as old as Islam in Indonesia itself, although essentially the same type of schools are/were found in Thailand and Malaysia (Lukens-Bull 2010). Further, they are strikingly similar to *madrasa* found elsewhere in the Muslim world. Before the establishment of a modern education system in the twilight years of Dutch colonialism, most education in Indonesia was Islamic. The only form of Islamic education in Indonesia until 1905 was pesantren (Dhofier 2000: 49). They taught an exclusively religious curriculum to a mix of students including future religious leaders, court poets (Florida 1995), and members of the ruling class (Adas 1979; Pemberton 1994: 48–49). Both in print, and in oral tradition, pesantren are closely tied to the *Walisongo* (the nine saints who brought Islam to Java). No pesantren claims to have been founded by one of the Walisongo, but all *kyai* are seen as inheritors of the role of the Walisongo. The kyai is a central figure in the pesantren milieu, part scholar and part mystic, a traditional kyai exercises sole control over their pesantren. In the nineteenth and early twentieth century, pesantren education was typified by each pesantren and kyai specializing in one area of knowledge. Hashim Ashari at Tebu Ireng was known for *Hadith*, whereas Pesantren Jampes of Kediri was well known for its kyai who were experts on Sufism (Dhofier

1980:11). Students would wander from pesantren to pesantren studying under each expert in the fields he wished to master. This tradition created *ulama* that had both a solid foundation of training as well as broad network of contacts, both horizontal (with classmates) and vertical (with teachers).

Traditional religious education in pesantren was self-directed and self-paced. It involved both individual and group study. Individual study may be used at the beginning of a student's time for remedial training in basic skills, such as reading and writing Arabic script. Advanced students work directly with the kyai on individual areas of specialization. One form of group lesson focuses on creating the basic study tools needed for the rest of a student's career as a religious scholar. These tools are called *kitab kuning*, or "yellow books" referring to the cheap paper upon which they are printed. The term refers to what van Bruinessen has called the classical texts of Islam (1990: 229). It should be made clear that "classical" refers not to the original Meccan and Medinan communities but roughly to the medieval period, specifically the twelfth to seventeenth centuries CE (Johns 1987) in which being Muslim and being Sufi were nearly synonymous. The pesantren community holds them to be of high importance in determining how to live as good Muslims in a globalizing and modernizing world. Kitab kuning are a defining component of traditional pesantren curriculum.

Kitab kuning start as printed pages of a text in what is called the bald script (*huruf gundul*), which is Arabic without the vowel marks. The student will fill in the vowel marks as the teacher reads the text. The teacher then gives the *makna* (formal meaning), which is more a translation than an explanation. The students write the verbatim meaning between the lines in their own copy of the kitab in fine Arabic script Javanese. This dictation method is only the beginning of the learning process. Students will review and repeat the lesson on their own or with a friend. Also, groups of students, particularly the advanced ones, are expected to gather and debate the meaning of the text. The addition of the government approved curricular schools during the day has put constraints on time. Those pesantren which have taken this step are attempting to teach two full, independent curricula and the schedule can be daunting, starting each morning at dawn and not ending until hours after dark. In fact, it is not possible for most pesantren to keep up the teaching of the traditional subjects at the same level as before. Therefore they shift the focus to graduating students with general knowledge (as contrasted with religious knowledge) but the morals of a religious teacher (Lukens-Bull 2005: 56–57).

An essential part of pesantren education is the inculcation of Islamic values. Pesantren teachers stress that while a day school can teach students about religion and morality, they cannot teach the students to be moral. Moral education, in terms of moral behavior, takes experience. Hence, pesantren strive to create an environment in which the morals of religion can be practiced as well as studied. The students learn about them in religious lessons and are then given the opportunity to practice them (Lukens-Bull 2001). The environment includes modest, even Spartan, communal living arrangements that are used to teach the value of simple living (*kesedehanan*). The meager meals are typically rice and vegetables. Further, while there is an acknowledgment of personal property, in practice, property is communal. Simple things such as sandals are borrowed freely. Other items, if not in use, should be loaned if asked for. The *santri* who habitually refuses to loan his property will be sanctioned by his peers and sometimes by the pesantren staff, which may include teasing or a stern reminder about Islamic brotherhood and the importance of being sincere and selfless (*ikhlas*, Lukens-Bull 2005: 60).

The term santri is usually translated as student, although it might be better translated a disciple (Effendi 2008: xxiii). The santri treat the kyai with much respect, never looking him in the eye, especially when spoken to. When the kyai passes, students should make way for him; some will even crouch down and bow their heads. They may greet him by kissing his hand. Traditionally, students did their own cooking, cleaning, and laundry. With the increase in time for study, there is not enough time for students to do all that they did in the past. A point is made to keep some of these tasks in place as a way to teach values including self-sufficiency as well, as compassion for those who will be doing these tasks for them throughout their lives. The behaviors of students are monitored and discipline is applied when needed. Beyond nurturing an environment in which values are practiced, many kyai talk about the need to set a good example and that modeling is the most effective way to teach values (Lukens-Bull 2001, 2005: 61).

In the twentieth century, an educational system focused on science, math, and other general subjects was promoted first by the

Dutch, then the nationalists, and later the Republic of Indonesia. The first Islamic school to integrate nonreligious subjects was Madrasah *Mandba' al-'Ulum* in Surakarta. The madrasah[4] style of education that grew out of this first model used European style classrooms with desks, blackboards, and grade levels (Dhofier 2000: 49). In response to the demand for this type of education, many pesantren engaged in curriculum revisions that later became the way through which they negotiated and engaged globalization. In the 1920s, Pesantren Tebu Ireng added a few nonreligious topics under the initiative of Wahid Hasyim and the permission of his father Hasyim Asyari. At this time, Muhammadiyah, the second largest Islamic organization in Indonesia started its own system of day schools. Starting in 1960, religious education became compulsory in public school at all levels as part of an effort to offset the expansion of communism (Kinoshita 2009: 6).

Starting in the 1970s, newer, general (nonreligious) education became an important part of the pesantren community's strategy for negotiating modernity. Pesantren added government-recognized curricula to schools, the vast majority of which were madrasah, which always had a high percentage of religion classes, although it has declined over time. Madrasah also existed outside the pesantren. A few pesantren opened madrasah following a national curriculum. In the beginning, this curriculum was 70 percent religious subjects, but the ratio switched in 1984 so that it was 30 percent religious subjects. In the closing years of the Suharto era, madrasah were in the process of being changed into general schools with an Islamic character (*sekolah Islam yang berciri khas Islam*), which only had about 5 percent religious subjects.[5] At each grade level, there would be one special cohort who was in an intensive madrasah program that not only returned to the original 70:30 ratio but also added the dimension that the language of instruction was Arabic (Lukens-Bull 2005: 63–64).

Pesantren educate both boys and girls, although this education is rarely conducted in mixed gender settings. As private institutions, pesantren and madrasah receive some government aid, but most of their funding comes from donations and tuition. Traditionally, pesantren did not charge tuition; students simply worked for their keep in the headmaster's fields or businesses. With a double curriculum, there is not enough time for most students to earn their keep, so tuition is charged. Even so, pesantren are sometimes the least expensive educational opportunities available. For the very poor, the old model of work for education is sometimes still used.

Negotiating Modernity and Tradition

In *A Peaceful Jihad* (2005), I examined how the Muslim community centered around pesantren is actively negotiating both modernity and tradition in the contexts of nation-building, globalization, and a supposed clash of civilizations. The preeminent study of pesantren was Zamahksyari Dhofier's *The Pesantren Tradition* (1999) that was based on research conducted in the late 1970s. Dhofier described a system in the early stages of change, as pesantren were taking on aspects of secular education. By the mid-1990s, madrasah were quite commonplace in pesantren and in some places, like Java, many if not most madrasah were run by pesantren (Lukens-Bull 2001; van Bruinessen 2009: 222). Some madrasah are run independently of pesantren and are simply Islamic day schools, lacking the boarding aspect critical to pesantren education.

Many pesantren found it increasingly difficult to maintain the balance between the traditional Islamic education and government schools. In fact, Tebu Ireng, the most famous pesantren of all was, according to some, no longer able to train religious scholars (Lukens-Bull 2005: 43) and many schools have refocused their purpose. No longer do they seek to train clerics and scholars, but now they seek to train people for the general workforce who have the morality of Muslim clerics and scholars (Lukens-Bull 2000). One result is that many of these pesantren were no longer able to produce graduates who have the knowledge and skills to become religious leaders. The pesantren community asked from whence the future leadership will come. One possible answer given in the mid-1990s was PhD holders.

In the 1990s, many *kyai* saw the bureaucratization of Indonesian Islamic leadership as inevitable, but they were not pleased by the education being received by future religious bureaucrats. To compensate for the perceived inadequacy of an IAIN education, some students, mostly from kyai families, endured a double education process, first attending a very traditional pesantren like Lirboyo or Al-Fallah and then obtaining a degree from IAIN. However, pursuing double education was long and difficult and few families could afford it. Therefore, an alternative explored by some was to combine the two. Given that the credentialing system centered on IAIN, several kyai have sought to supplement the education given there with a simultaneous pesantren education. Since IAIN students are free to take lodging wherever they wish, pesantren attract many students, in part because of the religious atmosphere and education and in part because they are cheaper than other options. This involved an adjustment to the traditional pesantren practice of not allowing students to leave on a regular basis. The prediction being made in the 1990s was that PTAIN would become the source of future Islamic leadership. There was the hope that maybe the PTAIN would become a higher level pesantren. The fact that PTAIN have not manifested this hope may be part of the reason for critiques of the system.

In East Java, the pesantren community has long been concerned about IAIN curriculum and the changes taking place. Concerning the future of Islamic education, Jabar Adlan stated in 1995 that he saw PhD programs as the final step, replacing such pesantren as Tebu Ireng, which he thought could no longer fill the role of creating leaders. Further, the roles of ulama and Muslim intellectuals would be combined. He predicted that, in the future, religious authority will come as much from advanced degrees as from community recognition. However, the vast majority of PhDs in religious studies and affiliated fields are held by PTAIN faculty members and more recently earned through an IAIN or UIN. Therefore there is a certain dimension of government control over this process.

The current debates about PTAIN echo discussions about pesantren education in the 1990s. As I have explored elsewhere, pesantren education has made a number of accommodations to modern educational demands (2005). This shift in educational goals means that it was no longer possible to give all students the same level of traditional skills and a "secular" education. Therefore, the emphasis in pesantren shifted to character development and moral education. In pesantren, the key methodology for this is to create an environment in which desired values are inculcated and reinforced. PTAIN in 2008 were facing some of the same issues and have proposed a similar solution.

History of PTAIN

In the 1970s IAINs were created, in part, to be tertiary education for pesantren and madrasah graduates. IAINs were not born out of nothing but was presaged by two institutions: one focused on the training of Islamic teachers for government curricula schools, called *Perguruan Tinggi Agama Islam Negeri* (PTAIN; not to be confused with the current usage of the acronym); and the other was designed to train government functionaries in MORA, called the *Akademi Dinas Ilmu Agama* (Government Worker's Academy of Religious Science) (Saeed 1999). Hence, the largest fakultas in IAIN, across all campuses, were Syari'ah (Islamic law) and Tarbiyah (education). These two fakultas provide the judges, teachers, and officials for Indonesia's religious bureaucracy and religious educational system (Steenbrink 1974: 159) including those for the marriage registration section of the Department of Religious Affairs. Azyumardi Azra, past rector of UIN Jakarta argues that the IAIN is not and has never been a "seminary" and has always had an agenda beyond simply training religious leaders (2011: 44).

The creation of PTAIN came at time when Islam was being pushed to the margins of Indonesian politics. A number of events in the early history of the Republic of Indonesia had placed Islam in the margins. Some would include removal of a Syari'ah requirement from the preamble of the Indonesian constitution, the so-called Jakarta Charter. Other important episodes include betrayals from both the Left (the Madiun Affair) and the Right (Darul Islam) (Pringle 2010: 69–70). During the 1965–1966 bloodlettings that followed an allegedly communist coup attempt, the Indonesian military recruited Muslim militias to help in the killing of an estimated 500,000 people. After this empowerment as partners with the state, Suharto understandably wanted to remove any potential threat to his own power. One way to do this was ensuring that the PTAIN system be explicitly apolitical.

Some have argued that the IAIN (in Jakarta and Yogyakarta) were "gifts" to the pesantren community to appease them after the "gift" of Universitas Gadjah Mada (UGM) was given to the nationalists (Saeed 1999: 182). These so-called gifts were given so that Suharto could garner support for what would become a 32-year regime. This interpretation is subject to debate. First it is questionable that there is, or has ever been, unified communities to be happy about their respective "gifts" (Meuleman 2002).

Second, it is clear that the establishment of the PTAIN system served a number of Suharto's political goals including the bureaucratization of Islamic practices such as family law, marriage, and inheritance. Suharto was arguably biased in favor of "progressive" Islam. The IAIN were to be depoliticized institutions that were removed from Islamist politics (Saeed 1999: 183). Suharto considered IAIN a center of the United Development Party (PPP), the Islamic "opposition" party. If there was ever such a direct connection, there is certainly no such one to one correspondence now. The reforms under a number of Suharto's handpicked ministers of religious affairs demonstrate how his agenda was carried out. These include moving away from a doctrinal focus to more critical and inquisitive approaches, engaging social science and historical perspectives, sending faculty members to Western countries for their doctoral education, and eventually becoming more than schools for studying religion.

Even if IAIN are not properly "gifts" to the pesantren community, there is a strong sense of historical continuity between pesantren and IAIN; many students and instructors have pesantren backgrounds. It is not uncommon to see undergrads line up after class to kiss the professor's hand (Woodward personal communication, January 2012), much like students do in pesantren. Even my doctoral students at IAIN North Sumatra, who are members of the faculty themselves, would not leave the classroom before I had. Meuleman argues that the strong connection remained even after the policy change in the 1990s that required all matriculating students to have a degree from a government-recognized high school; students simply then went to such schools inside a pesantren (2002: 285). IAIN graduates often become teachers at pesantren (Kraince 2008: 348). However, on Sumatra, while the connection still exists, a much smaller percentage of the students and instructors have previously studied in pesantren.

The connection to older Islamic traditions is marked by the full name of each campus, which includes the name of a local Islamic figure. For example, the full name of the Surabaya campus is IAIN Sunan Ampel, Surabaya. Sunan Ampel and the namesakes of many campuses at all levels on Java are one of the nine saints that brought Islam to Java (Walisongo). The Semarang campus is named after all nine and is called IAIN Walisongo. A campus can be known by its full name, its figure's name or its location, so that the campus in Yogyakarta can be known as UIN Sunan Kalijaga Yogyakarta, UIN Sunan Kalijaga, or UIN Yogyakarta or Yogya, following the common name of the city. There are a few exceptions to this pattern including IAIN North Sumatra, IAIN Surakarta, and IAIN Mataram,[6] which are known only by a place name. There is no consensus why some don't use the names of historical figures. For the same institution, some argue it is because there was no figure and others argue there were too many. I cannot find any published guidelines for who can be a namesake, but all the current namesakes are historical/legendary persons from no later than the seventeenth century. This certainly reduces the potential for conflicts between different understandings of Islam that might be represented by more recent personages.

In 2008–2009, the director of Islamic Higher Education was Muhammad Machasin, who reported to the Directorate of Islamic Education, which in turn reported to the secretary general who reported to the minister. Despite this high degree of centralization, on-campus governance runs according to a level of faculty governance unheard of on American campus. All administrators from department chairs to the rector are elected by a vote of what is roughly equivalent to the tenured faculty. To the American academic, the campus politics of IAIN, or any Indonesian university, may seem different. Patron-client relationships (cf. Aspinall 2013; Scott 1972) are extremely important in the development of a scholar's career. Until recently, the best students of each graduating class were selected to be junior instructors (*dosen muda*). They function much in the same way teaching assistants function in an American university, helping faculty with teaching and research. After a few years of service, they can pursue a master's degree and then start teaching. After a few years teaching, they may be able to pursue a doctorate. These opportunities, especially for study abroad, are intricately tied to the number and power of one's patrons. Conversely, gaining positions of authority like chair, dean, or rector require support of a wider base of people. So, people with such ambitions who are already well placed will act as a patron and cultivate relationships with clients. Clientage is sought not only among those who can vote in an election but from a wide range of people as well. Even junior instructors can influence the opinions of eligible voters. A common way to build such support is through hosting important ritual occasions such as fast-breaking suppers during Ramadan and post-Ramadan feasts. At one such event, junior instructors solicited my opinion of the host; it would be a significant coup for these clients to report the endorsement of a Fulbright scholar for their patron in his attempt to become rector. I fear I disappointed them because while I was happy to declare that I thought their patron was a good scholar and a really nice guy, I was firm that I did not want to lend my name to any party in campus politics.

Reform of IAIN

In recounting the history of the PTAIN system, Amin Abdullah, the rector of UIN Yogya from 2000 to 2010 said that from 1977 to 1997 PTAIN was focused on normative instruction or *ulum uddin*. That is, how best to practice Islam and how to teach others about these best practices. Even sometimes controversial work of some scholars, such as Harun Nasution's approach to the relationship between reason and revelation (Martin, Woodward, and Atmaja 1997) fit within what Abdullah called *ulum uddin*. Abdullah may be overestimating the recent changes as well as underestimating the influence of Harun Nasution, who is arguably the most important scholar and teacher in the history of Indonesian Islamic higher education and will be discussed in detail in chapter 3. For now, it is sufficient to note that Nasution encouraged students to examine aspects of Islam that they might not have previously considered. Some observers judge many of Nasution's students and others at PTAIN as merely repeating their teachers and not possessing a high degree of intellectualism themselves (Meuleman 2000: 289). However, to anyone familiar with any number of PhD-prepared PTAIN professors, this assessment seems inaccurate and misleading at best, and paternalistic and condescending at worst.

In the 1940s, long before the PTAIN system was established, the Institute of Islamic Studies at McGill University in Montreal started working with Indonesian graduate students (Webster 2009: 92). The number of students sent to McGill expanded in the 1970s with the establishment of the IAIN. Under the leadership of Munawir Sjadzali (1983–1988) as minister of religious affairs, the PTAIN system expanded beyond McGill and started sending professors to get advanced degrees in the United States, Australia, the Netherlands, and other Western countries. This is sometimes referred to as the creation of *ulama*-plus—people who are '*alim* (religious experts) but are more intellectual in their orientation. Before this time, the ties between IAIN and the Middle East were very strong with the faculty having a particular orientation toward Al-Azhar Mosque/University in Cairo (Saleh 2001: 7). Even though the shift toward critical studies informed by social sciences and humanities started almost from the beginning, Amin Abdullah argues that there was not a critical mass of PhD-trained faculty for the approaches to be mainstreamed until the 1990s.

The influence of such approaches is not spread evenly. Outlying campuses, like IAIN North Sumatra have only a small handful of faculty members with PhDs in the social sciences and humanities. The perspective has not achieved much breadth or depth. An important point stressed in the doctoral course that I taught to mostly faculty members was that one must bracket one's own beliefs when studying the religious beliefs and practices of others. This was hard for many of them to learn. By contrast, when I was invited, in a quite impromptu fashion, to sit on the MA thesis proposal review panel at UIN Jakarta, the resident professors told one student that he must bracket his own religious perspective in order to study the religious practice of villagers; when I was asked my opinion, I could only agree.

Evolution of Some IAIN into UIN

Starting in the late 1990s and early 2000s, six IAIN transformed from institutes to universities by adding at least two nonreligious fakultas. The motivation for these changes included concerns about employability of students and wanting to make sure that the Muslim community was not economically marginalized. Opinions about these changes are mixed both on and off campus. On campuses that have made the change, there is some concern about what will happen to the original religiously oriented fakultas; that the new, "secular" fakultas will provide too much competition and will eventually drive their fakultas out of existence. On campuses that have not made the change, there has been a call for a wider mandate. That is, they are adding programs like psychology, nursing, management, and public health under the existing fakultas. IAIN North Sumatra received the specific recommendation to create a public health program in their faculty of *Ushuluddin* (theology and comparative religion)[7] despite not having the staff to do so. Off campus, some are concerned about the quality of the nonreligious programs and conclude that at least for the time being these are not the best places to pursue nonreligious topics. The addition of nonreligious fakultas has introduced some debate about the supervision of PTAIN, with the Ministry of Education claiming oversight over the new programs.

Some critics go so far as to accuse specific PTAIN faculty members of apostasy. Some PTAIN instructors claim these accusations are because of the transition of several IAIN into UIN. However, the major work raising concerns about apostasy does not mention the transition into UIN (Jaiz 2005). Various aspects of the apostate accusations will be expanded in the next chapter. Hartono Ahmad Jaiz and Adian Huseini, two of the most vocal critics of the PTAIN system today, are part of what is called *Islam garis keras* (hard-line Islam) as well as IAIN graduates who were not selected to become junior instructors. The term "hard-liners" applies to a wide range of ideologies and organizations that, while not new, have gained greater prominence since the end of the Suharto era and the growth of democracy. While most of the hard-liners are nonviolent, violent groups among them have become more active in the post-Suharto era. Today, the PTAIN system is working in a context of the growing impact of hard-line Islam.

Debate and concern about the future of State Islamic Higher Education is not new. In the 1990s, it was not apostasy or even liberalism that was the problem. Rather, the worry was that IAIN might not be as capable of training future ulama as traditional (*salaf*) pesantren. IAIN graduates were not able to read the traditional religious commentaries (kitab kuning). This was especially true in East Java where the pesantren tradition is especially strong. Jabar Adlan, the acting rector of IAIN Surabaya in 1995, related the story of an IAIN graduate who entered the well-known *salaf* pesantren Lirboyo and was placed with the grade school–aged students. The IAIN graduate was judged on his ability to read kitab kuning; a mispronounced passage was taken to indicate that he had low religious knowledge, a standard with which Jabar did not agree. However, being able to read kitab kuning is an important measure in the pesantren world; it is the one used to criticize Tebu Ireng in the mid-1990s (cf. Lukens-Bull 2005: 58). Further, the private Islamic studies institute of which Jabar was also the rector required all the students to read and study classical texts in the traditional. Because Jabar saw the importance of students being able to read and have primary access to classical texts, he tried to institute a similar program at IAIN Surabaya. However, a complete lack of interest led to its quick demise. In the 1990s, Islamic studies at a few IAIN, like the Jakarta campus, were no longer defined by skill in recitation. The debates in the 1990s of whether success in Islamic studies should measured by traditional, some would say medieval, standards or by more modern and internationally recognized standards of scholarship gave rise to the debates taking place in the first part of the twenty-first century.

Chapter Summaries

Chapter 2 frames the discussion in terms of the variation found in the interpretation and practice of Islam. Theoretically, the chapter suggests that variation in religious practices is similar to dialect differences in language. The determination of which dialects are authentic and proper, like much of the construction of symbolic meaning, is inherently political. Within this theoretical frame, the chapter explores the broad outlines of the variation found in Indonesian Islam, namely the Classicalist, Reformists, Islamists, and Jihadists. Returning to the specifics of this book, the chapter will turn to the debates about Islamic higher education as they fit into the larger framework discussed earlier by examining accusation of liberalism and even apostasy on PTAIN campuses. While these accusations are not serious concerns for faculty and administration of PTAIN campuses, they have gained a small amount of traction in Indonesian society in general. Further, the accusations and the bases for them illustrate some of the key concerns in the debates about the future of Indonesian Islam.

In chapter 3, attention is drawn to the recent process of some IAIN becoming full-fledged universities by adding at least two nonreligious fakultas to the existing religious ones. Common additions have included science and technology, medicine, social science and humanities, and psychology. On the campuses that have become universities, some faculty members say that the central mission of the institution has been abandoned. There is also concern that the new fakultas will draw students away from traditional fakultas. Many of the campuses that have not made the transition wish to make it. They are aware that new programs will draw students away from the older programs, but they are also aware that this is already happening with students attending other institutions. Hence, PTAIN is losing overall enrollment and with it they are losing influence. To keep their influence, they must attract new students and retain their traditional pools of students. An alternative of a wider mandate has been proposed with nonreligious subjects integrated into the traditional fakultas. An important part of this transition has been defining a relationship between science and religion. Figuring out this relationship is an important component of negotiating a relationship with the modern world.

Chapter 4 turns to debates about where faculty members at PTAIN are best educated; whether it should be in the Middle East, in the West, or in Indonesia itself. The debates are not simply about where is best but about what is studied and how it is studied. It is in these debates that people position themselves vis-à-vis "orientalism." If the relationship between science and religion is problematic, even more problematic is the relationship between religion and the social sciences. It is also here that debates about authenticity emerge. Debates about authenticity take us back to a linguistic analogy. In language, speakers of power dialects often regard speakers on nonpower dialects to be speaking the language improperly. There is an assumption that those who pursue graduate training in the West are more liberal than those who study in the Middle East. The evidence for this is circumstantial and anecdotal at best.

Chapter 5 examines the hottest debate in modern Muslim societies, namely gender parity and explores some specific dimensions. At the UIN Yogyakarta and at other IAIN campuses, professors are using religious precepts to enhance the status of women in society. These efforts are typically coordinated through a *Pusat Studi Wanita* (PSW), or Women's Studies Center, which is a center for both community-based research and advocacy. These centers publish books, conduct seminars and training for women, for health specialists, and even for judges in the Islamic court system, which functions primarily as family court.

Chapter 6 draws the book to a close by exploring the ways in which people at PTAIN talk about the future and how they fit into the debates about the future of Islam in the Indonesian context. Given that the ways they talk about the future include topics covered in the previous chapters, this will serve as an effective conclusion to the book. The chapter also turns to the relationships between traditional Islamic education in pesantren and PTAIN. Some campuses are trying to establish on-campus pesantren whereas other are working with existing local pesantren to give students the experience of studying and living in a pesantren, which is thought to by its very nature to instill proper Islamic values. With this foundation, the chapter then reviews the ways in which various IAIN and UIN are seeking to redefine Islam. In the last analyses, the efforts are to define a higher education system as well as a form of Islam that serves the needs of the Indonesian people into the future by balancing (re)imagined forms of both tradition and modernity.

Chapter 2

Religious "Dialects," Variation, and Accusations of the Worst Kind

In January 2009, I sat in an office with Azyumardi Azra, former rector of Universitas Islam Negeri (UIN) Jakarta and then director of the graduate school. I raised the issue of a 2005 book, which accused many Perguruan Tinggi Agama Islam Negeri (PTAIN) professors of apostasy and described the campuses as a whole as cesspools of unbelief (Jaiz 2005). Azra was quickly dismissive of the work as trash and slander and the author, Hartono Ahmad Jaiz, as unintelligent and mentally ill. Azra asserted that the book has no real impact (indeed it has a small readership, cf. Weck, Hasan, and Abubakar 2011: 34) and then would speak of it no further. He was clear that Jaiz's book was not worthy of attention—his or mine. When I spoke about this book to other faculty members, they strongly recommended that I do not pursue this line of investigation. The sentiment was that by paying any attention to it that I would be granting it some level of legitimacy. In their minds, this aspect of the debates about PTAIN was best kept quiet. Further, they argued, this line of investigation would prove fruitless. I find that I must respectfully disagree with my friends. Although these accusations of apostasy come from a vocal minority in Indonesian society, they reflect a dimension of the debates that cannot be ignored. As Michael Gilsenan argues, the process of defining social elements as Islamic or non-Islamic is inherently political. He describes an overall process whereby,

> certain classes and groups that are politically and economically dominant in society legitimize a form of religion that increasingly relates to

a specifically class view of how Islam is to be defined, practiced, studied, taught, and authorized. This will be the "real" and legitimate Islam. (1982: 211).

In Indonesia today, the inverse is also true, declaring what is true Islam is part of efforts to gain political ascendancy. Convincing the general public that the State Islamic Institutes and Universities have gone astray is part of an overall attempt to establish a specific understanding of Islam and Islamic law as the single legitimate form to be endorsed by the state. To understand this debate we must begin by understanding the dynamics of variation in Muslim belief and practice.

An examination of variation must not only consider what distinguishes different Muslim cultures from each other but also what ties them together. To suggest that Muslim culture is synonymous with Islam is redundant (Roy 2004: 129) and ignores the cultural diversity in the global Muslim community (Davies 1988: 63) and even within a single village (Antoun 1989: 39; Loeffler 1988). Therefore, it is critical to consider the relationships between that which ties various Muslim communities together and what makes them distinct. This is what Talal Asad calls for when he suggests that the anthropology of Islam must devise a conceptual organization of the diversity in Islam (1986: 5). The most insightful contemporary theories regarding this relationship have attempted to explain variation within Islam by constructing linguistic analogies, including studying religion as discourse[1] (Asad 1986; Bowen 1993b). The discourse model has two central shortcomings. The first is that it is not very specific on the dynamics between a translocal or "universal" form and local forms. The second is that "discourse" sounds neat and tidy with equal participants trying to shape the outcome; it tends to overlook the political nature of such processes.

Linguistic Analogies

Indonesian discourse makes a distinction between *agama* (religion) and *keagamaan,* which literally means religiousness, but is often used to mean religious practice, or expression. When I tell PTAIN professors that I do not study Islam per se, but what Muslims do in any particular time and place as part of their religious practice, they tell me that I study *keagamaan.* Many scholars have identified a need to examine the relationship between Islam writ large and what actual people do with their religion in everyday life (Bowen 1993b: 7; El-Zein 1974a; Woodward 1988: 65, 87–88).

I wish to expand the linguistic analogy and draw a parallel between agama (religion) and *langue* (language as a system) and between keagamaan (religiousness) and *parole* (speech acts) (cf. Saussure 1972). The factors that shape religious expression include both idiosyncratic and social and historical factors. Idiosyncratic factors, those on the individual level, include factors such as the choice of how or whether to practice in a consistent manner. Idiosyncrasies, by definition, are hard to describe and model. More importantly then, idiosyncratic factors include choosing which social or historical factors to draw upon. Social and historical factors give rise to patterns of practice among groups of people that are analogous to dialects.

One way to distinguish between dialects is mutual intelligibility. In the context of religion, "intelligibility" does not simply entail mutual understanding but refers to recognizing someone as being on the correct path. However, claims of nonintelligibility may be exaggerated in religion as well as in language. Certain language communities may deny similarities with other communities as part of identity politics.[2] Similarly, it is common enough to encounter circumstances in which Muslims may deny that the practices of other Muslims are properly called Islam. Certainly the Ahmadiyya "dialect" is one that certain other Muslims would not recognize because of its acknowledgment of a prophet after Muhammad. Some groups draw on different concepts for the expression and practice of Islam, which produces some of the variation within Islamic societies, but what creates the distinctive variation in these religious practices are the cultural inflections placed upon concepts, words, and rituals.

Traditionalists and Modernists

One major division in Indonesian Islam is between what are commonly referred to as Traditionalists or Classicalists, and Modernists. This division in part references the question of *ijtihad,* which is most often translated as interpretation, but may be more correctly defined as "working with the sources of dogma" (Vikør 1995). Classicalists hold that the door of "interpretation" (*pintu ijtihad*) is closed and follow the broad outlines of interpretation set forth by earlier great scholars who did ijtihad of the Quran and Hadith (the sayings and actions attributed to the Prophet), which became the basis of the four schools of jurisprudence (*maddhab*). Later historical scholars, such as Imam Al-Ghazali, and even the fourteenth-century father of Islamic reformism, Ibn Tamiya were working as *mujtahid fil maddhab* (interpreters of a particular law school) (Federspiel 1996: 206). The Classicalist position does not mean a blind commitment (*taqlid*) to following established dogma, but means that forming opinions must be done within the frame of previous scholars. Indeed, Abdurrahman Wahid, former head of the largest Indonesian Islamic organization, favored a position in which the methods and general framework of previous scholars are used, rather than a strict observance of specific past decisions. One particular point of disputed interpretation concerns *wasilah* or the use of intercessors. Woodward reports that this is the primary "on the ground" issue between traditionalists and modernists (personal communication August 2012). I have no doubt that this is true. However, since at least some argue that all five maddhab allow *wasilah* (Raza 1997), to argue against intercessors means having to first take the position that the gates of interpretation are open and that scholars can work outside the maddhab.

The two largest Islamic organization in Indonesia are Nahdlatul Ulama (NU: Renaissance of Islamic Scholars) and Muhmamadiyah. NU is the largest Islamic organization in Indonesia, and the world, today. It was founded in 1926 in Surabaya, East Java. NU is closely linked with Islamic boarding schools (pesantren). The NU variant is centered around pesantren, and their headmasters (kyai) are hence the leaders of this religious community. The pesantren community practices and maintains classical Islam, which Zamakhsyari Dhofier sees as

> still strongly bound up with established Islamic ideas created by scholars, jurists, doctors, and Sufis during the early centuries of Islamic theological and legal development, sectarian conflicts, and the rise of Sufi movements and brotherhoods in the thirteenth century. This is not to say, however, that contemporary classical Islam in Java remains fixed in the molds created for it by the *ulama* (Muslim leaders) of the formative centuries (1999: xix).

Muhammadiyah can be referred to as Reformist because it seeks to reform Indonesian Islam so that it draws primarily on scriptural sources (Peacock 1978), which is why it is sometimes also called scripturalist. Muhammadiyah was established November 18, 1912 by K. H. Ahmad Dahlan. It is a nonpolitical organization that sponsors schools, hospitals and clinics, colleges, and orphanages. It has a women's auxiliary, *Aisyah,* and its own scouting organization. Muhammadiyah takes a position that the basis of Islamic Law (syari'ah) is the Quran, Hadith, and personal interpretation. They thereby reject historical developments in Islam and classical Islamic scholarship, but also take moderate positions vis-à-vis the Indonesian state and the place of syari'ah law, non-Muslims, and categorically reject the use of violence.

Salafis and Islamists

Several positions taken up by "modernists," or scripturalists as Geertz (1968) calls them, were first formulated by the fourteenth-century thinker, Ibn Tamiya. First is his use of *qiyas* (reasoning by analogy) in reading and understanding Quran and Hadith. Second, he bitterly attacked the practice of *ziarah,* or pilgrimage to the tombs of saints and called these practices *bida* (innovation). It should be noted that similarities between Ibn Tamiya and Muhammadiyah in Indonesia are not accidental as Ibn Tamiya's teachings were used by the founders of the Wahhabis (Cheneb 1974: 152) and Muhammadiyah. Reformists favor the position that the door of interpretation is open and that a properly qualified scholar must have the right to perform *ijtihad* at all times. They also reject any use of an intercessor between the believer and God. Noorhaidi Hasan argues that "the contemporary *salafi* movement is a form of reconstituted Wahabism" (2011: 95). Another term used for the scripturalists is *salafi.* However, in Indonesia, this term is ambiguous. The International Crisis Group (ICG) is not quite right when they say the term is used in two ways (2004: 2). In Indonesian discourse, a distinction is made between *salaf* and salafi, with the former referring primarily to pesantren which teach only religion and the latter to Islamists. More specifically, salaf, identifies pesantren with a strong emphasis on mysticism; students frequently meditate by the founder's grave to absorb *barakah* (blessing but with a physical quality). Therefore, in Indonesian discourse, one letter changes the meaning 180 degrees. *Salafi*s seek to follow what they understand to be the Islam practiced by the

Prophet and the two generations after him. It can be confusing to have such a drastic difference in meaning depend on a single letter, especially when in the original language, Arabic, there would be absolutely no difference in meaning. Djohan Effendi equates Modernists with *Salafi*s (2008: 64), however, Modernists like those associated with Muhammadiyah, would not identify as salafi and do not consult Saudi sheiks like most salafis, which are referred to by some as Saudi-Wahabis (Woodward personal communication, August 2012) which is consistent with Hasan's assertion that the spread of Wahabism is inexorably linked to the foreign policy of Saudi Arabia (2011: 96).

The Bali Bombing in 2002 brought international attention to the activities of jihadis in Indonesia. For those unfamiliar with Indonesia, this seemed to be a sudden rise of an element of Islam not previously seen in the country. However, the Bali Bombing was preceded by Laskar Jihad, a salafi jihadi militia that went to Eastern Indonesia in 2000 to take sides in ongoing conflicts between Muslims and Christians. While democracy and its attending freedoms did allow jihadi ideologies to be spread and discussed more openly, both jihadi ideologies and actions were not absent under Suharto. Julie Chernov-Hwang shows that church burnings increased exponentially in the closing years of the Suharto regime (2009: 64).

Olivier Roy defines Islamism as a political movement that uses (particular interpretations of) Islam as its ideological foundation (Roy 1996: 28–48). I would narrow this definition to those who have the political agenda of establishing particular, if contested, understandings of syari'ah law as civil law. In the Indonesian context, those who argue for a syari'ah state often refer to the Jakarta Charter, a statement in the original draft of the Indonesian constitution, which would have required the observance of syari'ah law for all Muslims as part of the national ideology of *Pancasila* (Sukma 2003: 346). This statement was removed from the draft by the Preparatory Committee for Indonesian Independence (Panitia Persiapan Kemerdekaan Indonesia [PPKI]) at the behest of Muhammad Hatta, later the first vice president of Indonesia (Elson 2009). An International Crisis Group report about Islamism in the Middle East/North Africa identifies three strains of Sunni Islamic Activism: political Islamism, proselytizing Islamism, and jihadist Islam (ICG 2005; Weck, Hasan, and Abubakar 2011: 15). In that report, the ICG makes a distinction between salafists as having primarily a religious orientation and Islamists as having primarily a political orientation. Azra (2005) identifies a range of *salafiyah* movements including those that focus on preaching (*dakwah*), education, and social welfare as well as those who use violence to achieve their goals.

The ICG makes a distinction between salafis and salafi jihadists. Salafi purists reject compromising religious purity for the sake of political gain and with associating with those who do. They also have little tolerance for those willing to acknowledge some "deviant" teachings hold some good (2004: ii). They also distance themselves from groups like the Prosperous Justice Party (PKS), which can be considered the Indonesian branch of the Muslim Brotherhood (Hefner 2009: 74), *Hizbut ut-Tahrir, Jemaah Tablighi*, and *Darul Islam*. The purists typically seek advice from Saudi sheiks closely aligned with the Saudi government. ICG suggests that the more "radical" the salafi the less likely they are to be drawn to Jihadi movements (2004: ii). ICG identifies four differences between salafis and salafi jihadis. First, salafi jihadis allow for rebellion against a Muslim government. Second, salafi jihadis prefer to define jihad in exclusively violent terms whereas salafis define it as whatever actions are needed to strengthen the faithful. Finally, although both groups argue that violent jihad must be defensive, salafi jihadis use a wider definition of defensive; they seem to subscribe to the adage "the best defense is a good offense."

Under the repression of the Suharto era, or New Order, political Islam, in all its forms, was kept out of political power and even pushed underground (Abuza 2004: 6). However, Islamism was never far from the surface. Muhammad Natsir, considered by some to be the elder statesman of Indonesian Islamism (Woodward et al. 2012: 3) was active throughout the Suharto era and even established Dewan Dakwah Islam Indonesia (DDII; Indonesian Islamic Missions Council) when he was not allow to revive the Islamic political party, Masyumi (Liddle 1996). DDII, a key portal for Saudi influence (Hasan 2011: 96), was a way of doing politics with dakwah (van Bruinessen 2002) and propagated salafism when politics and armed struggle were restricted by New Order policies (Woodward et al. 2012: 175). In the mid-1980s, salafi communities started expanding and becoming more assertive through the establishment of salafi madrasah (Hasan 2011: 95). The growth of the salafi movement in Indonesia was, in part, a backlash against the widespread impact of the Iranian Revolution. To counter the influence of Iran, the Saudi kingdom built upon the efforts of *Dewan Dakwah* and established the Institute of Islamic and Arabic Studies (LIPIA), which graduated hundreds of students who continued their studies in Saudi Arabia. Many of those who studied in Saudi Arabia felt the need to volunteer for the anti-Soviet Jihad in Afghanistan and with this experience formed the leadership for post-Suharto salafi jihadis (Hasan 2006: 48–51).

The transition to democracy and greater civil society opened the space for "uncivil society" (Abuza 2004: 6; Sukma 2003: 343, 350), but it is misleading to suggest that democracy radicalized certain groups. The roots of their radicalization came during the Suharto era. Suharto was deeply concerned about Islam as a political force (Sukma 2003: 343) and even to depoliticize Islam through the *Institut Agama Islam Negeri* (IAIN) system. In general, Islam was not allowed to play a preeminent role in politics and policy making and the state was suspicious of Islam as a political force until near the end of the New Order (Chernov-Hwang 2009: 47; Sukma 2003: 343). Suharto did not distinguish between violent and nonviolent groups; all forms of political Islam were seen as a threat to the state (Chernov-Hwang 2009: 47). Suharto disbanded the popular Islamic party Masyumi and folded all Islamic parties into the United Development Party (PPP), which was one of two "opposition" parties to the ruling party, Golkar (Abuza 2004: 14; Chernov-Hwang 2009: 48; Sukma 2003: 344). The PPP was structured in such a way to be politically impotent; by combining groups with conflicting religious views, the Suharto regime hamstrung PPP from the start. Further, neither opposition party was allowed to have a societal presence outside of the month prior to elections (Chernov-Hwang 2009: 50); they could not have offices, hold rallies, or even provide social services to stay in the public eye between elections. It was not the last time Suharto would neuter an Islamic organization. Before Ikatan Cendiakawan Muslim Indonesia (ICMI, Indonesian Muslim Intellectuals Network) became co-opted by the Suharto regime, it was an independent organization founded by students and professors at Brawijaya University, according to a young man who bore a certificate of appreciation as a founder from the organization.

Under Suharto, all mass organizations including NU, Muhammadiyah, and PPP had to accept the national ideology, *Pancasila* as their sole philosophical basis. The first point of the *Pancasila* was belief in one great God; all the officially recognized religions (Islam, Protestantism, Catholicism, Hinduism, Buddhism, and Confucianism) are imagined to fit this mold. This point therefore established Indonesia as a religious but multi-creedal state. The other points concerned democracy, justice, and prosperity for all Indonesians and were not as challenging to religious organizations as the first. Therefore PPP, the party into which all the Islamic parties were folded could not proclaim itself as Islamic (Abuza 2004: 15). However it used the *kabah* as its symbol and was seen as the Islamic party by many conservative Muslims.

In the immediate post-Suharto era, over 141 parties were formed, 48 were certified to participate in the elections. 18 of those parties certified were Islamic (Chernov-Hwang 2009: 77), some of which, saw political involvement as a way of keeping their religious message in the public eye even if they never enjoyed much success at the polls. This was explicitly stated by the head of the Sufi-oriented Peace and Love Party in an interview I conducted in June 2000. Also dozens of new Islamic organizations emerged that purportedly are nonpolitical but influence political discourse.

One of the first radical Islamist organizations in post-Suharto Indonesia was Laskar Jihad (Jihad Troops) that was responding to a perceived inability of the government to control Christian-Muslim conflict (Chernov-Hwang 2009: 90). In 2000, a communal conflict in the Malukus in Eastern Indonesia was recast as a religious conflict (Hasan 2011: 93). In the summer of 2000, young men stood on the corner of Jalan Mataram and Jalan Malioboro and other major corners of Yogyakarta in an interpretation of Arab attire collecting funds and distributing pamphlets titled "Maluku Today" ("Maluku Hari Ini"), which included battle reports from the "front." Many, if not most, Yogyakartans expressed dismay about this group's fund-raising, marching practice, and even their very presence. However, no one publically spoke against them and some drivers put a few coins in the buckets. My friends who observed this claimed that those who donated did not really understand the nature of the group. The emergence of Laskar Jihad gave rise to concerns about the resurgence of radical Islam (Sukma 2003: 345).

The New Order history given above only explains the emergence of radical groups, it does not explain their turn to violence. Radicals want quick and dramatic changes in the social, economic, and political life of Indonesia (Sukma 2003: 345). Sukma identifies four major aspects of the agenda for radical Islam in Indonesia. The first is the adoption of the Jakarta Charter, or the requirement that Muslims follow syari'ah. The second is the eradication of social ills and vices. Some groups, like the Islamic Defenders Front (FPI) have raided and vandalized bars, karaoke lounges, gambling houses, and brothels. However, their concerns about these vices have entered mainstream political discussion so that a law was passed closing all bars during the month of Ramadan. Further, the 2008 passage of the antipornography law that was featured prominently as a common goal at a 2008 Kader Alumni Himpunan Mahasiswa Indonesia (KAHMI, Indonesian Students Association Alumni Group) gathering in which a number of Himpunan Mahasiswa Indonesia (HMI, Indonesian Students Association) who were running for office from different parties came together to gather support. This is not the only time that Islamist parties have formed issue-based alliances (Chernov-Hwang 2009: 83). The antipornography law was so vaguely worded that some people were concerned that it would effectively ban some forms of traditional dances including those of predominantly Hindu Bali (Allan 2007; McGibbon 2006; Setiawati 2008,). The third is social and political justice and the force is the worldwide solidarity of the Islamic community (*ummah*).

Some Islamists argue that things have gotten worse under democracy and even reject democracy outright (Weck, Hasan, and Abubakar 2011: 97). For example in January 2009, Hizbut Tahrir Indonesia had hung banners around the UIN Jakarta campus that asked whether it wasn't time to try Islam, after ten years of democracy with no improvement. On Sunday August 12, 2007, Hizbut Tahrir Indonesia organized and hosted a conference in the Bung Karno arena in Jakarta attended by 90,000 people. The point of the rally was to express a deep-seated sentiment that democracy had failed and that is now time to try syari'ah as the basis of the state. The media reported that the increase of attendance from 5000 in 2006 was proof that this sentiment was growing (*Jakarta Post*, Monday August 13, 2007). In a 2007 interview, Hasyim Muzadi, general head of NU, argued the number 90,000 cannot be taken as meaningful because the organizers bused in attendees from the countryside and were able to attract mostly young women with a promise of a day in the big city, including money for lunch and transportation. Further, the promoters listed him as one of the speakers, which gave the event the NU seal of approval even though it was patently untrue and he was forced to publicly repudiate his alleged association with the event (interview, August 14, 2007).

Mainstream Muslim leaders such as the late Nurcholish Madjid, Syaafi Maarif of Muhammadiyah, and Hasyim Muzadi of NU have stressed the need for the government to be restrained and not be heavy-handed toward militant groups because such an approach will only serve to increase radicalization (Sebastian 2003: 361). Some claim that Indonesia was slow to enter the War on Terror but that this cannot be explained by the influence of Islamist groups on the government (Sebastian 2003). While fear of offending mainstream Muslims by associating Islam with terrorism may have played some role, others suggest that Megawati was under pressure to follow the example of President Musharraf of Pakistan who "extracted financial benefits in return for his support for the American attack on Afghanistan" (Hafidz 2003: 388). The implication is that Megawatti waited until after the promise of American aid before becoming fully engaged. The Indonesian government passed two strong antiterror laws after the 2002 Bali Bombing (Sebastian 2003: 363, 364). After the passing of these regulations, hard-line groups saw the writing on the wall: Laskar Jihad, disbanded; *Fron Pembela Islam* (Islamic Defenders Front) temporarily "froze" its organization, and other groups decided to lie low (Hafidz 2003: 384). Of course the repeat bombings in 2005, suggests that the deterrent effect was limited.

According to Hafidz, the reason Umar Jaffar Thalib, the leader of Laskar Jihad disbanded his well-structured and armed organization was because the organization's patron, a Saudi sheik felt that there was no longer a threat facing Indonesian Muslims (Hafidz 2003: 393). In the more common version of this story, it is Thalib's Yemeni teacher who told him that violent jihad was not necessary in Indonesia because it is a Muslim majority country. In fact, in August 2007, Richard Daulay, the secretary general of the Indonesian Council of Churches, the largest ecumenical Protestant organization, told me that he is personally on good terms with

Thalib and that he, Thalib, and VP Yusuf Kallah had recently traveled together to Eastern Indonesia in a show of collaboration to put down renewed sectarian conflict (interview, August 2007).

The growth of extremist Islam in Indonesia is shifting the discourse in Indonesia. Hard-liners are still a small minority but they have been able to influence public notions of morality and religiosity. As more conservative elements were becoming more prominent in society at large, PTAIN were working toward a more progressive, open, and intellectual expression of Islam.

Pillars of Moderate Islam

PTAINs are often referred to as the fortress (*benteng*) of Islam by those who are critical of some of the developments; they wish for PTAIN to be solid and unchanging like the walls of a fortified city. Most PTAIN faculty will not use the fortress/walled city metaphor. They prefer to identify the system as one of the pillars of moderate Islam along with the socioreligious organizations of Nahdlatul Ulama and Muhammadiyah, which together represent just over half the Indonesian population (van Bruinessen 2009: 219). It might be more appropriate to call State Islamic Institutes and Universities the engines of moderate or progressive Islam to the vehicle comprised of NU and Muhammadiyah; PTAINs are dynamic moving systems that are central to the continuation of moderate Islam. They are intricately connected to both NU and Muhammadiyah, as both NU and Muhummadiyah high schools are important sources of IAIN students. Further, many, if not all, religious teachers in NU and Muhammadiyah high schools are IAIN graduates.

Sukma suggests that there are number of reasons to believe that Indonesia will remain resilient to the challenge of radicalism. First, radical groups are only a tiny percentage of the Indonesian Muslim community. Islamists, more generally, are still a minority. In 1999, for example pro-syari'ah parties only gained 14 percent of the votes. However, they have been able to insert aspects of their agenda, such as the antipornography law, part of the agenda of other political parties. Even though PKS pushed for the law, it needed the backing of non-Islamist parties to pass (Tomsa 2010: 152). Second, NU and Muhammadiyah continue their historical opposition to the Jakarta Charter (Sukma 2003: 348). Hasyim

Muzadi, then general chairman of NU, flatly denied the possibility that anyone in the NU organization could be pro-syari'ah (interview, August 14, 2007). He may have been overstating the organization's ability to monitor and control the political opinions of its membership (cf. Bush 2009: 2), however, he did describe the general sentiment of NU's members and affiliates.

After 1971 and the consolidation of political parties, both NU and Muhammadiyah focused more on being socioreligious organizations. In this environment, cultural Islam, best exemplified by Nurcholish Madjid's slogan, "Islam Yes, Islamic Party, No", was able to prosper and flourish (Kersten 2009: 93). Greg Barton suggests that because of their greater familiarity with Arabic and the classical texts, the NU Classicalists have been better able than modernists to participate in the critical reexamination of Islam found on many IAIN campuses (2002: 66). Muhammadiyah has never been directly involved in politics. The *Kembali ke Khittah* movement in NU, led by Abdurrahman Wahid starting in 1984 took NU entirely out of politics. However, both Muhammadiyah and NU each founded political parties after the fall of Suharto, Partai Amanat Nasional (PAN, National Mandate Party) and Partai Kebangkitan Bangsa (PKB, National Awakening Party) respectively. Even with an indirect turn to politics, NU and Muhammadiyah are strongly, even stridently, opposed to a syari'ah state. In 2008, two think tanks—the Wahid Institute, affiliated with NU, and the Ma'arif Institute, a Muhammadiyah affiliate, coedited and published a book titled, *Ilusi Negara Islam (The Illusion of a Islamic State*, Wahid 2008). In brief, this book rejects the idea of a syari'ah state and details some of the ways Islamist are trying to subvert Islamic institution like village and campus mosques. Perhaps the most striking example of NU's commitment to a pluralist state came in the summer of 2000 as Laskar Jihad was conducting a violent jihad against Christians in Eastern Indonesia. Hasyim Muzadi of NU declared that, pending presidential approval, NU would send *Banser*, its sergeant-at-arms security group to the Malukus to fight a violent jihad in defense of the Christians (*Siar News Service* 2000). Although President Wahid did not give them permission and they never went, their readiness to fight a violent jihad against Muslims in defense of Christians marks NU as a group with a strong commitment to religious pluralism. Both NU and Muhammadiyah have consistently rejected syari'ah law, and key figures from both organizations were on the committee that removed the syari'ah provision from the 1945 constitution. Weck, Hasan, and Abubakar see NU and Muhammadiyah as the most visible forces for cultural Islam as opposed to Islamism. Further, cultural Muslims still have a dominant role in religious discourse (2011: 10, 79). It is common to think of these different expressions or streams of Islam in terms of organizations. The dialect model proposed here allows us to consider the relationship between variants; there may be considerable congruence between organizations suggesting that they are either part of the same dialect or minor variations thereof. Conversely, within large organizations such as NU or Muhammadiyah there can be considerable variation of expression, which again points to the linguistic analogy; not all speakers of the same dialect speak exactly the same.

Apostasy Accusations and Dialects

Another way in which thinking of different expressions of religion as dialects is useful concerns the dynamics between standard and nonstandard forms. Prejudice toward nonstandard languages is common enough. It leads to a number of problems in education; nonstandard languages are not recognized as separate dialects but as "broken" forms of the standard (Labov 1972; Rickford and Labov 1999). In religious discourse, terms like syncreticism, superstition, or even apostasy are used to denigrate nonstandard forms.

Ada Permurtadan di IAIN (There Is Apostasy at IAIN) was published in 2005 by Hartono Ahmad Jaiz, a 1970s graduate from IAIN Yogyakarta. He accused many famous alumni and instructors of leaving the true path of Islam. His reasons range from the absurd (Nurcholish Madjid receiving a liver transplant from a Chinese person) to what he would consider socially subversive (equal rights for men and women) to the theologically serious (stating that all religions may lead to paradise). The accusation of being an apostate (*murtad*) is consequential and Jaiz lays out what he understands the consequences to be. The apostate is to be warned and given three days to repent. Failing repentance, Jaiz says that they should be killed, denied a proper burial, and have their property confiscated from their heirs and the proceeds used to advance the Muslim community (2005: 95ff in e-book version). I personally know of one death threat arising out of the accusations. Of course, it was delivered in a truly Indonesian (Javanese) fashion. My friend received a phone call from someone who said, "it would be best if you did not walk in front of my mosque." My friend was adamant that this was no mere warning but was clearly a threat on his life. Fortunately, no one has taken Jaiz's rhetoric to its conclusion and tried to murder an alleged apostate.

Jaiz himself never compiles or categorizes his reasons into an organized scheme. To understand larger patterns of Islamic discourse, I found it necessary to find some semblance of order in Jaiz's sometimes rambling series of accusations. The first category of accusations can be described as "guilt by association." The most significant of which is having a connection to Harun Nasution (Jaiz 2005: 42), who was an influential scholar in the development of the IAIN system. It might almost be impossible to identify anyone in the system who was not influenced by his ideas. Therefore, although not articulated as such it means showing support for Nasution's ideas. Another act that might get one labeled as apostate was to vote for Azyumardi Azra in the 2002 UIN Jakarta Rector elections (2005: 36), presumably because Azra himself was so accused.

One way to look at these accusations is to take a step back and consider the different ways the linguistic analogy adopted here illuminates the debates. The chief value of this analogy is the ability to model the relationship between what differentiates believers in different settings and what ties them together (Table 2.1). In specific, it is useful to look at how the concept of apostasy finds expression in different dialects. Cultural Islam, the mainstream "dialect" in Indonesia, would limit apostasy to converting to another religion or denying Islam. When the discussion of apostasy occurs on PTAIN campuses no one is willing to make such an accusation; they will say that someone is too liberal but that they are not an apostate because they still keep the required rituals (*ibadah*). The salafi "dialect" agrees with the three basic ways of being an apostate used by Cultural Islam but would add many other ways including anything that smacks of feminism such as gender parity in employment, disagreeing with polygamy, or women's rights quickly leading to accusations of apostasy from Jaiz and his ilk. We will return to gender issues in a later chapter but for now it is sufficient to note that gender issues is one of the most hotly contested issues in

Table 2.1 What makes for an apostate

"Universal"	Expression	Dialect	Elements
Apostasy	Apostate/Murtad	Cultural Islam	+converting to another religion +denying Islam +forgoing Ibadah
Apostasy	Apostate/Murtad	Salafi	+gender parity +feminism +shia −polygamy −Syari'ah state +Pluralism +Hermeneutics +democracy +getting a liver transplant from Chinese person

the debates about the nature of Islam in the modern world (Mir-Hosseini 2006: 81).

The aphorism "a language is a dialect with an army and a navy" highlights the theoretical importance of standard, or power, dialects. Similar relationships exist within Islam, although it may not be armed forces but petrodollars that define the power dialect or "orthodoxy." Debates over orthodoxy and apostasy are negotiations over power relations. The interplay of power and symbols is found in the social construction of symbol systems, which is the process of defining shared meaning. All conscious efforts to construct, maintain, or alter meaning constitute politics (Sederberg 1984: 7; Urban 1991: 12). Disputes about shared meaning of political expression and competing ideologies are not epiphenomenal to politics, but *are* politics itself (Cohen 1979; Fairclough 1989: 23).

Foucault rejects both symbolic and dialectic analyses of power relations. He prefers an analysis of what he calls, "the genealogy of relations of force, strategic developments, and tactics." He argues that the model for power relations (i.e., politics) should be that of war and battle rather than of language (*langue*) and signs. He sees dialectic analyses of power evading "the always open hazardous reality of conflict by reducing to a Hegelian skeleton." Symbolic analyses of power, according to Foucault avoid the violent, bloody, and lethal character of power relations by suggesting that they could be understood in terms of "the calm Platonic form of language and dialogue" (Foucault 1980: 114, 115). Foucault is clearly arguing against the kind of theoretical framework I would favor. I think he is mistaken. If there is a war between the dominant and subordinate groups it is often a hidden, quiet, guerilla war. As James Scott suggests, the struggle continues even when the public discourse suggests that each group "knows its place" (Scott 1990). Furthermore, the weapons in the war are often symbolic; when the subordinate group cannot wage a physical war it wages an ideological war (Scott 1990). Gal argues that control over the representation of reality is more than a source of social power; it is also a locus of struggle and conflict (1989: 348). However, it is important to remember that the "playing field" in a symbolic war is uneven.

Relationship with the State

Another set of accusations concerns accepting the Republic of Indonesia as a secular state and opposing the establishment of a syari'ah state in Indonesia (Jaiz 2005: 20, 64). Even worse, in Jaiz's book, is being supportive of the idea of *jihad nusantra,* meaning that the struggle for national development counts as a form of jihad. If there were any doubt about Jaiz's religio-political orientation, none remain after his scathing attacks on Muslims who are also Indonesian nationalists. He is clearly influenced by Sayyid Qutb, the father of modern Islamic radicalism, who argued that all forms of nationalism were blasphemy or attributing an equal to God (Woodward 2001), which suggest a dialectal commonality between them. Harono's position concerning the Indonesian state clearly marks him as a fringe author. However, he is not alone; Islamist groups have capitalized on society's frustrations with government corruption to argue for a syari'ah state.

If anyone on PTAIN campuses might agree with Jaiz's accusations it would those be those associated with PKS, DDII, and other Islamist groups; but none concur. At most, they allow the possibility of apostates on other campuses but deny any on their campus and reject the label when asked about specific individuals on other campuses, such as Azyumardi Azra. I asked a PKS affiliated faculty member, what would make someone an apostate. He said that it would take a clear statement of rejection or a lapse in ritual practice (*ibadah*). He makes a distinction between apostasy and liberalism and holds that being liberal on worldly issues does not make someone an apostate. Imam Suprayogo, the rector of UIN Malang, similarly limits apostasy to converting to another religion, "There are no IAIN professors who have become Christian or Hindu" (interview, February 2009).

Reaction to Accusations

Saeed suggests that PTAIN faces hostility mainly from "scripturalists" for historical reasons, namely the Soeharto regime's agenda to use IAIN to create an apolitical Islam in service to the state (Saeed 1999: 178). As of yet none of the alleged apostates have met their untimely demise. As long as that remains the case, which is most likely, the culture wars about Islamic higher education remains at the level of discourse. Such concerns and criticisms are not new. Martin van Bruinessen suggest that graduates of UIN Syarif Hidyatullah in Ciputat, Jakarta, sometimes refer to themselves as followers of the Ciputat maddhab, suggesting a position neither quite in line with either Muhammadiyah or NU when it comes to relating to traditional Islamic scholarship. Further, UIN Jakarta (Ciputat) has been seen as a threat to conservatives and fundamentalists for over 35 years (2006: 193).

There are three basic reactions to the apostasy accusations. The first is to dismiss them as the ravings of an uneducated lunatic. They are called trash and even "bullshit" (using the English term). The arguments are dismissed as lacking an understanding of Islam, the goals of higher education, and even the facts about what is happening on PTAIN campuses. Not surprisingly this reaction comes from those who have been accused of apostasy by name or those who take positions similar to those who have been directly accused.

The second response is to deny that there any true apostates on PTAIN campuses. The ways to do this include defining apostasy narrowly as converting to another religion or becoming an atheist. Another approach is to defend freedom of thought both in an academic setting and in Islam in general. People who take this position frequently disagree with the positions taken by their more liberal colleagues but are unwilling to engage in *takfiri* (calling others *kafir*, or unbelievers). However, they also defend academic freedom and the right for people to make arguments and for others to judge for themselves, which distinguishes them from those who take the third response.

The third response also refuses to call anyone an unbeliever or a murtad. However, it calls into question the value of academic freedom. Those who take this position argue that all PTAIN academics should first and foremost position themselves as Muslims, and must make all their arguments based on Quran and Hadith, or at least make them all consistent with Quran and Hadith. They even argue that if the findings of social science are inconsistent with the revealed text, they must be subordinated to scripture. They do not argue that the "liberals" are apostates but suggest that it might be best that they no longer serve as IAIN teachers if they want to base their arguments on social science perspectives. It is telling, however, that even the most "liberal" IAIN academics consider themselves and their opinions as consistent with the sacred sources, thus suggesting that those who take this third response are taking narrow interpretations of the sacred texts and insisting that all their colleagues follow suit.

Azyumardi Azra argues that Jaiz is not interested in dialogue or understanding. Azra says that similar accusations came from people associated with Dewan Dakwah (DDII). He related the story of encountering a DDII leader whose child graduated from the psychology program at UIN Jakarta. Azra asked the DDII leader if his child had become an apostate yet and the leader just stood there dumbfounded. Azra said that certain people just cannot stand seeing Muslim organizations succeed if they do not profit from it themselves and that is the reason for these accusations. Azra suggests that Jaiz has had no impact. It is possible that Azra underestimates the impact of the accusations. Either that, or the impact is greater outside of Jakarta. At the very least, Jaiz keys into issues and concerns that are current in society, or to use the analogy employed here, he is using a particular religious dialect that is understood by a particular community. I had a doctoral student in my class at IAIN North Sumatra who made a point of taking me on almost anything I said. His behavior was explained to me as being due to the fact that he was a Friday preacher and that it was important that he maintain certain appearances. Since, "sitting pretty in front of Orientalists" is one of the signs of apostasy; he was making sure that no one remembered him "sitting pretty" in my class.

Another example of how Jaiz has had an impact is the case of a professor from a small IAIN campus on one of the outer islands who faced accusations of being an Orientalist pet after studying abroad. The accusations were not direct attacks per se but someone had called for the removal from the faculty anyone with exclusively Western graduate training. In order to shut down these criticisms, he completed his doctorate at UIN Jakarta. Before going abroad he had completed all the coursework, and only had the dissertation left. The UIN dissertation was on the same research material but was written to the expectations held for a UIN dissertation: less social science references and more Quran and Hadith quotations. When I related this story to Azra, he dismissed the idea that my friend did this because of apostasy accusations, although he did not really know the reasons, but remembered advising him that since he only had the dissertation to complete that he should do so. It is likely both versions of the story are true. Azra made a practical recommendation and my friend accepted it for the reasons he gave me.

A former dean of the *Fakultas Ushuluddin* in Yogya, which Jaiz says is the center of these alleged problems, said that they Jaiz's ideas are being consumed (*dimakan*) by many people, especially those in pesantren and this has impacted recruitment efforts. Another professor asserts that she needs to position herself carefully; she said that whenever she wants to do an event, she has to start by saying that she is from UIN from the fakultas of *Tasfir-Hadith* and that she was raised in a pesantren. She leaves out entirely her time in the United States. She simply says that she was educated through Madrasah Aliyah in pesantren and then went to a larger pesantren, namely IAIN, in a "pesantren" department, namely Tasfir-Hadith.

The differences of opinion around IAIN are much more than that; they are reflections of differences in expression much like dialects of a language. The last place this should take us is a return to a Geertzian mode of analysis of the forms of Islam. There is no benefit in imagining *abangan, santri,* and *priyayi* nor in Wahabi, Sufi, Muhammadiyah, or NU dialects and stopping there. If we use those labels to explain behavior, then this approach has not moved us forward. The labels may be useful in identifying major dialect families, but to really understand the dynamics involved in various expressions, we will need to understand the ways in which the variation in religious practice is affected by a number of factors and how expressions of religion can be diglossic, polysemic, and even idiosyncratic. I develop my linguistic analogy further in the Theoretical Epilogue to help address some of these difficulties.

Chapter 3

Becoming Universities: Old Traditions, New Directions

In November 2008, I was back at the Annual Conference of Islamic Studies (ACIS) this time in Palembang, South Sumatra. The event was just three days before the inauguration of a new governor. The incoming governor gave a speech on the second day of the conference. During this speech he said that he wanted the local State Islamic Institute, Institut Agama Islam Negeri (IAIN) Raden Fateh to become the best. Immediately following the speech, a representative of this campus thanked the governor for his commitment for Raden Fateh to become a Universitas Islam Negeri (UIN). This hope was expressed despite the fact that there was a moratorium on IAINs converting to universities.[1] The transformation of six IAIN into full-fledged universities since the late 1990s excited and captivated the imaginations of many IAIN instructors and staff. Many IAIN faculty expressed concern about the declining impact IAIN had on Indonesian society. Without expanding the programs beyond the traditional religious fakultas, they fear that State Islamic Higher Education will lose its relevancy. To answer the question of where PTAINs are going, we must consider from whence they came. The basic structure of any Perguruan Tinggi Agama Islam Negeri (PTAIN) is said to be modeled after Al-Azhar University in Cairo.

Many of IAIN's founders had studied at Al-Azhar, which has a one thousand year history (Kinoshita 2009: 1; Zeghal 2007: 108). Al-Azhar is a preeminent institution of Islamic scholarship, one which is subject neither to the Ayatollahs of Iran nor to the royal Saudi family. Malika Zeghal argues that Al-Azhar seeks to build a public Islam related to an Egyptian national identity (2007: 109). This role expands beyond Egyptian society—during the controversy around the banning of the headscarf in France, the Mufti of Al-Azhar declared that, to avoid difficulty, Muslim women in France do not have to wear the headscarf (Samuel 2003). The three oldest faculties (comparable to the Indonesian fakultas), all male, are located by the Al-Azhar mosque in old Cairo (Zeghal 2007: 110) are the most popular for Indonesian men. Indonesian women are exclusively enrolled in the Dirasat al Islamiyah faculty on the new campus in Nasr City.

Because Indonesians have studied at Al-Azhar for a long time, the structure of IAIN is said to have been deliberately modeled after Al-Azhar and included a Fakultas of Syari'ah (Islamic Law), Adab (Islamic civilization and history), and Ushuluddin (Islamic theology and comparative religion). However, as Meuleman notes, this was not mere imitation. Indonesia sought to deal with local needs by adding a Fakultas of Tarbiyah (Islamic Education) and a department, and later a Fakultas of Dakwah (Missions). Meuleman suggests that the current curriculum and structure of Al-Azhar has changed from the one that first inspired IAIN; it now has large fakultas in nonreligious subjects (Meuleman 2002: 296). However, that assessment ignores the fact that by 1961, Al-Azhar had nonreligious schools such as medicine and engineering. The partial modeling is in part due to the fact that none, or nearly none, of the Indonesians studying at Al-Azhar enroll in the nonreligious schools. Even when writing about Al-Azhar University, Indonesians tend to ignore the Nasr City campus where the more secular programs and the religious-oriented program which admits women are located, and simply refer to the campus next to the old Al-Azhar mosque, which at one point in history was the entirety of this educational institution (Burhanudin 2008: 13). The omission of nonreligious fakultas in the original IAIN charter suggests two issues for further consideration. First, it may be that connections and continuities with the pesantren community may have as much to do with the original structure of the IAIN as modeling after Al-Azhar. Second, the transition of IAIN to UIN actually brings the institutions closer in structure and purpose to Al-Azhar. Kinoshita argues that while it is inappropriate to suggest that the PTAIN system as a whole is Al-Azharized, she suggests that institutionally it has been, while in practical terms it has not (2009: 22). I am not certainly what she means by this distinction nor am I convinced that even that it is true. Only the Jakarta campus has the *Dirasat Islamiyah* faculty. Further, it seems that the addition of nonreligious fakultas is more related to being on equal footing with other Indonesian universities than trying to be like Al-Azhar.

Adian Husaini, an Islamist author and speaker, states that the presidential order that established the PTAIN system was intended to further the agenda of the Jakarta Charter (2008: 54). Husaini highlights the presidential order's goal to enrich the Muslim community in order to make the argument that the primary function of IAIN is to strengthen the practice of syari'ah. Husaini concludes that the intention, purpose, and spirit of those involved in the founding of IAIN was to create knowledgeable and faithful Muslim intellectuals and ulama. He argues that the PTAIN system was never intended to create faith-neutral scholars as is common in the West (2008: 56). Many, if not most, IAIN faculty would disagree with Husaini; not about the original purpose of IAIN as much as the idea that it should maintain that purpose. They would argue that IAIN must adjust its curriculum and even its vision and mission to meet the needs of Indonesian Muslims in an ever-changing world. Further, other scholars suggest that the establishment of the PTAIN system and the subsequent enrichment of the Muslim community was part of the military's strategy to counter the growing influence of communists in the waning years of the Sukarno regime (Kinoshita 2009:6).

History and Trends

For Abdullah Saeed, a missing component of the original IAIN curriculum was any critical, social, or historical study of Islam. He argues that this had led to the jealous preservation of "purity" of Islamic scholarship and hostility toward Western modes for the study of Islam, at least on the part of some faculty. Soon, IAIN introduced a new element, the inclusion of the humanities and the social sciences. In time, this allowed for the development of critical studies of Islam and the Muslim community (Saeed 1999). The general outline of these changes as well as some of the specifics can be traced to the efforts and ideas of Mukti Ali and Harun Nasution. The early IAIN efforts were influenced by Fazlur Rahman, the Pakistani scholar who taught at the University of Chicago Divinity

School until his death in 1988 (Kraince 2008: 350). Rahman defined the modernization of Islamic education as,

> rendering it capable of creative Islamic productivity in all field of intellectual endeavor together with the serious commitment to Islam that the madrasa system has generally been unable to impart (Rahman 1984: 134).

Fazlur Rahman briefly mentioned the PTAIN system as a praiseworthy experiment in creating exactly this kind of institution (1984: 126). The question of how best to study Islam is a debate that was not settled with Nasution and remains part of the ongoing discourse. Even in situations where the faculty members are in agreement that Islamic studies must move beyond doctrinaire review and a faith-based approach, it sometimes proves difficult to get students, even at a graduate level to do so.

Another important influence on the shape of IAIN was the Institute of Islamic Studies at McGill University in Montreal. From 1951 to 1963, it was headed by Wilfred Cantwell Smith who insisted that Islam could modernize itself and that Orientalism should become a "project in intercultural communications" instead of an "essentializing project of knowledge" (Webster 2009: 92). Cantwell Smith's successors continued his quest to act as a modernizing agent for the Islamic world. David Webster observes that this effort was most effective in Indonesia (2009: 97). Over the years, hundreds of IAIN faculty members have studied at McGill.

The first Indonesians arrived at McGill in 1955–1956. Mukti Ali was among the first to earn his master's degree. Mukti Ali returned home with the charge to develop comparative religious studies at the IAINs—which was aimed at both developing religious studies as an academic field as well as to foster greater religious tolerance (Kersten 2009: 94). Later, as minister of religion (1971–1976), Mukti Ali developed a "Weberian" policy in which all religions contributed to the socioeconomic growth of the nation (Kersten 2009: 94; Steenbrink 1999: 285). He sought to reform Islamic education by revamping the underlying values of the pesantren. This policy lead to the kind of curriculum reforms that allow pesantren to actively engage development and globalization (Lukens-Bull 2005) and to become a seedbed for "hybrid" Muslim intellectuals (Kersten 2009: 95; Raharjo 1985; Rumadi 2008). Mukti Ali appointed his fellow IIS graduate, Harun Nasution as the rector of IAIN Jakarta (Webster 2009: 99), who became easily one of the most influential figures in the history of the PTAIN system (Meuleman 2000: 288).

Harun Nasution was born to a kyai (traditional Islamic leader) who sent him to a Dutch primary school and later to an Islamic secondary school. Nasution pursued more education in Mecca and Cairo. At Al-Azhar, he studied a form of Islam he considered modern and rational. When Harun's mentor, Mohammad Rasjidi was hired by Cantwell Smith in 1958, Harun followed him to McGill. Harun earned his master's in 1965 and his doctorate in 1968 (Webster 2009: 98–99) with a dissertation titled "The Place of Reason in Abduh's Theology, Its Impact on His Theological System and Views." Nasution's emphasis on rationality in theological thought was not an end in itself but seen as the foundation for advancement in science and technology (Meuleman 2000: 288). He was quite contented at McGill and said that he found an Islam unlike that taught at Al-Azhar (Husaini 2008: 59). Harun said that his time at McGill strongly influenced his view of Islam (Webster 2009: 99). For some critics, like Adian Husaini, Harun's engagement with Western scholarship about Islam was a shortcoming and not a strength (2008: 58). However, for most professors currently affiliated with the State Islamic Higher Education System, Nasution was, and is, a model *par excellence* for Muslim scholarship, in his breadth and depth, even if they do not concur with his conclusions.

Harun returned to Indonesia to become the rector of IAIN Jakarta (1973–1984), where he instituted a number of curricular reforms that were soon adopted across the PTAIN system. More precisely, he was tasked by the Minister of Religious Affairs, Mukti Ali, to reform Islamic higher education as part of his "Weberian" project to have all religions serve in the socioeconomic development of the country (Kersten 2011: 95). Some of Harun's former students said that his purpose was to move Islamic Studies (*Kajian Islam*) from a review of doctrine, such as is found in pesantren, to being a fully developed academic field of study. After Nasution finished his term as rector, he founded the graduate programs at several PTAIN campuses.

Given Nasution's importance, it is useful to summarize some of his key ideas, particularly as found in his book *Islam Ditinjau dari Berbagai Aspek (Islam from Different Perspectives*, 1977).

Nasution promoted a framework in which Islam was seen as a culture and a civilization as well as a religion. The framework distinguished between absolute Islam, which is defined as Quran and Hadith and is eternally true and cannot be modified, and relative Islam, which can be modified as circumstances change and includes philosophy, Sufism, and "deviant" perspectives (Cone 2002: 58; Kersten 2009: 95; Saeed 1999). Meuleman (2000: 288–289) identifies four aspects of Nasution's perspective. The first is that the primary difference between Islamic theologies is not on basic tenets, but on the relative place of reason and revelation in knowing these tenets. Second, unlike the compartmentalized specialization Dhofier ascribed to the pesantren community (1999: 8), Nasution took a more holistic approach to Islam. The third feature of Nasution's approach, according to Meuleman, was his effort to move beyond the exclusivity and defensiveness of the Muslim community. Finally, for Nasution education was for the growth and development of the Muslim community (Meuleman 2000: 289).

Nasution's book *Islam Ditinjau dari Berbagai Aspek* was quickly criticized by other Muslim intellectuals, such as Muhammad Rasjidi, a PhD from Sorbonne, and Nasution's former mentor (Saleh 2001: 201). Rasjidi wrote a special report for the Ministry of Religious Affairs (MORA) opposing the use of Nasution's text. Despite this, it became a standard text at nearly all PTAIN campuses for decades. Rasjidi objected to Nasution's approach on the grounds that it could weaken one's belief (Saleh 2001: 201). Rasjidi's objections were not given much credence. Adian Husaini attributes this either to an outright endorsement of Harun's views or a gross incompetence on the part of the ministry (2008: 57).

Harun's former students and others who knew him describe a much more complex man than the single-dimensional Neo-Mutazalite that he is often depicted as being. He was "very Sufi" according to his former students and even belonged to a Sufi brotherhood (*tarekat*). In fact, Harun is credited with instituting and requiring two fields previously "forbidden" (or at least, absent) at IAIN: philosophy and *tassawuf* (Sufism).

Several components in the Nasution curriculum continue to have significant presence on IAIN campuses; his influence is everywhere in the system (Kartanegara 2010: 107). The first is freedom of religious thought, particularly the ability to study all the *maddhab*. This academic freedom even extended to the margins of Islam including the so-called heretical rationalism of the Mutazilates, the sometimes excessive mysticism of Sufism and the less orthodox views of Ibn Arabi (Kersten 2009: 95; Saeed 1999: 188). More than just studying different approaches, Azra argues that this aspect of Nasution's curriculum encouraged students to learn different perspectives within Islam's scholarly traditions and taught them that such studies did not oblige them to follow the perspectives which they studied (Azra 2011: 51). This approach was a key reason given by Malaysian students studying at IAIN North Sumatra as to why they prefer to study in Indonesia rather than on clearly nicer campuses in Malaysia. The second component was paying greater attention to historical and sociological approaches (Azra 2011: 51). As a consequence, an increasing number of IAIN faculty were sent to Western countries to take graduate degrees; this was especially true when Munawir Sjadzali led MORA from 1983 to 1994 (Feener 2007: 138–139; Kinoshita 2009: 7). Sjadzali, who had served for a time as an instructor at McGill, held up Mukti Ali, Harun Nasution, and Muhammad Rasjidi as examples to be emulated, and therefore pushed for intensifying the practice of sending IAIN instructors to the West for graduate education (Kasdi 2003: 3). We will return to a discussion of the impact of such programs in the next chapter. For now, it is sufficient to note that Western academic approaches to religion and culture entered the PTAIN system through these Western graduates and fundamentally changed the very questions being asked. No longer were Islamic studies exclusively concerned with eternal truths but also became concerned with local wisdom (*kearifan lokal*). The third change was a general introduction course in Islamic Studies required for all students. It is no longer required but it figures into the debates about what Islamic Studies is and should be. Overall, the reforms introduced under Nasution aimed to have PTAINs "become institutes for the development of religious sciences, rather than centers of Islamic doctrine" (Meuleman 2002: 286).

From Religious Institutes to Full Universities

Starting in the early years of this century, several IAIN transformed from institutes to universities by adding at least two nonreligious fakultas. The transition of IAIN to UIN may have a wide range of motivations ranging from dropping enrollments and employability concerns for graduates, to concerns about graduates of "secular" universities lacking a moral compass. Azyumardi Azra, the rector of UIN Jakarta as it made the transition from being an IAIN, argues that this process started in the 1970s but the Suharto regime, in part, hindered this process. The liberalization after the fall of Suharto that contributed to the proliferation of political parties also allowed greater autonomy for PTAIN, which gave momentum to the movement to create Islamic universities (2011: 43).

In the 1980s, while more and more IAIN faculty members were studying in the West, some IAIN fakultas started undertaking a wider mandate. During this time, five new majors opened in the Dakwah Fakultas at IAIN Bandung including Islamic Counseling, Communication and Islamic Broadcasting, and Journalism. This allowed students to have broader training and skills development compared to the older Dakwah curriculum (Kinoshita 2009).

Amin Abdullah said that the vision for UIN Yogya under his administration was not solely his own. When the Yogya campus first became a UIN, he gathered 200 faculty members to discuss the vision for the "new" university. Out of that meeting came very clearly a desire for integration (*perpaduan*) between Islam (*keislaman*) and science (*keilmuan*) to yield a particular kind of civilization (*perabadan*). He was very clear that this vision came from the faculty, who designed the curriculum around this vision, so that it could actually be achieved and be more than a statement. Amin argued that to achieve this "marriage" of science and Islam, what is needed is far more than interdisciplinary or multidisciplinary approaches but rather the "interconnectedness of disciplines" (he used English).

Yudian Wahyudi, dean of Syari'ah at UIN Yogya in 2008 felt that the change from IAIN to UIN was an absolute necessity. By becoming a full university and adding nonreligious programs Muslims can be better integrated in the nation, whereas the previous limited focus of PTAIN marginalized graduates. UIN graduates on the other hand, can build bridges with graduates of secular public universities. This greater integration also heads off extremism. Yudian asserts that no PTAIN graduates, and certainly no UIN graduates, become extremists. He asserts this is because they are taught to feel responsible for nation-building and economic development, as part of their duties as a Muslim as well as a college graduate. Yudian said that the purpose is to prepare quality people who will enter the system but not as opposition, but as an integral part of the system (interview, September 2008). This may reflect a shift how Islamic education positions itself vis-à-vis the state. In the 1990s, some educators expressed the specific desire to use government-recognized Islamic education as a way of placing opponents of the Suharto regime into the system (Lukens-Bull 1997: 209).

Opinions about these changes are mixed both on and off campus. On UIN campuses, many if not most instructors support the changes, but some from the original religiously oriented fakultas are concerned that over time, that the new, "secular" fakultas will provide too much competition and will eventually drive their faculty out of existence. The logic is essentially "by giving students a choice, they might not choose us, so we should not give the students a choice." Those opposed to the change find that justifying it based on the changing needs for the Muslim community to be disingenuous and that such needs (like for rural doctors) are being met adequately already.

On campuses that had not yet become universities in 2008, there was an almost desperate desire to do so. This is well illustrated by the excited response to the incoming governor's announcement mentioned at the top of this chapter. However, MORA had put a freeze on new UIN and there was a sense that the success of these institutions in integrating Islam and general sciences still needed to be evaluated. Off campus, some are concerned about the quality of the nonreligious programs and conclude that at least for the time being these are not the best places to pursue general topics. As part of becoming a UIN, in addition to adding nonreligious fakultas, the original (religious) fakultas had to open up to more general aspects related to their field.

At UIN Jakarta, the traditional fakultas have created awkward names in order to accommodate a wider mission. The Faculty of Adab became the Faculty of Adab and Humanities and to its original curriculum on Islamic History and Arabic Language and Literature added Library Sciences and English Language and Literature. Ushuluddin became Ushuluddin and Philosophy by adding comparative religion and broader philosophical perspectives to its curriculum. Tarbiyah added teaching sciences so that it became the somewhat redundantly named Tarbiyah and *Keguruan*, since both the Arabic and the Indonesian can be translated as "Pedagogy." Syari'ah and Hukum is another fakultas with a redundant name. The faculty members and I would joke it was the Faculty of Law and Law, translating each word from its original language into English. This awkward name reflects the transition process. It was not possible to keep the old name; keeping an exclusively Arabic name would have required that they become part of *Dirasat Islamiyah* (Islamic Studies), the only faculty to teach in Arabic and to have an exclusively Arabic name. On the other hand, there would have been too much resistance to go straight to Fakultas Hukum (Faculty of Law); it would have been taken as signifying the abandonment of the traditional foundations of the faculty. The double name also reflects different fields of study: state law (*hukum*) and Islamic law (syari'ah), and implicitly supports a continuing separation of the legal traditions in Indonesia. This by itself can be a sore spot for some of the more conservative elements in Indonesian society.

At other UIN campuses, name changes were being debated for the older fakultas to reflect developments within them. Sometimes this leads to conflict not unfamiliar to American academics. Proposed names suggested overlapping, even competing areas of interest. For example, at the Yogya campus, the Ushuluddin (Theology) Fakultas wanted to become Ushuluddin, Budaya, dan Masyarakat (Theology, Culture, and Society) whereas the Adab (Islamic Civilizations) Fakultas wished to become Adab, Ilmu Budaya, dan Sejarah (Islamic Civilizations, Culture Studies, and History). In 2009, the dean of Ushuluddin told me that the overlaps are more in name than in mission or context; Ushuluddin uses the term culture to mean local culture in a broadly anthropological sense, whereas Adab uses it in the culture studies, literary criticism sense. However, the various deans are concerned with possible, or even perceived, overlap. There seems to be local autonomy in working out the new designations; MORA is staying out of the process, except perhaps for final approval. In the end, they became *Ushuluddin, Studi Agama, dan Pemikiran Islam* (Theology, Religious Studies, and Islamic Thought) and *Adab dan Ilmu Budaya* (Islamic Civilizations and Culture Studies).

Debates on Campus

One faculty member in the Fakultas Tafsir-Hadith at UIN Yogya was one of the few UIN instructors opposed to the reforms who would speak with me. He disagreed with the transformation because the religious fields would be marginalized. He was also concerned that the students who come to UIN to study in the general fields are those who did not have the academic qualifications to be accepted at more established universities. He questioned why PTAIN don't simply mange smaller programs with deliberate intent rather than be overly concerned with large numbers. He held up the example of a seminary or divinity school in the United States[2] that only admits a few students and every department remains rather small. He argued that popularity should not determine educational strategic planning (interview, January 29, 2009). A counter argument was made by Yudian Wahyudi, dean of the Syari'ah Faculty at UIN Yogya in 2009, argued that in order for the Muslim community to be fully integrated into the nation that IAIN needed to become UIN. If not, the Muslim community will continue to be marginalized (interview, January 30, 2009). Komaruddin Hidayat acknowledged that some people question whether becoming an UIN was an advance or a decline for UIN Jakarta. There is a fear that religious scholarship will be lost and the general fields of study will dominate the university. He argued that the fears are based on understanding the mission as being the creation of ulama, but, he argued there is a limited need for Islamic scholars. Further, there are other institutions capable of creating ulama, such as pesantren and madrasah. He said,

> Everyone who studies here, even those in non-religious fields, receive basic education in Islam as well as Islamic character development. So we can say to parents, your child can come here to become ulama or to possess skill and potential and still have belief and faith (*berkhlak dan beriman*). What I see as of now is that the children of *kyai* often want to become modern academics and still have a expertise, a character, and a view point that is Muslim; but they don't want to become *ulama* (Hidayat 2008: 91).

He wants to be able to say to parents "your child can come here to become ulama or to gain skills and knowledge in a general field and maintain belief and faith" (interview, February 2009).

In regard to the process of IAIN becoming full universities, Katimin, a graduate professor at the IAIN in Medan, said that they should not force students to pursue religious majors. He acknowledges the common fear that religious programs will become less important. Rather than fearing this, Katimin argued that IAIN and the wider community must accept this as inevitable. Furthermore, he argued that the traditional programs do not adequately prepare graduates for work outside the limited number of jobs in government offices and schools. The focus of PTAIN, therefore, should be on ethical guidance and the creation of a "moral mind." The traditional programs should become limited access programs. Katimin is advocating an approach that was taken by the government curricular madrasah in the 1990s. One consequence of that change in the 1990s was that madrasah graduates were better prepared for science and general higher education than for Islamic higher education (Kasdi 2003: 3), and more interested in continuing in similar subjects at PTAIN (Azra 2011: 45).

In May 2009, I was again an invited plenary speaker, this time at a regional conference in Jambi, South Sumatera. A few months earlier I had completed the bulk of the research for this book but was still reflecting on how best to interpret my data. Over an official dinner at the Mayoral (*Bupati*) residence, I had a discussion with a Muhummadiyah official and a graduate student from IAIN Jambi. The student repeated the common concern that the new programs draw students away from the older religion-focused departments. In the course of this conversation, I discovered that at IAIN and UIN, each faculty must be financially independent. The intensity of the opposition I had seen, finally seemed to have a rational foundation. Decreasing enrollments threaten the health of programs and the job security of faculty and staff in those programs. The Muhummadiyah official said that this was not the case at universities run by his organization, which have been mandated to keep the religion programs whether or not they have many students and to subsidize them from the more popular programs.

An important episode that illustrates part of the debates is the tale of IAIN Sunan Ampel in Surabaya, which is an interesting counterexample. It was offered the opportunity to become one of the first UIN. After a discussion with the faculty, the administration, and the community, the consensus was that becoming UIN would risk losing the campus' historical basis in the pesantren tradition, which is strongest in East Java. In the decision-making process, local kyai opposed the change and wanted IAIN Sunan Ampel to remain true to its roots. Similar pressure gave UIN Malang its particular form and focus with an on-campus pesantren and mandatory Arabic studies for all students; remaining true to those roots and still becoming a university.

Abd Ala, the first vice rector at IAIN Surabaya in 2008, related to me how Effendi Ghozali at the University of Indonesia asked him why so many IAIN wanted to be UIN. Abd Ala suggested that it was simply the desire to follow the trend. He also said that a few, like Jakarta and Yogya, really had the vision and mission and needed to develop in that way, but that the rest were just being opportunistic (interview, April 30, 2009).

In late 2009, Abd Ala was elected rector and shortly thereafter, even before he was formally installed, he asked Dr. Muzakki, an Australian educated professor to lead a committee to discuss (and later write the proposal for) becoming an UIN. Ala did not change his position; his point in early 2009 was that in order to become an UIN, an IAIN campus must have very clear reasons and a well-articulated vision and mission for doing so. In his vision of UIN Sunan Ampel, Ala sees Islamic Studies remaining the core mission but wished to add the mission of enriching Islamic Studies with other disciplines. He was clear that Islamic Studies needs to maintain a position of prestige on campus and even to have greater prestige than general studies. A key way to do this, he argued, will be to increase funding for scholarships for students in the traditional core faculty.

One Western-educated professor who opposes this transformation feels that Islamic Studies in Indonesia is already dying and by becoming a UIN, Sunan Ampel will contribute to its demise. He says that those who favor becoming a UIN point to UIN Malang's enrollments being close to 14,000 whereas Surabaya's are in the 7,000s. Since Malang was once a branch campus of Surabaya, this might be a matter of pride. He points out that in the last decade or so (2000–2012), IAIN Sunan Ampel has grown from about 2,500 students to its current size. He is also concerned that the nonreligious fakultas will give rise to radicalizations on campus. This concern might have a reasonable foundation—the Science and Technology Faculty in Yogya is known for students and professors affiliated with International Islamist organizations Hizbut Tahrir Indonesia (HTI; Hizbut al-Tahrir) and PKS (Muslim Brotherhood).[3]

This is a case where religious dialect does not determine opinion; a commitment of a progressive vision for Islam and Indonesia does not necessarily mean total agreement with the transformation of IAIN into universities. He does not object to some campuses becoming UIN, his position was simply that there is a need for both kinds of institutions. This demonstrates the value of using the dialect analogy and not parties and organizations; why it is important not to let the analogy devolve into broad categories used to explain behavior whether we use Geertz's tripartite divisions, more current ones like Progressive, Islamist, Western-educated, or even organizations like HTI, PKS, *Nahdlatul Ulama* (NU), or Muhammadiyah. This professor is in agreement with conservatives on this issue, but not on any others.

In the IAIN Sunan Ampel case, the change is not coming from the outside but once the decision was made to become UIN, those who had been opposed felt that they had no choice but to support the policy. Yudian, at the Yogya campus, associated some of the antagonism about IAIN becoming UIN with traditional NU and Muhummadiyah divisions. On the one hand, he argued that in the general discourse, UIN is more associated with Reformists (e.g., Muhummadiyah and Himpunan Mahasiswa Indonesia [HMI]) and IAIN is more typically associated with Classicalists, or NU. This is because of the association of NU with pesantren and hence a greater focus on religious rather than general education. On the other hand, he argued that Muhammadiyah's educational system has been better integrated with the state and general education system. He suggested that some of the critiques come from NU people because they fear it will marginalize them. In direct contradiction with Yudian's assessment, other NU people on some campuses saw Muhummadiyah people as reactionary and not very open-minded toward multidisciplinary approaches in the study of Islam. However, most faculty members self-identifying with each group have nothing but positive things to say about each other. Some of these rumblings might reflect interpersonal conflicts[4] rather than a significant return to the historical rivalry between these groups.

Learning from Others

The proposed UIN Sunan Ampel in Surabaya attempts to directly address some of the concerns that have arisen from the other campuses and even openly admits to learning from their missteps. When the other campuses became UIN, it was common for the new programs to be made from whole cloth and hire all new faculty members. This gave rise to a feeling that new fakultas were not part of the campus community. The argument that Dr. Muzakki gives is that IAIN Sunan Ampel is already a university and so it is just a matter of adjusting the name and the organization to match the reality. Of the three proposed new fakultas, two are being created out of existing programs. The Faculty of Economics and Business will be created by moving the Islamic Economics department out of its current home in the Fakultas of Syari'ah. To it will be added Islamic banking and Islamic accounting. To offset its loss, the Fakultas of Syari'ah will add a program in philanthropy (*Zakat* and *Waqf*) management and in secular law (*Ilmu Hukum*). The School of Political and Social Sciences will be made up entirely by moving old programs from their original homes: political science from Ushuluddin and sociology, communication, and psychology from Dakwah. Dakwah will develop a new social work program to offset its losses. The new School of Public Health will have programs in nutrition, midwifery, and nursing and will have to draw almost on new hire. However, the likely candidate for dean is a woman currently teaching in Dakwah. By building the new schools as much as possible out of existing programs, the hope is to prevent the feeling that they are disconnected from the older fakultas (interview, May 2012).

Other concerns that have arisen on the first UIN campuses include that students in the nonreligious schools lack key competencies expected of graduates from what were once (and still considered by many to be) institutions of Islamic knowledge and leadership. Another concern is that they are easily radicalized. To deal with these concerns a number of new certificates will be required of all students in the new fakultas. The placement of these certificate programs under existing centers on the campus will also serve to keep the new students integrated with the more traditional student body. The first certificate program will be under Student Affairs office in Islamic Studies Mainstreaming. It will require 20 credits in religious studies and is designed to teach the students a moderate, tolerant Islam in line with the spirit of Sunan Ampel, and will be required of all students in the new fakultas. Students from the older fakultas are already exposed to these perspectives and material. The second certificate, also designed to fight the radicalization of the students, will require the general students to live in the campus pesantren, which will house 1,000–1,500 students initially. The close monitoring of students in the pesantren is a big part of forestalling radicalism (cf. Lukens-Bull 2001). The plan is to eventually require this of all students. The final certificate in this category is in Quranic recitation—that is being able to have a physical copy of the Quran and to read it aloud at a level expected of IAIN students. If asked, all graduates would be able to publicly recite the Quran effectively. This program will be under the supervision of the campus mosque. There will be two more certificates designed to address different kinds of competencies and will start as being required of students in all fakultas, old and new. The first is the international language certificate which will require all students to demonstrate competency in both English and Arabic by achieving a minimal performance on standardized exams.[5] It will be placed under the current language lab. The final certificate will be under the information system program and will be a collaborative effort with Microsoft, in which Microsoft will train and offer a certificate in using all aspects of Microsoft Office, blogs, and e-learning.

There is also concern that new lecturers in the general fakultas will not have the basic Islamic knowledge or Quranic recitation skills the community expects of IAIN faculty. There will be training and workshops to strengthen Islamic knowledge and in the recitation of the Quran for these instructors. The hope is that if they are asked for an impromptu prayer (*do'a*) or recitation, they will not disappoint.

Islamization of Knowledge

The Islamization of knowledge is a critical aspect of addressing how to be a truly Islamic university. To become a UIN, each campus had to add at least two nonreligious fakultas. At most UIN, at least one of the fakultas added is a hard science faculty such as science and technology, medicine, or biology. Each UIN has created its own model of how religion and science come together. UIN Malang uses the model of the tree of knowledge. In the lobby of the administration (*Rectorate*) building are two large decorative versions of this model: one in English and the other in Arabic. It is an important part of a typical campus tour to show visitors these trees. IAIN Surabaya, as part of its application for becoming an UIN, developed the model of twin towers—religion and science. UIN Bandung uses the model of a wheel of knowledge. UIN Yogya does not use a metaphor but emphasizes the importance of the integration and interrelation of science and religion. UIN Jakarta likewise does not use a metaphor but talks about the development of integrated knowledge. Regardless of the model used, the point is to find a relationship between natural sciences, social sciences, humanities, and religion. This is such an important dimension of the process of becoming a UIN that each UIN and those currently in the process convened a conference and published an edited volume that addressed different dimensions of the Islamization of knowledge (e.g., Kusama 2006, Syam 2010a; Zainuddin et al. 2004). In some cases, internationally known scholars who specialize on the relationship between science and Islam are represented in the edited volumes, including scholars from Malaysia, Iran, Pakistan, and Palestine. Some them started in the sciences and then took advanced degrees in Islamic philosophy. Yatsir Nasution, rector of IAIN Medan felt that this was easier for the exact sciences rather than the social sciences and that there are four focal points in Islamizing science: ontology, theology, epistemology, and axiology. In other words, what is the nature of science, how is it related to God (especially in concern to scientists developing God complexes), how do we know what we know, and more important the use of science, and what are its appropriate uses (interview, November 2008)?

The discourse about the Islamization of knowledge is by no means limited to Indonesia. There are at least three common approaches found outside Indonesia. The first is identified with the Malaysian philosopher, Naquib Al-Atas who founded the International Institute of Islamic Thought and Civilization (ISTAC) at the International Islamic University of Malaysia (IIUM) in Kuala Lumpur. Al-Atas argued that the Islamization of knowledge is a twofold process. The first stage is de-Westernization, which involves the isolation of scientific knowledge from the culture-bound dimensions of science specific to Western culture. The second stage is Islamization or the infusion of Islamic elements and key concepts into all branches of knowledge (Kartanegara 2010: 104). In Indonesia, this approach is associated with the journal *Islamika*, the Institute for the Study of Islamic Thought and Civilization (INSIST), a research institution in Jakarta and Universitas Islam Sultan Agung in Semarang. The second major approach is associated with Isma'il Farouqi (d. 1986), a Palestinian-American philosopher who founded the International Institute of Islamic Thought in a Washington, D.C. suburb. His approach requires the mastery of modern sciences, traditional Islamic scholarship, and Islamic scientific heritage. Next, he recommends determining the specifically Islamic relevance to modern science as well as the critical reexamination of both modern-scientific disciplines and Islamic heritage. Then modern-scientific disciplines have to be put into an Islamic framework and the distribution of the Islamized science in the form of textbooks. The point of the process is to address the problems of both the Muslim community and humanity, in general (Kartanegara 2010: 105). Farouqi sees *tauhid* as the basis for Islamized science. In general, tauhid is the idea of the unity, or oneness, of God. Both Osman Bakar of Malaysia and Nur Syam at IAIN Surabaya take up this idea of tauhid as the bases of all scholarship (Bakar 2010a: 44; Syam 2010c: 20). Syam interprets the place of the concept of tauhid in science as the idea that the omniscience and omnipotence of God should underpin all scholarship (Syam 2010c: 20, n.). This is related to the idea that God created all knowledge and that God can be known through all pursuits of knowledge. This is clearly a Sufi understanding of tauhid; the oneness of God means that God is in everything including everything that science can study.

The third major approach is associated with the Iranian Muslim philosopher Sayyed Hossein Nasr and his close friend and disciple Osman Bakar. Nasr argued for the reassertion of the immutable principles of Islam and their application to modern knowledge. He argued that authentic and contemporary Islamic education must neither reject modern disciplines nor surrender to modern theories. Nasr also subscribes to the idea of tauhid in science and argues that knowledge cannot be separated from the sacred because everything has a profound religious charter; every type of knowledge is created by God (Kartanegara 2010: 106). Bakar seeks to underpin science with Islamic values and spirituality, very similar to the efforts in pesantren in the mid-1990s (Lukens-Bull 2005). Bakar says that to find such a foundation there is a need to see religion as an "ally" of science. However, he argues that even Muslim scientists and technologists see religion as unnecessary and any attempt to bring science back in as a backward move. For him, this is something that needs to be corrected (2010: 38).

Within Indonesia, an important approach has been the integration of science and religion closely tied to Harun Nasution. In this view, science is universal, objective, and rational, therefore there is no reason why there cannot be an open and "dialogical" integration of science and religion. Kartanegara says this approach engages an uncritical acceptance of secular sciences. If this was true of Nasution, and I am not convinced that it was, it is certainly not true of his former students. However, we can see the influence of this approach in the models adopted by several UIN most explicitly Yogya and Jakarta.

Another approach I have seen in both Malaysia and Indonesia is referred to as "Ayatisasi," or the quoting of relevant Quranic verses and Hadith to justify modern science. It is perhaps the most popular form of the Islamization of knowledge and is associated with UIN Malang, Bogor Agricultural Institute (Institut Pertanian Bogor), and MORA. Kartanegara says that the approach does not criticize science but seeks to justify it. Therefore Islam is not antiscience. However, if something found in science cannot be justified by religious texts, it must be rejected. Many books using this approach have been written in many fields including biology, mathematics, physics, and others (Kartanegara 2010: 108). If on the one hand this approach uses the Quran to justify science, on the other hand, it also uses science to "prove" that Islam is true. Sometimes this kind of work devolves into facile statements that affirm that the Quran knew the health risks of dog and pork meat before science could verify it (Qamar and Raza, n.d.). This is, of course, not a uniquely Muslim thing. Christians also use science, including archaeology, to "prove" their faith. Both Muslim and Christians even delve into pseudo-science to make their points (Berlitz 1987; Ruse 1982; Scott and Cole 1985).

The prominent Muslim intellectuals who were involved with the PTAIN system since near the beginning and into the twenty-first century, most notably Nurcholish Madjid, Harun Nasution, Abdul Mukti Ali, and Munawir Sjadzali encouraged the integration of secular sciences with Islamic studies. According to Azra, this was a primary motivation for creating the UIN (2011: 45). They based their advocacy and policies on the argument that the early Muslims did not make a distinction between religious and secular knowledge (Kraince 2000: 180). However, traditional dichotomization of knowledge is between the revealed knowledge (*al-'ulum al-naqliyyah*) and reasoned knowledge (*al-'ulum al-'aqaliyyah*) (Bakar 2010b: 71). Osman Bakar reviews classical divisions of the sciences to look for places where the modern dichotomous relationship can be overturned. He looks at classical scholars in both the natural and the social sciences namely Qutb al-Din al-Shirazi (1236–1311) and Ibn Khaldun (1332–1406), respectively.

Nur Syam says that the Islamization of knowledge is not easy because there are theological dimensions that sometimes cannot be approached or understood (*didekati*) empirically (2010: 20). Syam is not really interested in the relationship between Islam and the natural sciences, but is only making explicit the connections between social science/humanities and religion. In the end, he concludes that social science can make contributions to the study of religious life and that Muslim intellectuals can and must safeguard against potential dangers that may come from using the social sciences (Syam 2010c: 30). One way to find said safeguards was explained to me at UIN Malang. A PKS leaning professor drew a distinction between two kinds of knowledge: *ilmu kauniya* (discoverable knowledge) and *ilmu kauliya* (revealed knowledge). The hard sciences, biology, mathematics, and information technology are part of discoverable knowledge. Revealed knowledge includes all of the traditional disciplines at PTAIN. It is firmly based on the foundation of Quran and Hadith. What was most telling was the placement of social sciences under revealed knowledge; meaning that if data counters the teachings of doctrine, doctrine wins. For example, he argued that social science data about gender relations cannot be used to reinterpret doctrine and canon.

Research at PTAIN

Part of becoming a full-fledged university is the development of robust research agendas on the part of the professorship. Arief Furqan who was responsible for Islamic higher education circa 2004 as the Director of Islamic Higher Education and later (2008) as the Secretary of Islamic Agencies within MORA, wrote a rather dismal assessment of research at Islamic college and universities in Indonesia (n.d.). His main critique is that the research is not widely read and frequently does not benefit the populace. Whether research must have an applied dimension, as implied by Furqan, is subject to debate. Applicability is not the only measure of research productivity. Marzuki Wahid argues that IAIN must continue to make contributions to both society in general, as well as to scholarship (2003: 1). Furqan is correct; PTAIN research is not widely distributed. Each PTAIN publishes at least one journal and distributes these paper journals to other campuses. Once distributed, it is quite difficult to find copies. Furqan identifies several causes for low-quality research in the PTAIN system: (1) professors not having strong research skills, (2) not enough administrative attention to research, (3) poor support facilities, and (4) a lack of research funding. It is not possible to fully assess Furqan's evaluation; it is nearly impossible to examine the full corpus of research coming out of Islamic institutes and universities. Based on what is available it is fair to say that the quality is wide-ranging and some of it fits Furqan's assessment of being low quality. However, it is not at all a fair assessment of research at IAIN and UIN in their totality. The flagship universities at Jakarta and Yogyakarta have produced scholars and scholarship of the highest international caliber. At each are research centers known for high levels of research quality and productivity. Further, there are professors at smaller campuses who publish in international journals and who have international reputations.

Conclusion

According to some, the desire to make IAIN full-fledged universities is not new but there were many hindrances along the way (Azra 2011: 44). Certainly for some, the establishment of UIN reflects long-term goals. There are others for whom there was never any intention of become anything more than an institution for studying normative forms of Islam. The debates about whether or not the PTAIN system should engage in more than its original mandate are not only ideological in their orientation. There are real financial consequences for these changes. The financial aspects of these changes are on both sides. Opening up other fakultas can draw new students and increase enrollments. Wider mandates also allow IAIN to compete with nonreligious educational institutions. The core question is whether Indonesia still needs to produce large numbers of religious specialists, or if there is a need for a fully

Islamic but broader trained intellectual cohort. On the other side there is a concern that the new fakultas will draw students from the traditional fakultas and will negatively impact their enrollment and budgets, and thereby their ability to continue to function. The concern is while there may not be as much need for religious specialists, that there is still a need whether or not such programs are profitable or even self-sustaining.

There are other practical dimensions in the debates, namely mission creep: a sense in which PTAIN is moving away from its original purpose. According to Azra, IAIN were not and is not a seminary but rather a liberal institution that prepares teachers for madrasahs, pesantren, and public schools not only in Islamic studies but also in English, mathematics, and other nonreligious subjects (Azra 2011: 44). These concerns naturally transition the debate to the ideological elements of the debate. In the older metaphor IAIN is the fortress of Islam, to take on other tasks weakens the ability to defend traditional Islam. The arguments for change address new ways to better serve the Muslim community and to help it not be relegated to a marginal position in Indonesian society.

The ideological dimensions of the change concern the relationship between religion and science. The Muslim world has not faced a Copernican Revolution, or if it has, philosophers influenced by it have had no impact on the discourse in Indonesia. There has been a traditional dichotomization to be sure but not the sort of compartmentalization that would allow for something like Steven J. Gould's "Non-Overlapping Magisteria" (1997) which, in part, cites two papal encyclicals that basically argue that evolution does not contradict Catholic doctrine. Gould's point is that religion and science deal with two entirely different realms, or magisterium, and that there is no need to try to make them compatible in a narrow sense. Of course, Gould's model has proven controversial in the West, and while subscribed to by both religious and scientific thinkers and organizations, it is also criticized by other thinkers, both religious and scientific. The proposed solutions discussed by Muslim philosophers and intellectuals who primarily influence the debates in Indonesia, do not render to science the things of science, and to God the things of God. Instead, they assert that all knowledge belongs to God. There are different degrees of sophistication in these approaches. The most promising return to the resolution reached earlier by the pesantren milieu as expressed in the saying, *al-muḥāfaẓa ʿala al-qadīm al-ṣāliḥ wa al-akhdh bi al-jadīd al-aṣlaḥ* (keep what is old that is good and take what is new that is better). The solution is then to focus on infusing science with the ethical and moral dimension of Islam. If the core of Islam is to submit to the will of God, then to Islamize science is submit it to the will of God (to do good and prevent ill), and not the subservience of science to dogma.

Chapter 4

Splitting the *Kiblat*: Consequences of Alternate Strategies for Educating Faculty Members

Inayah Rohmaniyah, a faculty member at Universitas Islam Negeri (UIN) Yogya who teaches a course on Orientalism reported that students begin the course thinking that Westerners who study Islam have a limited number of motivations. Either they want to convert or they want to destroy Islam. At first the students are very resistant and emotional. So much so that when confronted with fact that Edward Said was a Christian, they hoist him on his own petard. They understand Said's thesis to be that Westerners study Islam to colonize Muslims and therefore Said, as a Westerner (his being born a US citizen and his US education taking precedent over his Palestinian birth and his boyhood in Cairo) must write about Islam in order to colonize Muslims. The course then focuses on the wide variety of methods, goals, and even individual scholars. Typically after two or three months, the students have come to see the complexity in Western Islamic Studies. Rohmaniyah finishes her course with a reflection paper that traces the students' intellectual journey in the class.

On Perguruan Tinggi Agama Islam Negeri (PTAIN) campuses, the long relationship with Western scholars has created a backlash. There is a deep concern about "Orientalism"—seemingly defined as a sense that the West is out to destroy Islam—and that Western scholarship about Islam was and/or is part of it. This distrust can be seen in the concerns about PTAIN faculty members studying in the West. There are two main traditions on PTAIN campuses: one comes out of Middle Eastern universities and the other comes out of Western universities (Azra 2011: 47). Starting in the 1980s, the Ministry of Religious Affairs (MORA) promoted graduate work in Religious Studies and Islamic Studies in the "West" rather than the Middle East. The idea was to send equal numbers to the Middle East and the West. The factors determining who went where included language ability. Those who were more proficient in English went to the West and those who were more proficient in Arabic went to the Middle East. Some argue that this is correlated with educational background; those with pesantren backgrounds (and hence better Arabic) were more likely to head to the Middle East (Fadhil Lubis, interview, December 15, 2008). Of course, *Pondok Moderen Gontor*, with its focus on teaching both English and Arabic yielded students who went against this trend, including Nurcholish Madjid. Further, one friend and colleague of mine started his education memorizing the Quran at an uncle's pesantren and finished with a PhD in History from UCLA. The general trend has a number of implications. First of all, if there is an association with liberalism or at least a conciliatory attitude toward the West and studying in the West, it may precede going there. There had to be some desire to study English and perhaps even a greater desire to learn English, than to gain proficiency in Arabic. Secondly, once someone has started down a track of studying in the West or in the Middle East, enough investment has been made in language and disciplinary perspective, that it is impractical to switch. This may contribute to the polarization of these two broad categories of alumni. However, it is common for high-ranking PTAIN administrators who did not study in the West to have had short study tours hosted by the United States. This indicates a clear effort on the part of Western governments to reach out to the current leadership and to bridge this perceived gap.

Further, surveys have shown that the close intellectual connection between PTAIN faculty members and other Indonesian Muslim intellectuals and the West is in part due to the fact that they felt marginalized by the Middle Eastern Islamic hegemony—a sense that Indonesian Islam is less real than Middle Eastern versions (Kraince 2000: 184). If there is a general trend that graduates from Western institutions are more liberal, and this is by no means certain, this might have to do more with self-selection rather than anything that occurs during their education. Those who are worried that the West might corrupt their faith are less likely to study in Western universities.

Fadhil Lubis, a PhD alumnus from UCLA, says that those who studied in the West returned to their campuses with the desire to make some changes. These reforms encouraged people to use rational methodology and to read books by non-Muslim scholars that significantly influenced their scholarship. This led those educated in a more traditional way and those who went to the Middle East to bemoan a loss of religious authority at PTAIN (interview, December 15, 2008). In a sense, the Nasution-Rasyidi divide has continued through the development of the system. However, it is crucial to note that some of the most important "Western" scholars inspiring Indonesian students are expatriates from Muslim countries. They include Fazlur Rahman from Pakistan who taught at the University of Chicago Divinity School until his death in 1988 and Machmud Ayoub from South Lebanon who teaches at Hartford Seminary. Therefore, the influence on Western graduates include forward-thinking Muslims in addition to Western scholars.

While some see a split orientation on PTAIN campuses, this may be overstating the point. It is clear that some graduates from the Middle East are quite progressive and even liberal. This is also seen in Malaysia where Middle East graduates strongly oppose neo-Islamist government policies (Woodward, personal communication, May 2011). A simple East/West division overlooks many levels of variation; simple logic dictates that some of the variation arises from differences in which country and at which university they studied as well as with whom they studied.

Under Minister Basyuni (2004–2009), MORA policy restricted studying Islam in the West, favoring the Middle East as the place where one should study Islam. Through the 1990s, great numbers of PTAIN faculty continued to take graduate degrees in the United States, Canada, Germany, the Netherlands, Australia, and other Western nations. This was justified by the fact that these nations offered scholarships and that similar funding was not available for PTAIN faculty from Middle Eastern countries and those that were available were administered by Islamist organizations like DDII. Some scholarships are available to study in the Middle East and yet, on any given campus, PhD (or other terminal degree) holders will comprise mostly of graduates from the flagship programs in Jakarta and Yogyakarta, which have become very credible PhD-granting institutions. This is according to plan; the flagship schools were designed as an Indonesian source of PhD holders. The remainder includes graduates from both Western and Middle Eastern universities. When we include MA graduates, there is a growing parity between these two groups. However, there has been at least one case of a professor taking a doctorate both abroad and at UIN Jakarta because each degree carries their own cache.

Kiblats

The inclusion of Western social science and humanities in the study of Islam, its texts, and practices can be thought of as a change in *kiblat*. Literally, kiblat is the direction of prayer of which there is only one, the Kabah in Mecca, although there is more than one way to calculate the kiblat. The traditional Javanese kiblat is due West. In legend, it was established by Sunan Demak, one of the *Walisongo* who placed one hand on the central pillar of the mosque he built and the other on the Kabah in Mecca. Modernists use specific compass point directions for each locale.

The term kiblat is frequently used in the pesantren community to speak about the center of spiritual leadership (Lukens-Bull 2005: 106, n. 5). In the 1990s, the debate in the pesantren was whether the kiblat of the pesantren community had moved from Tebu Ireng to another pesantren. Then, as now, kiblat is used as a metaphor. Sometimes it is used directly (cf. Zarkasyi 2008: 9) and sometimes it is used implicitly. In this current debate, the struggle over whether or not Islam is most authentically learned in the Middle East is rarely, if ever, discussed explicitly as a debate over the "kiblat." However, the passion of the debate suggests that this metaphor underpins it. To accuse someone of being an apostate (*murtad*) merely because they have studied in the West, or in the terms of the accusers "sat at the feet (*duduk manis*) of Orientalists" (Jaiz 2005: 13, 49) clearly illustrates what, in their minds, is at stake is the very heart of Islam. The question becomes whether the developments on PTAIN campuses really represents a split kiblat or merely two ways to calculate it. Johan Meuleman suggests that the combination of drawing on both Al-Azhar and Western scholarship and universities has meant that PTAIN has had plural orientations throughout its history (2000: 286). Azra suggests that rather than a conflict between these two approaches to Islamic

Studies, PTAIN has become a meeting place for them. The desire to study in the Middle East, Azra argues, has not decreased due to the increase of degrees sought in the West (2011: 52).

As faculty members on the Surabaya campus explained, the Muslim community has certain expectations of PTAIN. For example, there is the hope that the Tarbiyah fakultas will graduate good religious teachers. They noted that the community does not desire State Islamic Higher Education to be ideologically neutral; the question is what PTAIN should be: a place for Islamic Studies or a missions center (*pusat dakwah*). Society wants PTAIN to be the center for studying Islam and for graduates to be pious, but there is another orientation among the intellectuals—for Islam to be an object of scholarship.

Islamic Authenticity

The more conservative elements involved in the debate about the future of PTAIN are concerned with a loss of Islamic authenticity and orthodoxy. This loss of authenticity may also include a loss of the pesantren tradition, so that it is not enough, at least on some campuses to be Muslim, there is a need to be grounded in pesantren. Another factor in the loss authenticity is the inclusion of Western approaches to religion in general and Islam in particular. The threat from the West is typically given the label of "Orientalism," which is understood as both any Western attempt to study Islam and an attempt to control, limit, or destroy Islam.

An interesting incident happened during the opening banquet at the 2008 Annual Conference of Islamic Studies (ACIS), which is illustrative of the competing models for PTAIN. M. Maftuh Basyuni, the minister of religious affairs called for using an Arabic name for the conference instead of the English currently in use, as if somehow Arabic was more authentic for the study of Islam than English. This is not mere linguistic wrangling, it is part of the debate over the nature of Islamic Studies in Indonesia. I was told by other participants that ACIS was deliberately modeled after Middle East Studies Association (MESA) annual meetings. The minister's call challenged that model. This simple matter of using Arabic to name the conference was part of a larger discourse on Islamic authenticity. MORA had recently issued a policy regarding the standing of Ahmadiyah, a rather controversial sect because it recognizes a prophet after Muhammad. Prior to the minister's speech, the hosting governor (the banquet was in his official residence) had spoken for 45 minutes—it was a humorous speech peppered with references to his connections with well-known kyai and other religious figures. It was clear he was trying to establish both his likability and his religious credentials, even if in a secondhand way. In the closing minutes of his speech (made prior to the buffet line being opened) the governor used the symbolic capital he had built (or at least made an accounting of) in the prior 30 minutes to address the issue of Ahmadiyah. He was the governor who had brought the issue of Ahmadiyah authenticity to the fore. He had outlawed Ahmadiyah in South Sumatra, only to have the MORA policy recognize freedom of religion for followers of Ahmadiyah granting the right to exist but restricting them from spreading its teaching. So, in response to this challenge, the minister not only explained the policy but also turned to other issues of authenticity like his recommendation that an Arabic name should be used for the conference.

"Authenticity" regardless of what it concerns is imagined. Discourses around authenticity seek to take an imagined tradition (cf. Hobsbawm and Ranger 1992) and reify it. It paints a picture of what it would like to be the truth and proclaims it as such and holds it as an eternal standard. It denies the dynamic nature of any human endeavor. Authenticity discourse marginalizes certain groups. Discourse about authentic Native American whale-hunting techniques marginalizes the Makah and says that if they want to keep their traditional hunting rights they must give up modern technology (Dark 1999). Concerns about authenticity in a foreign tourist destination seek to deny access to global trends in food, culture, and technology to locals; it is best they remain as they are because we did not travel for endless hours to see ourselves. Authenticity in language and dialect marks correct and incorrect forms. Being able to use the correct form may grant one access to greater opportunities; being unable to do so can be a hindrance. Authenticity discourse in religion is even more serious because those who are inauthentic are witches, heretics, and monsters.

Although Islam originated in the Arabian Peninsula, the idea that authentic Islam is best found there today is subject to considerable debate. There was a time (nineteenth century) where

Southeast Asian scholars and Sufi masters were well-respected leaders in Mecca (Dhofier 1978b: 86; Kartodirdjo 1966: 185, 192; Snouck Hurgronje 1931: 273, 278). There are elements of the pesantren and PTAIN community who have ridiculed *ke-arab-arab-an* (pretensions of acting Arab) and attempts to make Indonesian Islam more Arabic. I have previously discussed how Jabar Adlan, the rector of Institut Agama Islam Negeri (IAIN) Surabaya and of IKAHA, the college at Tebu Ireng in 1995 was of the opinion that *jilbab* (head covering) was a misplaced imitation of the Arabs. What is required in Islam is the covering of the *aurat* (those parts of the body that are erotic). For men, this is minimally the area between just below the knees to just above the belly button but in practice typically covers more. For women, the minimal *aurat* extends over her breast but again in practice typically covers more. Adlan made the argument that just how much more is covered really depends on culture. To have women totally covered and even restricted from reciting the Quran is part of Arabic culture because Arab men are easily aroused. Javanese culture does not lead men to be so easily aroused, so women do not need to be so covered (Lukens-Bull 2005: 82).

As part of the controversy about studying Islam in the West, some people ask why not study Islam in the Middle East, where it originated. For example, Syeh Marbun, the headmaster of Pesantren Al-Kautsar in Medan discussed with me this controversy and argued that Islam does not have a real presence in the West and hence there are no real experts (*ahli*) there. Perhaps because I was accompanied by an IAIN professor with a PhD from Germany, he allowed that there may have been a time when the community benefited from having scholars study in the West, but argued that there is no longer such a need. For Syeh Marbun, the best choice was to remain in Indonesia and to go to the Middle East, only if there was a real need. This is a common response from traditional religious leaders.

No More Studying Islam in the West

The United States, Australia, and Germany, and other countries, have programs that bring faculty members from the State Islamic Higher Education system to pursue graduate degrees in Islamic Studies, Religious Studies, and sometimes other fields such as education and anthropology. From these kinds of programs have come people like the late Nurcholish Madjid, Abdurrahman Mas'ud, Inayah Rohmaniya, Fadhil Lubis, and many others. Madjid is famed for his efforts to guide Indonesian Islam toward a more tolerant, pluralistic, and even liberal perspective. These professors daringly engage the West as well as controversial Muslim thinkers such as the Egyptian Nasr Hamid Abu Zayd, who was convicted of apostasy by an Egyptian court, and some have faced professional repercussions for such associations. Rohmaniya ran the gender studies program at the UIN Yogyakarta. All of these things, liberalism, pluralism, feminism, and so on have come under attack as part of a Western conspiracy to destroy Islam. Nur Fadhil Lubis has a PhD in History from UCLA and is criticized as being too liberal on the grounds that he cites historical and social scientific literature and data rather than religious texts to make his arguments.

In mid-2008, MORA released a new policy restricting PTAIN academics from taking advanced degrees in Religious Studies and Islamic Studies in the West. The sentiment of those who supported this move is best expressed as "why study Islam in the West? If you want to know Islam, go to where Islam is strongest, the Middle East." The concern is that those who study religion scientifically can become doubtful about their own religion. Muhammad Machasin, the Director of Islamic Higher Education within MORA in 2008–2009, understands that fear but did not agree that the solution was sending more faculty members to the Middle East. He felt that if the desire was to study Islam, then it is sufficient to stay in Indonesia. However, if there is a desire to study about Islam scientifically, then there is no choice but to go to the West. However, Machasin saw no reason to go to the Middle East, other than to improve one's skills in conversational Arabic (interview, January 14, 2009).

The policy seemed to be based on understanding Religious Studies as faith-based training in how to be religious rather than an academic, non-confessional study of religion. This misunderstanding is best demonstrated by a conversation I had with an instructor in the *Fakultas Tafsir-Hadith* at UIN Yogya. In general, this instructor was opposed to the evolution of his campus into a full university, for fear that it will weaken the religious authority of the institution. He also opposes faculty members who use social science perspectives to illuminate the meaning of sacred texts. He felt that those who, in his estimation, position themselves as social scientists first and Muslims second are no longer fit to teach at an Islamic institution of higher learning. He was very wary of the Western tradition of the study of religion. He had pursued a doctorate at McGill University but did not successfully complete the program. He says that he was asked to leave for unstated and undecipherable reasons. Others say it is because he spent too much time in extracurricular activities and was not making adequate progress in his program. He was quite adamant that the study of religion in the West requires a distinctly Christian perspective and that the study of other religions must be done in reference to Christianity. He came to this conclusion after a discussion with a professor at Harvard Divinity School. In Indonesia, Harvard is the poster-child for the religious institution that lost its way, and so is seen as the model for how religion is studied in the West. A review of the Harvard Divinity School website shows it to be a multi-faith "seminary" committed to an interfaith dialogue tradition more than the Religious Studies model found less at divinity schools and more at state universities. The mistaken conclusion that Harvard is the model for how religion is studied in the West reflects the distrust of Western doctoral programs and those who study in them.

There is considerable debate on the PTAIN campuses on how best to understand Islamic Studies, whether it is best understood as a faith-based pursuit of deeper religious truth or an academic discipline.

Under the new policy, going to the West to study "supporting" disciplines like sociology, anthropology, and other social science and humanities disciplines was still permitted. This is significant because there are not yet any policies restricting instructors to teaching within the area of their graduate degrees. Therefore, it is possible for someone to have her undergraduate degree in English education, and her graduate degree in history with a focus on the Middle East and Islam to teach both English composition and Islamic law. Because in the past, teachers were hired upon graduation from their undergraduate program, it is consistent to allow them to keep teaching in the fields in which they started. As for their advanced degrees, what is most relevant is the topic of their research rather than the academic discipline in which they received their training. This means that by shifting from Religious Studies programs to social science or even education programs, PTAIN academics could continue to study in the West. While the specifics of the government policies regarding PTAIN faculty studying in the West will shift with each administration, the general concerns and debates remain.

The debate about studying in the West is not new. In 1995, then Director General of Islamic Education Directorate in MORA, Zamakhsyari Dhofier responded to criticisms about sending more PTAIN instructors to the West than to the Middle East by arguing that the West provided scholarships and the Middle East did not. In a published interview, he countered the challenge by saying that Western countries were making scholarships available and Middle Eastern countries were not (1991: 3). Middle Eastern countries do make scholarships available now but as Muhammad Sirozi and others at IAIN Palembang noted that these scholarships are for high school students or at most people who have just an undergraduate degree. They are explicitly not for people who have advanced degrees (master's) and are seeking more education. Similarly, a leader at the *Ahlul Bayt* (*Shia*) library and community center in Medan, 700 Indonesians are sent to Iran each year on full scholarships (for as much education as they wish to receive). The preference is for high school students, but some bachelor-level applicants are also considered. The implication is that these programs want to target people who are still young and who still do not have their worldview set. This means PTAIN faculty who are under consideration for scholarships to the West are not eligible for scholarships to Iran. Occasionally, study abroad can be self-funded, or in one case I know personally funded by a father-in-law. In these cases, the Middle East is the most common destination. However, some academics argue that Indonesia needs to abandon its position of receiving what it is given, decide what it needs and pay for it itself.

In a 1991 article, Komaruddin Hidayat, then a young PhD, foreshadowed many of the issues debated more recently. He suggested a dichotomy between liberal Western graduates and conservative Middle East graduates that has taken on a life of its own. However, he did not assign value to the terms "liberal" and "conservative." He did, however, suggest why the difference existed. He associated "liberalism" with the critical thinking that arises from studying Islam as an object of study (*obyek studi*) rather than as a religious conviction (*keyakinan agama*). Students who studied in the West were commonly drawn to the social sciences. It is not that

Middle Eastern universities do not have social science programs but rather that Indonesians drawn to the Middle East are much more attracted to traditional Islamic Studies, are more conservative, and hence, do not study social sciences (1991: 38). Hidayat himself occupies a middle position between Western and Eastern graduates as he holds a doctorate in Western Philosophy from the Middle East Technical University in Ankara, Turkey. Despite his area of training and the secular nature of Turkey, he is considered by many to be a Middle East graduate.

Reaction to Policy

Nur Kolish, a professor at UIN Yogya, argues that Basyuni was a diplomat to the Middle East (Syria and Saudi Arabia) before becoming minister of religious affairs and that may explain, in part, his favoring of Middle Eastern universities for the training of PTAIN faculty. Imam Suprayogo at UIN Malang was of the opinion that people should be able to study anywhere, and even cited the Hadith that Muslims should pursue knowledge anywhere, even in China. "Has the air disappeared in the West?" he asked sarcastically. "Why then can we not study there?" He suggested that the idea that students who went to the West would lose their Islam was ridiculous; to have such fears is to have basic doubts about Islam. If Islam is true, there is no reason to fear going to the West to study (interview, February 2, 2009).

Azyumardi Azra, former rector of IAIN Jakarta argued that this policy was based on ignorance, misunderstanding, and not even wanting to understand (*ketidakmaumengertian*). He argued that those who called for it do not understand the nature of Islamic Studies or related fields in Western countries, nor did they make any attempt to learn about them. He also suggested that the policy was motivated from fear of criticism by people who may bear some resentment against PTAIN, such as failed academics. Indeed, some critics of PTAIN openly admit their unrealized aspirations of being a professor. Azra recounted how people can be hypocritical in these matters. He once gave a speech to Indonesian students studying in Melbourne. They asked, accusingly, why do PTAIN people take advanced degrees in Western countries? He pointed out their hypocrisy by pointing out that they were studying in Australia. The justification that those students made was that they were studying engineering not religion. He told the students that they were applying a double standard and if the Islamic Studies students should not study in Australia, neither should they. He also challenged the students on the fact that they are critical of the Australian government and its policies but are happy to accept its scholarship money (interview, January 16, 2009).

Muhammad Machasin, then director for Islamic Higher Education told me that although he did not agree with this policy, he had to do his duty and enforce it. Although the concept of the policy was developed by Basyuni, Machasin was tasked with drafting the written policy. He constructed the policy in such a way that what was restricted was going to the West to study religion (*belajar agama*), but not studying about religion (*pelajari agama*). The written policy, hence, allows PTAIN faculty to study in the West as long they understand they are not going to study religion but study about religion. It also expresses a preference for "escort sciences" (*ilmu pengantar*). Under Basyuni, this policy was interpreted in such a way to disallow any study in the West. However, Machasin constructed it so that another minister would have the freedom to change the interpretation (interview, January 4, 2009).

Studying in the Middle East is often put forward as a panacea. The hope is that graduates from Middle Eastern universities will be less liberal, more orthodox, and more focused on religion qua religion. Machasin argues that while those who study in the West are accused of having liberal ideas, those who study in the Middle East can be liberal as well. For example, there are several professors across the system who were educated in Muslim countries but have so called liberal perspectives. There is no better example of a Middle East graduate who had progressive views of Islam than the late Abdurrahman Wahid, who long before becoming president of Indonesia was well loved by Indonesians of all religions. Even scholars in the Middle East can be so liberal that they have been accused of apostasy. For example, Egyptian scholar Abu Zayd, who was educated at Cairo University, was denied tenure and convicted of apostasy because of his views on how to interpret the Quran. When Abu Zayd was invited to the ACIS conference in 2007, enough controversy was stirred up that in the end he could not enter the country. Machasin disagrees with the very idea that where one studies makes one a liberal. He argued on the one hand that for the study of Islam, there is no need to leave Indonesia and certainly no need to go to the Middle East. On the other hand, he suggests that studying in the West will allow Indonesians to learn how to study religion and Islam scientifically (interview January 14, 2009).

According to Nur Kholish at UIN Yogya, a fundamental problem with studying in the Middle East is that the scholarships provided by them are not very generous. Many who have studied in the Middle East had to take on jobs that interfered with their studies. He argued that although equal numbers may depart for the Middle East and the West, only a handful have completed advanced degrees in the Middle East (interview, January 27, 2009). Finally, he was critical of undue pride in studying abroad. He says that pride in being alumni from a Western university shows that Indonesians are a colonized people. The same is true for alumni of the Middle East, it means that Indonesians are colonized by Middle Eastern nations and lack self-identity. It is critiques from within Indonesia about intellectual colonialism that supports the efforts to train more PhDs within Indonesia itself.

Islamic Studies—Definitions Are Models of Reality

Amin Abdullah argues that Muhammad Basyuni, then minister of religious affairs was mistaken when he issued the policy restricting or rather forbidding studying in the West. Further, the policy was based on not properly understanding the nature of Islamic Studies. Both before and after the release of the policy, PTAIN scholars wrote and spoke at length about the nature of this discipline. Azra enumerated four trends in the development of Islamic Studies. The first is to increasingly integrate religious science with natural sciences, social sciences, and humanities. The second is to increasingly employ sociohistorical approaches and analyses. Third, Indonesian Islamic Studies must consider local context, cultures, and knowledge in a more distinctive way. Finally, it must use a comparative approach toward local practices to identify differences and similarities (2011: 54). Komaruddin, the rector of UIN Jakarta, said in a published interview that specialization is the basic nature of science and this is the source of the basic fakultas found on PTAIN campuses. Komaruddin also made a distinction between Islam as a scholarly pursuit and Islam as a religious outlook. He suggests that for most of society Islam is only a worldview, but on campus that is not enough, Islam must be studied in scholarly manner. He affirmed that in the Quran itself there is no dichotomy between religious and general knowledge (2008).

In part, the debate about studying religion, or Islam, in the West is based on a linguistic disconnect. The (apparently) Arab terms *dirasat Islamiyah* and *dirasat diniyah* are the literal equivalents of Islamic Studies and Religious Studies respectively. But the connotations of these terms could not be further apart. In common usage, the Indonesian-Arabic terms, *dirasat Islamiyah/diniyah* refer to a faith-based study of the divine's interaction with humanity. Dirasat diniyah is a term that covers the religious education received in pesantren or madrasah. It is the basic education need to be an '*alim* or other type of religious leader. While dirasat Islamiyah has a more intellectual connotation, it remains a faith-based endeavor. In the history of the PTAIN system, there was once a core curriculum designed to ensure that all students had the same basic doctrinal knowledge and orientation, that core program was referred to as dirasat Islamiyah.

What is meant by Religious Studies or Islamic Studies in the West could not possibly be further in meaning. At an international conference in May 2009 in Jambi, Jamhari, the then academic vice president at UIN Jakarta, made a distinction between how and why Muslims study Islam and the study of Islam in the West. He stated that the Muslim study of Islam is focused on strengthening spirituality and the spread of Islam. On the other hand, in Western universities Islamic Studies comes out of area studies, comparative Religious Studies, and even anthropology (where the focus is local practice and society) (interview, May 2, 2009).

Religious Studies and Islamic Studies programs at least at secular, and certainly at state, universities in the West, while they do not require or even encourage the abandonment of one's faith, typically require an analysis of religion based on something other than personal faith. Religious Studies and Islamic Studies in the West are, by design, hodge-podge disciplines. They draw on history, linguistics, textual criticism, anthropology, sociology, literature, and any other social science or humanities approach that can contribute to an understanding of their subject. These fields are not defined by their methods or by their central theories, but by what they study. That is the central difference between Islamic

Studies in the West and Islamic Studies as it is understood by many Indonesians.

Amin Abdullah, former rector, at UIN Yogya makes a distinction between three levels of Islamic Studies, namely, *ulum uddin*, *Al-Fiqrih Islami*, and dirasat Islamiyah. *Ulum uddin* is basic religious education and is therefore focused on ritual texts including kitab kuning (literally, yellow books, mostly fiqh commentaries), and scripture. It is by definition canonical in its focus. This is the form of education at which pesantren have excelled. *Ulum uddin* can create actors in society: teachers, preachers, missionaries, politicians, and social workers. He avers that *Al-Fiqrih Islami*, or Islamic thinking, is more conceptual and philosophical and anchored to the humanities. *Al-Fiqrih Islami* is still faith-based, although it engages reason to process and understand matters of faith. The third level is dirasat Islamiyah. Because it is the literal Arabic translation of Islamic Studies, his category shares a label with the more common usage that places dirasat Islamiyah at the level of faith-based learning. Ulum uddin is canonical but Islamic Studies, or dirasat Islamiyah, for Amin, must be critical. There is no critical perspective in the canonical approach. It is difficult for these two perspectives to meet. This disconnect is part of what led to the MUI decision forbidding secularism, pluralism, and liberalism. For the most part, he says that Indonesians mix up the three levels he has identified.

Amin is unwilling to surrender the term dirasat Islamiyah to the "right." He insists on understanding dirasat Islamiyah as based in the social sciences using field work and taking seriously local experience; it is not merely the application of doctrine. He wishes to redefine dirasat diniyah as well and wants it be equivalent in its connotations to the English "Religious Studies." For dirasat diniyah there must be approaches from sociology, anthropology, history, psychology. He argues that what pesantren do is ulum uddin and not at all dirasat diniyah, in the way he wishes to redefine the term. He sees no difference between Islamic/Religious Studies and dirasat Islamiyah/diniyah other than geography.

Amin did not want to distinguish between the levels above based on the degree to which each was based on faith, but rather in terms of balancing the participant and observer roles. He said that the debate over whether PTAIN should teach ulum uddin or Islamic Studies will continue indefinitely. Amin clearly argues that that ulum uddin belongs in the lower levels of education, but once at the university level it should be exclusively Islamic Studies (Amin Abdullah, interview, September 9, 2008). He was clear that Islamic Studies is based on social sciences like anthropology rather than religious texts and religious understanding and that this is a good thing. He was firm that ulum uddin alone is simply not adequate. For some, like Adian Husaini, Amin's approach is part of a project to ruin PTAIN and thereby Islam by ruining the methodology for studying Islam by making it more like Western approaches (2008: 62) reflecting a basic difference in religious dialect.

When I spoke about these issues to Masdar Hilmy, a faculty member at IAIN Surabaya, he argued that Islamic Studies should be something accessible by Muslim and non-Muslim alike as long as they use good methodology and epistemology. PTAIN are not interested in the ritual study of religion (*mengaji*) but want the scholarly examination of religion (*kajian*). He argued that Islamic Studies needs to have some distance from the object and must not start with the normative aspect. Those who are unable to achieve that distance will never become professional researchers at IAIN Sunan Ampel (interview, April 30, 2009). With the change to UIN, the methodological orientation in the study of religion changed from normativity to historicity with an emphasis on empirical research (Bagir and Abdullah 2011: 59).

Comparative religion as a field of study in the PTAIN system started in 1981 with Mukti Ali as the chair of the department. Mukti Ali's approach has been criticized by some for taking a clearly Muslim worldview and assessing other religions from that perspective (Bagir and Abdullah 2011: 58). This approach to other religions is still common enough especially among faculty members with only a master's degree. Those with doctorates, especially from Western universities tend to write in more neutral tones. The very presence of a comparative religion program was an important step forward toward encouraging religious pluralism. Over time, comparative religion department faculty became associated with interfaith organizations and efforts to design civic and peace education.

The Center for Religious and Cross-cultural Studies (CRCS) at Universitas Gadjah Mada (UGM) is an interesting development in the creation of an Indonesian discipline of Religious Studies. It offers a master's degree in Religious Studies and its affiliate, the Indonesian Consortium for Religious Studies (ICRS) offers a PhD. CRCS drew on faculty from a number on religious universities from all recognized faiths because UGM did not have an undergraduate program in Religious Studies (Bagir and Abdullah 2011: 59). Bagir and Abdullah identify three clusters within CRCS that seemed to have continued through into the ICRS PhD program, namely, interfaith dialogue, religion and local cultures, and religion and contemporary issues. The multi-religious dimension of CRCS was institutionalized in ICRS, which is a consortium between the secular UGM, Duta Wacana Christian University, and the National Islamic University of Yogyakarta (2011: 60). The consortium was possible because of the interactions and the trust built between professors from all three universities who were teaching at CRCS. Together CRCS and ICRS represent a significant development in the study of religion in Indonesia, a program that takes all religions seriously but not as foundational. In fact, some outsiders have accused ICRS of trying to Christianize students. This accusation is congruent with the apostate accusation aimed at UIN and are made by many of the same people. The ICRS PhD program is becoming a viable alternative to studying abroad.

An "Orientalist" teaches at IAIN

In 2008–2009, I taught at IAIN North Sumatra in Medan. Before I arrived, there had been eight other Westerners to come to this campus in a five-year period. When Fadhil Lubis started inviting Westerners to campus, there were protests. Later Westerners were accepted as long as they stuck to teaching English. A watershed was the third scholar, a female sociologist, who worked hard to adapt, wearing long skirts and a *slendang* head cover. After her, the next four were all English teachers. When asked if they wanted me to teach at IAIN North Sumatra, the rector had said that more than wanting, they needed me there, especially given my fluency in Indonesian, so few previous Westerners on that campus had been. They needed the exposure to social scientific approaches in the study of religion.

It is interesting that I taught in the graduate program in Islamic Thought but the original plan to have me teach undergraduates did not come to pass. The given reason was to allow me more time for research. Although it is possible to interpret this to mean that they did not want the students exposed to me, I think the reverse is more likely. They did not want to suffer the embarrassment of having undergrads respond negatively to me. There was sufficient embarrassment about the doctoral student who started out in a very antagonistic mode. Outside the classroom, however, undergraduates were by and large pleased to see me and even eager to talk to me and help me in various matters. IAIN North Sumatra had visiting scholars from Saudi Arabia and Egypt previously also, but most of them only taught Arabic. Only one or two taught religious subjects. Among students that I interviewed said that the Western scholars were more open and approachable than the Middle Easterners.

My teaching assignment was in the Islamic Thought track of the Islamic Studies doctoral program. Originally, I was asked to teach a course called *Teologi Agama-Agama* (Comparative Theology); it was a required core-course for third semester students. Comparative Theology is far beyond my expertise and training and so I negotiated with the graduate dean to teach instead *Teori Agama-Agama* (Theories of Religion). Because of the rarity of international scholars to this campus, the graduate dean doubled the class size by having the first semester student take that core-course a year early. The majority of the students were faculty members teaching in undergraduate programs at IAIN-SU. Others taught at other universities in town, and still others were employed in the local offices of MORA.

In addition to teaching this class, I was asked to conduct a faculty seminar for mid-level faculty. These were faculty members who have earned a master's degree (many from Western universities) who are not currently enrolled in a doctoral program. The focus of this faculty seminar was on research methods and the question of how to apply anthropological theory and method to the study of Islam. Aside from the one student already mentioned who expressed concerns about my trying to Christianize them through reading about atheist Jews (Durkheim, Marx, Freud), my reception was extremely warm. I was accorded so much respect as a scholar-teacher that I experienced some reverse culture shock upon returning to my home university.

Discussion

Amin Abdullah expressed concerns about the development of violent expressions of Islam. He said there needs to be two dimensions each with its own set of players in the counter-discourse against radical Islam. The first is the cultural dimension. This is where pesantren play a role. The other dimension is higher education and this is where PTAIN play a role. With both of these dimensions, Islam in Indonesia can be balanced and can avoid the extremism and violence found in Pakistan. He also spoke at length how transnationalist jihadis are a less spoken about dimension of globalization. One dimensions of this is the Saud family working with the Wahibis to maintain the status quo in Saudi Arabia. He argued that the conflicts in Pakistan, Palestine, Iraq, and Afghanistan are the breeding grounds of transnational jihad and then it is exported to the rest of the world (Amin Abdullah, interview, September 9, 2008).

All of this is part of the debate of what PTAIN should be and what the future of Islamic Studies should be. Some argue that the real future of Islamic Studies graduate training needs to be in Indonesia; that the best option is to take the best from the West and the Middle East and make a homegrown program for training Indonesian scholars with Indonesian sensibilities and Indonesian scholarly agendas. One outcome of having PTAIN professors pursue their doctoral education in both the West and the Middle East has been the development of a distinctly Indonesian form of Islamic Studies that draws on both traditions.

If the primary ideological concern about the new nonreligious fakultas is the relationship between religion and science, then the concern about developments within the traditional fakultas is about the relationship between religion and the social sciences and humanities. Some of the concern is about the Western origin of modern social science and humanities disciplines and that those disciplines can draw models of reality that contradict religious principles. For those who engage them, social science data and theories do not contradict religious principles but merely challenge traditional understanding of such principles. In no area is this clearer than in gender studies. Feminism and gender equity are seen by some as the fruit of Western social science and in contradiction to a traditional gender hierarchy, which they believe to be ordained by God. In the next chapter, we turn to gender issues as they are debated in the PTAIN environment. It also examines the implications of gender debates for Indonesian Islam.

Chapter 5

Women Pushing the Limits: Gender Debates in Islamic Higher Education

In November 2008, I had driven for a few hours to attend a wedding of a friend's relative. I have attended Indonesian Muslim weddings before and I thought I knew what to expect. I knew I would be a special guest and would be posed with the bride and groom and other members of the wedding party for pictures. I knew that there would be the formal wedding (*nikah*) ritual and plenty of speeches. I knew the *penghulu* (the marriage officiate and registrar from MORA) would give a short sermon. What I did not expect was some of the content of that sermon. He spoke at length against spousal (really, wife) abuse. He admonished the groom not to be tempted to take out stress on his wife; of course, there may be tensions, but they must be dealt with by talking and not by striking out. It wasn't his speaking against abuse that was striking, it was the length at which he stressed the importance of nonviolent conflict resolution and that violence against the wife was grounds for divorce. In fact, he spent quite a bit of time enumerating the wife's rights within the marriage. A few weeks later, I learned that North Sumatra was one of several regions that had sent *penghulus* to training about the rights of women in Islam according to Quran and Hadith. The training had been carried out by the Women's Study Center at Universitas Islam Negeri (UIN) Yogyakarta with funding from the Asia Foundation. The literature on women in Indonesia suggests that gender issues are not simple or static but subject to contestation (Brenner 1995, 1996, 2011; Rinaldo 2010). Recent work has looked at the place of Muslim women activists in the gender debates (Hamdi and Smith 2012;

van Doorn-Harder 2006, 2008). As might be imagined, efforts to increase gender parity being carried out by faculty members at UIN have not set well with certain critics. Hartono Ahmad Jaiz is quite clear that any effort to improve the status of women in Islam is tantamount to apostasy (2005). Debates about gender equality are among the fiercest in Islam since the beginning of the twentieth century (cf. Kersten 2009: 98; Mir-Hosseini 2006: 81). This is particularly true in Indonesia even though it grants women far greater equality compared to other Muslim countries. However, as Subhan points out, despite women being 38 percent of the civil service, only 16 percent of the higher level positions are held by women (2006: xxi). Understanding the place of gender studies and gender parity in these processes is not only important for understanding the future of Islam in Indonesia but also for examining emerging models of gender relations that might be exportable to other Muslim societies.

Background of the Pusat Studi Wanita (PSW)

Women's studies centers at government institutes of higher education were mandated by the Suharto regime starting in the 1980s as part and parcel of "State Ibuism" (Motherism) project that mated the roles of wife and mother (*Ibu*). During this period, the centers were part of the effort to implement these roles on a national level. In the 1990s, the discourse about women's issues started to shift away from the "motherism" ideology to a more "feminist" tone (Qibtiyah 2010: 152). Today, some of these centers are called gender studies centers in order to acknowledge that the issues involved are more complex; however, the focus remains on male-female relations.

In 1995, what had been a small working group within a larger research center at IAIN Sunan Kalijaga was transformed by a rector's decree into a Women's Studies Center. The PSW, or Women's Studies Center is a center for both community-based research and advocacy. In all their efforts the faculty and researchers at the Women's Studies Center seek greater gender parity through finding an Islamic basis for it. This center has undertaken a number of efforts to improve the status of women including seminars about reproductive rights, leadership in the household, as well as educational programs for judges who preside over divorce hearings.

There is sufficient evidence in the textual tradition to support such positions. This particular center has had important partnerships with McGill University, the Canadian International Development Agency, the Ford Foundation, and the Asia Foundation.

Five years into the PSW operation at UIN Yogyakarta, the president of Indonesia, Abdurrahman Wahid, pushed forward the idea of "Gender Mainstreaming into National Development" by issuing Presidential Instruction (Inpres) number 9/2000 (Qibtiyah 2010: 153). In this shifting context, the PSW at UIN Yogyakarta developed the specific focus of gender in Islam, which distinguishes it from other centers especially those at secular universities like Universitas Gadjah Mada (UGM). It is now one of the preeminent research centers on Islam and Gender in Indonesia (Doorn-Harder 2006: 12). Ruhaini Dzahayatin, who was the head of the center from 2000 to 2006 said that when she started the discussion about gender in the 1990s there was considerable resistance, and that one can see progression in the publications over time. Ruhaini and Ema tell the story of one man who was particularly resistant at IAIN Surabaya, Kyai Dr. Ghozali, who was both the head of a pesantren and a professor at IAIN Surabaya. After long discussions about source texts, he made a 180 degree turn and became an advocate and partner in their work, often speaking at workshops. For younger faculty, they held workshops on gender issues but senior faculty members would not attend trainings or workshops. Such things were for younger, less experienced, less expert scholars. Other campuses have experienced similar issues in reaching senior faculty. To some extent this has more to do with the idea that trainings and workshops in general are more for junior faculty rather than the fact that these are gender-focused workshops. The center addressed this problem by holding a three-day "expert meeting," which the rector attended. During the three days they had very deep discussions about human rights, women's rights, and children's rights. This was an important milestone in the development of the PSW and its acceptance on campus. Some of the centers, such as the one at IAIN Surabaya, have an uncertain position in the budget and structure of the institution. This means that the work can be difficult to maintain at a consistent level. The center in Yogyakarta is recognized as the most active of all the centers in Indonesia and it cannot be separated from its structural position in that it reports directly to the rector.

The PSW has pushed for important considerations on the UIN Yogya campus that may seem small to an outside observer, such as a day care center and a nursery room for breastfeeding mothers on campus. Another consideration in this category was pushing for a maximum rise of 10 cm on stairs in all new buildings on campus so that pregnant women can safely climb stairs (in the absence of any elevators). Although the rector had agreed because it benefits older faculty as well as the pregnant faculty, it was still a hard-fought battle because the contracted architect was resistant. This episode illustrates that the center is not narrowly focused on women's issues and that they have paved the way for others. Specifically, the center supported the establishment of a Difable (differently able) Studies and Support Center, the first of such centers in Indonesian Higher Education, which started by making the campus more accessible and friendly for the 34 visually impaired students already enrolled at the university. Keeping with the pattern established by the PSW, the new center conducted sensitivity workshops for faculty (www.ahed-upesed.org/projects/indonesia/, accessed July 3, 2012.) Other than moral support, the PSW does not have an ongoing relationship with the Difable Center.

The first thing that might be striking for a Western observer unfamiliar with Indonesia, is that several men (nearly half of PSW faculty) are active members of the center. Although PSW UIN Sunan Kalijaga has the highest rate of male involvement, other gender studies and women's studies centers have several men on the faculty. I have been told by an American university administrator that they would not trust anything a male researcher had to say on women's issues. And while this may not be a widespread opinion, women's studies as an academic discipline in the United States and women's centers as service centers on American university campuses do not involve many men. Susilaningsih, the director, was a bit incredulous when I described the common situation in the United States and she sardonically replied, "This is an academic field and it can be done by anyone. Why would it be the domain of women?" (interview, June 2012).

For Indonesian gender activists, cooperation between men and women is a highly effective strategy for challenging the structural inequity that arises out of traditional, misogynistic teachings (Doorn-Harder 2008: 1022). The faculty members at the Gender Studies Center (PSG) at IAIN Sunan Ampel in Surabaya suggest that it is important to have men involved in the efforts of the center because if only women presented on gender equity, especially as it applies on campus, they would be seen as only trying to advance their own careers and interests. Men will listen to other men on issues of gender parity more than they will listen to women, according the PSG director and staff at IAIN Surabaya.

Men who work at these centers often say that they are involved in this work because it benefits the women in their lives (wife, sister, mother, and daughter). Muhammad Sodiq, a senior researcher, says he is following the example of the Prophet Muhammad by being an activist for women's rights. In Sodiq's view, the Prophet greatly improved the status of women over pre-Islamic Arabia; women went from being heritable property to inheriting property. He is far from unique in making this argument. Asma Barlas, a Pakistani whose work proposes a liberatory Quranic hermeneutics (2002, 2004), argues that the story of Abraham and his first born son shows that the rule of God overrides the rights of fathers. She writes:

> That I didn't see the Quran as privileging fathers or fatherhood and, indeed, read it as subverting the concept of father-right and father-rule which is at the heart of traditional patriarchies was a building block in my claim that the Quran is anti-patriarchal (2008: 18).

For Barlas then, the Quran does not endorse patriarchy.

When I asked Sodiq about the fact that only women have been directors of the PSW in its brief history, he said that because of the limited opportunity for women to occupy leadership positions in the university without prior experience, the men deliberately seek to correct that imbalance by keeping the position for women (interview, June 2012). Another structural dimension of the PSW that Susilaningsih said was part of their original charter was that it includes people from both Muhammadiyah and Nahdlatul Ulama (NU) so that they can speak to the broadest range of Indonesia's Muslims.

There are considerable difficulties with the labels "feminist" and "feminism" in the Indonesian discourse about gender. The usage of the term "feminist" shows both dialectal and idiosyncratic factors. Even among gender activists, these are problematic terms (Doorn-Harder 2008: 1022). Elsewhere, it is not uncommon for Muslim women activists to reject the feminist label (Barlas 2008:

15; Kynsilehto 2008: 9). Being at an Islamic university versus at a secular university does not affect whether they identify as "feminists"; women faculty members at secular state schools also avoid this label (Qibtiyah 2010: 156). Even though equal percentages of men and women at PSWs and PSGs self-identified as feminists, the label is more commonly applied by others to women, rather than to men. When used as an epithet, the term "feminist" in Indonesian discourse implies someone who accepts lesbianism, hates men, and wants to dominate them (Qibtiyah 2010: 158). Also, to be feminist means for women to reject their God-given nature (*kodrat*). For these reasons, many more women than men working as gender activists and advocates explicitly self-identify as nonfeminists. Qibtiyah reports that 22 percent of the men working in six different PSW or PSG in Yogyakarta self-identify as feminists and suggest this helps us understand why each of the centers had a core of male members from the beginning (2010: 158).

Facing off Hizbut Tahrir

If Islamic "feminism" is one aspect of Muslim discourse on gender, then another critical aspect is women who embrace conservative forms of religion (Brenner 1996; Rinaldo 2010; Smith-Hefner 2007), which is not unique to Islam (Ingersoll 2003; Jacobson 2006). A focus on piety helps to explain some of the reasons why women embrace more conservative interpretations (Brenner 1996; Mahmood 2005); the seeming regressive positions advocated by these women are expressions of their piety and faith.

One Friday, I attended a faculty meeting at Women's Study Center at the UIN in Yogyakarta. After the men had left for Friday prayers, there was scheduled meeting with some women from Hizbut Tahrir Indonesia (HTI), which is part of Hizbut ut-Tahrir (an international Islamist organization). What followed was a debate between different interpretations of piety. Neither party was arguing for an impious form of Islam, neither was arguing for a more secular or even less strict interpretation of the texts. The argument was between different ways to read the texts and different ways to be pious.

Two professors, Ema Marhuma and Ruhaini, had stayed to meet with them. The time was selected by the visitors specifically so the men would be at Friday prayers. Ema's interpretation was that perhaps they thought the men would be more expert in religious matters and that it would be easier to convince the women, but they were in for a surprise. When the three women from Hizbut Tahrir arrived, they seemed a little uncertain about my presence. I considered leaving but stayed at Ruhaini's insistence. Ruhaini put the women at ease by saying that I was her friend from America. One of the visitors had an infant in a sling and a helper who watched the infant after she had fallen asleep. Consistent with the center's philosophy and agenda, they found space for the little one to sleep, and were very accommodating to the needs of mother and child.

The Hizbut Tahrir women all had bachelor-level degrees, one from UIN Yogyakarta, consistent with Rinaldo's observation that women in another conservative movement tended to be well educated (2010: 425). The HTI women said that their purpose was to exchange information and to let people know about information that came out of an international conference about women hosted by Hizbut Tahrir. They said they want humanity to return to *fitrah*—the purposes of "He who created us." The conference affirmed the need to create an Islamic solution because Islam not only sets out the nature of the relationship between husbands and wives but also between men and other men and between women and other women. It is telling that the only kind of relationship between men and women they mentioned was marital. The way the HTI women framed the discussion placed them firmly within a religious dialect and discourse that espouses gender inequality by embodying the assumption of classical fiqh that biology is destiny and focuses on woman's role as mother and wife (Mir-Hosseini 2006: 83–84).

Ema and Ruhaini listened politely for about 10 minutes before responding. What ensued was a lively and sometimes even heated discussion. Ema's initial response was to suggest that they did not come for a discussion but to give them a *fatwa* and for that they were thankful. Even though she said this without the slightest hint of sarcasm, she confirmed later she felt more annoyed than thankful. However, she continued that this kind of discussion needs a comprehensive review of the Quran and Hadith. Her implication was that a thorough examination of the text would counter the visitors' position.

To explore another aspect of the gender debates, Ruhaini asked the visitors about whether women could lead the prayers. After confirming that they were all in agreement that this is not mentioned in the Quran, Ruhaini asked them what particular Hadith mentions it. They did not know the specifics and simply said that the question of leading the prayers was already set forth by Islam. So Ruhaini said that of the three Hadith that concern women leading the prayers, one permits it in the context of family if the wife has memorized the Quran better than her husband. The only one which clearly states that women cannot be imam is considered *daif* (weak), meaning that it is of questionable origin and should not be trusted. Further, Ruhaini argued that this Hadith only became widely used because of the cultural context of the patriarchal societies in which Islam first took root. The visitors had no response to this. The difference between the two groups was dialectal and can be diagrammed in order to show the factors involved in each religious dialect (table 5.1). Obviously, there is a difference between the kinds of activism each group of women engaged in. The PSW professors are clearly gender activists and opposed to the establishment of a syari'ah state. It is also obvious that there is a difference in their level of education and understanding. However, the differences in how they understand the Hadith on the issue does not come only from these factors but also a basic understanding of how to interpret the texts. The very concept of strong and weak Hadith is not part of the vocabulary used by the HTI women to talk about religion. For them, Islam is one and immutable, whereas the PSW professors have a fundamentally different way of conceptualizing Islam and its texts. This is a difference in religious grammar that must be considered before the other variations involved in the two different expressions.

Table 5.1 Dialect differences and women as imam

"Universal"	Expression	Dialect	Elements
Imam/prayer leader	Women as imam not expressly forbidden	PSW	+strong/weak Hadith +pro-woman activism −pro-syari'ah activism +advanced scholarship in the study of religious texts
Imam/prayer leader	Women as imam expressly forbidden	HTI	−strong/weak Hadith −pro-woman activism +pro-syari'ah activism +HTI conference talking points

Mir-Hoseini argues that Islamist efforts to codify classical fiqh notions created blowback in the form of critiques of the gendered notions of classical fiqh and increased activism among women (2006: 90). She identifies this discourse as reformist in nature. A new element in this discourse was disconnecting the gender inequality found in classical fiqh from ideas of divine justice so that classical fiqh is not understood as a sacred text but a construction of male jurists based on sacred texts. The point is that gender inequality is not because of divine will but male abuse of power (2006: 91). The PSW professors have been part of this discourse through efforts to reinterpret the Quran and Hadith. Margot Badran identifies the Moroccan sociologist, Fatima Mernissi as the first to expose the fraudulence of misogynistic Hadith (2008: 30) in Mernissi's book *Women and Islam: An Historical and Theological Inquiry* (1991). Misogynistic Hadith are the basis of popular understandings of gender relations.

Islam, Women, and Violence

The HTI women moved the conversation to women and violence. Although Hizbut Tahrir is opposed to violence and injustice against women, they are also opposed to the UN Convention on the Rights of Women. HTI's position is that the UN Convention is imposing concerns from outside of Muslim societies. This is consistent with Margot Badran's observation that feminists in the "East" are branded as traitors of their own culture because feminism was labeled as inextricably Western (2008: 26). The visitors implied that the data would not support the idea that violence and injustice against women exists in Muslim countries. Ruhaini had two responses to this. The first is to reject the assertion that the convention comes from outside of Islam because many Muslim countries participated and were signatories included Iran, Egypt, and Saudi Arabia and it was based on data coming from all over the world. The second was to show the women specific data that speaks to discrimination and violence against women in Indonesia; over 23 percent of Indonesian women and girls are abused physically, and 48 percent are abused emotionally, in their own homes (Hakimi et al. 2001: 23–24).

Ruhaini stood up to a large note pad and moved into lecture mode. She argued that are a number of basic rights including life, safety, health, education, and full participation in politics, economics, and social-cultural matters. These are the rights of all humans regardless of race, creed, or gender. And that the safeguarding of these rights is the responsibility of the state. The Hizbut Tahrir group asserted that if this is indeed an international conversation, then it needs to come from all countries and we to see if there is a need for our country. They argued that if the government cannot do it, then the religion should and Islam has a way to protect women—for example, wearing covering garments.

Ema said that she objects to Hizbut Tahrir using "Islam" as if they own it. Ruhaini admonished the visitors not to use "Islam" as a reason for their position but rather to say, "according to Hizbut Tahrir or even Islam as Hizbut Tahrir understands it." One of the Hizbut Tahrir women said that there is only one Islam and they all have the same one. At this point, Ruhaini put her in her place by saying, "Don't tell me this, I am a professor of Syari'ah." Ruhaini continued that if you say "Islam" you have to say what sources, which ritual/legal school (maddhab) is being referenced. And then to make a point she reminded them that each maddhab says that if women leave the house they have to be accompanied by a related man (*muhrim*) and so, "we are all sinners." To this the Hizbut Tahrir women said that it is the government that is sinning for "allowing us to leave the house without male chaperones." The irony of this seemed to be lost on the young women but not the professors, that if such institutions were in place then the conversation they were having could not have occurred. Perhaps it did not seem ironic or contradictory at all to the HTI visitors. As Rinaldo observes, such political activism is an expression of faith and piety and not merely instrumental (2010: 423); they do not need to achieve the goal of restricting their own movement without a chaperone, working for it expresses their piety all by itself.

The PSW professors tried to explain the difference between *kodrat* (God-given nature), sex, and nature on the one hand, and gender, social expectations, and culture on the other. *Kodrat* cannot change and no Indonesian women's activists argue to change this, but rather accept it as a condition of working in this cultural context (Doorn-Harder 2008: 1029). Ruhaini also very openly discussed genitals, menstruation, pregnancy, and lactation as factors that are innate and unchangeable. It is likely that the visitors openly addressed *kodrat* because of the perception that gender activism is anti-*kodrat* (cf. Qibtiyah 2010). Ruhaini was adamant that claiming that gender is a Western concept is nonsense since the Arabic language marks words as feminine and masculine and even has a term for describing gender markers in language.

Ridha Saleh, a leading woman in Hizbut ut-Tahrir, argued that genderism is part of secularism, pluralism, and liberalism (Kersten 2009: 98, Robinson 2008: 126). The Hizbut Tahrir group said they are working for women to be primarily mothers and housewives. Ruhaini agreed that the primary role for women is to be a mother (pregnancy for nine months and nursing for two years, stressed Ema) but did not agree with the role of housewife. She argued the husband's religiously mandated responsibility to provide sustenance (*nafkah*) made him responsible for keeping the household. She argued that even nursing is the husband's responsibility: if the wife nurses then he must provide two times the sustenance (*nafkah*) and if she does not nurse, it is the responsibility of the husband to find a milk mother (*ibu susu*) for the infant and to provide her with the extra food needed. Further, she argued the responsibility for men to provide sustenance to their family, as well as they can, does not mean women cannot work. Working is not the same as providing. It is not even required for men to work, only to provide for their families. If they can do it without working, then there is no need for the husband to work. Ruhaini continued that negotiating the relative contributions of the husband and the wife is a private matter.

Marriage and Family Law

Although Indonesia is not a syari'ah state in the common usage of that phrase, since 1974 it has enforced syari'ah in the areas of marriage and family law, including inheritance. The Marriage and Family Law of 1974 was a uniform marriage law for all Indonesians even though it follows Islamic law. This was justified by arguing that most Indonesians (87%) are Muslims, but Ruhaini Dzuhayatin questions the application of this law to non-Muslims (2006: 95). The government makes the argument that this is Islamic law with new procedures but the traditionalists are not convinced. The law did enhance the status of women by effectively outlawing all forms of interfaith marriage that was previously allowable only to Muslim men. Further, under this law the court must approve any polygamous marriages. A requisite of this court approval is a signed affidavit from the first wife. Government employees must also seek their supervisor's approval for all marriages and hence effectively they are barred from polygamous marriages (Dzuhayatin 2006: 96–97). A third improvement was a requirement that all marriages had to be registered and that parental consent was required for marriages before the age of 20. The law also effectively outlawed *talaq* divorce (the husband saying "I divorce thee" three times in any setting) by requiring all divorces to be declared before the court. The law was criticized by new women's movements because it also established the husband as the head of the family and the wife's role as housewife and mother, and not as breadwinner. This leads to differences in earnings between men and women especially when employers offer supplements for dependents—men receive such supplements but women do not, even when they are single mothers (Dzuhayatin 2006: 97). This law, and others similar to it, is part of a neo-traditionalist trend that emerged in the early twentieth century partially as a result of colonial and postcolonial contexts. This opened up the discourse on the status of women, which became a key battle ground in the struggle over the future of Islam and its relationship with the modern world (Mir-Hosseini 2006: 87). A major component of this discourse was attempts to work aspects of syari'ah into the legal codes in Muslim countries; it rejected "gender equality" as a Western import and instead focused on the complementarity of rights or "gender equity."

Judge Training

At present, one of the most important activities of the PSW is training for religious court judges. In practice, the religious courts are first and foremost family courts dealing with issues of divorce, child support, child custody, spousal abuse, and child abuse, including incest. Since 2002, they have trained hundreds of lower court judges from the religious courts system. PSW worked with judges and marriage registrants in workshops in 12 provinces. Sodiq told me that because marriage law has many gaps that they also train the judges in the laws and other considerations about the welfare of the children involved (often in divorce cases) (interview, June 2012). One goal was to have the judges think about how it feels to be married under polygamy. The center also produced a book of wedding sermons that address power relations within marriage and the potential for violence. This is the likely source of the sermon I heard in Sumatra, however, one faculty member in the center said that such sermons are one in a thousand. The training also addressed children's rights.

In mid-June 2012, there was training for religious high court judges from all over Java. I was able to attend this three-day event. The structure of the workshop was designed to move from the least controversial in terms of gender issues to the potentially controversial. The opening speech emphasized the importance of "client satisfaction," which meant that litigants felt that they were heard and dealt with fairly and that there was public trust. The keynote speech the next morning was by Amin Abdullah, former rector of UIN Yogya that dealt with an orientation toward syari'ah that has changed and should change with time to fit the time and place. While there was some resistance to this idea from one participant, it was clear that by the end of training most of the judges agreed with the idea that they should not use interpretations of syari'ah past their "expiration date," to use the phrase used by Amin. This was followed by discussion of rights and responsibilities in the family which was a general discussion and did not strong-arm gender issues. The last presentation of the day was a discussion of the rights of children and the international convention on the rights of children. If there had been some dissent about rights in the family, the rights of children carried no controversy. In Indonesian society in general, children are cherished, and even if there was a judge who did not agree with the ideas presented from the international convention, no one would be as crass as to say so in public.

Polygamy is allowed under Indonesian and Islamic law. The male judges were firm about this when discussing polygamy in the workshop. To prompt more thought on the matter, Sodiq asked them how they might feel if they had a daughter with a master's degree whose husband wanted to take a second wife. When put this way, the male judges were less supportive of the idea. This is a small part of contradictions faced by Indonesian women. Another is the disconnect between the role women play in the public sphere as politicians and even religious leaders, and their private lives where traditional teachings can be used to control them (Doorn-Harder 2008: 1030). The fact that the male judges would be uncomfortable with their own daughters in polygamous marriages further illustrates the ways in which the traditions are manipulated.

Polygamy

The center published an edited volume on polygamy (Rahmaniyah and Sodik 2009). Many of the authors received small grants from the PSW for the research that led to the papers. Polygamy is addressed by a small number of Quranic verses (al-Nisa 4: 2–3, Al-Baqarah 2: 129). Historically, ulama have interpreted these verses in three basic ways: (1) allowing it unreservedly, (2) allowing it with specific limitations, and (3) forbidding it unreservedly (Marhumah 2009: 6). Hasibuan, at Institut Agama Islam Negeri (IAIN) North Sumatra, told me in an interview, that polygamy[1] is part of the teachings of Islam that were for the time and place in which they were taught. Polygamy was allowed in seventh century Arabia but the situation in Indonesian today is different. Hasibuan suggests that it is important to remember that polygamy is not a commandment (*anguran*) but permission (*pembolehan*). The normal mode of marriage is monogamy; polygamy is the exception (interview, January 2009). Murhamah argues that the Quran teaches the proscription of some behaviors in a gradual way (*tadarruf*). For example, the earliest verses concerning alcohol only forbid drunkenness, whereas later verses forbid all uses of alcohol. The argument is that the Quran approached polygamy in a similar fashion, although there may not be an abrogating verse, per se (Marhumah 2009: 8). I have heard traditional Islamic teachers (kyai) make similar arguments. This is not the kind of argument that is limited to gender activists but is rather a more mainstream Muslim perspective in Indonesia. This is well illustrated by the fall of popular TV preacher, A. A. Gymnastiar, because he took a second wife in 2006 (Hoesterey 2008).

Marhuma argues that while the Quran sets out the rules for polygamy given that it was an established practice in the time and place of its revelation, that does not mean that it endorses the practice (2009: 12), much as both the Quran and the Bible describe the limitations and proper practice of slavery without endorsing the practice. I have heard Javanese kyai explain in sermons that the requirement allowing polygamy if the husband treats all his wives equally is actually a prohibition because no man can divide his affections equally. Marhumah attributes a similar position to an UIN professor who goes farther to suggest that it also difficult to divide time and finances equally (2009: 28). Marhumah also draws on Indonesian law, which in U/U 1 (1974) 4: 1 restricts polygamy to cases where: (a) the wife cannot carry out her obligations as a wife; (b) the wife is physically handicapped or terminally ill; (c) the wife cannot give the husband descendants. She summarizes in general, UIN professors fall into two categories regarding polygamy. The first opposes polygamy in all forms and the second allows it only under special conditions. Noticeably there are none who adopt the position of the classical ulama and allow polygamy with only the Quranic limitation of no more than four wives (2009: 36). In other contexts, I have heard Indonesian women argue that polygamy should be practiced as the Prophet did: after being married to one woman for the rest of her life and then after marrying a young bride, marrying widows needing social support, although marrying a widow did not help Gymnastiar.

Reproductive Issues

Since control over reproduction is considered a fundamental aspect of women's rights, the center has put considerable effort on reproductive issues. At a basic level, PSW has worked to create an environment at UIN where women faculty members, many of whom are of reproductive age, can both work and be mothers. A more academic project concerned reproductive health and was done in partnership with the Ford Foundation. It yielded a bilingual book *Men's Involvement in Reproductive Heath: An Islamic Perspective*. The book opens by observing that serious health problems are created by the lack of men's involvement in reproductive health. Men frequently restrict their wives access to health services like prenatal care. Men are also insensitive to the potential risk of pregnancy and put full responsibility for contraception on their wives. This often leads to women using potential risky device like IUDs, which are made more risky by limited access to gynecological care (Iyas et al. 2006). Women's health advocates have told me that it is not uncommon for IUDs to remain in place far beyond medical recommendations, sometimes for as long as ten years. It also appears that government efforts have not significantly influenced the behavior and attitudes of men and that reproductive health does not get the attention it deserves (Ilyas et al. 2006: 2, 3).

The book reviews a number of religious justifications for treating women equally and particularly for men to be equally involved in reproductive health. The book states quite clearly that the duties and rights of husbands and wives are culturally constituted and therefore should differ by time and place. By combining religious justification with culturally postulated ideals for men's behavior, the authors are advocating for a culturally inflected expression of Islam.

Membina Keularga Barokah (*Creating a Blessed Family,* Ilyas and Hidayat 2006) is a short book(let) of 60 pages. It is intended as an educational manual that includes a review of what Islamic texts say about marriage and then reviews a basic social science summary about the nature of family, bringing in Quranic references when appropriate. The third chapter is 20 pages of basic sexual education. It includes detailed diagrams of both the internal and external reproductive organs of men and women, including the location of the clitoris. It gives and defines the scientific names for different parts of male and female genitalia and relates them to Indonesian colloquial terms. In defining Islamic (marital) sex, the book lists the following:

- Sex between a husband and wife is not just for having children but the happiness and pleasure of both.
- It is to be done when both parties want sex and the wife is not menstruating or having postnatal bleeding.
- It is to be done using perfume so as to arouse both the husband and the wife.
- So that it becomes a religious act (*ibadah*), sex should be done with the stated intention (*niat*) to guard self-respect and to please each other.
- Sex should begin with this prayer: *Bismillah Allahuma jannibas syaithana wa jannibis syaithan mimma razaqtana.* In the Name of God, oh God distance us from Satan and distance Satan from the children you have given us (2006: 29–30).

The sex-ed chapter goes through a number of birth control methods including natural methods, condoms, diaphragms, medication (including emergency contraceptive pills), IUDs, and surgeries and uses diagrams and pictures to illustrate. It ends with a brief review of the risk factors for HIV/AIDS and other STIs. The fourth chapter is nine pages on how to reduce domestic violence and its definition includes abuse toward domestic workers as domestic violence.

I had been given a copy of the first book in 2008, but misplaced it. When I asked for another copy, I discovered that neither of these publications is meant for distribution. The frank nature of the discussions in both books along with the diagrams may be sufficient reason to keep them internal; there are certainly elements within Indonesian society that would object to an Islamic university distributing such materials, even if their intended use is as a marital relations manual. However, when asked why the book could not be distributed, one professor said because it was *modal* (capital) and as such has not been distributed even to other PSW. It is clear that the books could easily be misconstrued by those who might want to put the PSW in a bad light. These materials occupy a very interesting position. They are not supposed to leave, but the center leadership had no problems with my summarizing them here when I specifically asked for permission to do so.

Parity in Education

Creating gender parity in education at all levels (K-20) is another important mission for the center. That this kind of effort is necessary, came home to me when I gave a public lecture at another Islamic university. The audience was mostly graduate students and roughly equal in gender distribution. After my talk, the floor was opened to questions. All the questions were from men. Having been made sensitive to this issue through my conversations with the PSW professors, I pressed for a woman to ask a question. When no woman stood to ask a question, the moderator—with every good intent—tried to goad the women into speaking. He asked whether men were just naturally smarter; he was clearly hoping that he would irritate a woman into asking a question. A woman finally stood to ask two questions. Unfortunately, her first question was essentially the same as three similar questions that I had already answered. I was willing to hear her out and answer it again, just so that a woman would have participated in the forum. However, the moderator and some male students interrupted her to say that I had already answered that question. After this embarrassing outcome, she was not willing to ask her second question.

When I recounted this event to the center faculty members, they were naturally distressed. It became clear that good intentions were inadequate; deliberate strategies were needed.

An important goal is the development of a gender inclusive curriculum for the university. PSW has produced a number of resources about mainstreaming gender in the university. The term mainstreaming is translated at *pengarusutamakaan*, a fairly literal translation. In practical terms, it seems to mean having women on equal footing with men in the classroom, in the governance of the university, and being aware of the different learning styles that men and women have. *Gender Best Practice: Pengarusutamakan Gender dalam Universitas Islam Negeri Sunan Kalijaga* (Hidayat, R. 2005) is a *buku panduan*, a book that sets standards of practice for the university. It was born out of the perceived need to standardize approaches for dealing with gender issues in the classroom and in the management of the university. Hidayat gives specific suggestions on how to actively include women students in classroom activities and how to give equal time to examples using women and to women of historical importance (Hidayat, R. 2005).

The book assumes that women have a different way of learning than men and includes an appendix which summarizes a 1987 paper titled "Women's Way of Knowing: On Gaining a Voice." In the appendix, and in the book itself, there are several generalizations made about how women learn. For example "women are passive, reactive and dependent on those in authority which are usually men" (2005: 102). Further, women are said to be less likely to make problems in the classroom. The book advises professors to give women more time to respond to questions because they are more careful and take more time before they speak. Some of these suggestions and generalizations may sound a bit odd to a Western audience. However, the book points out that gender differences in learning styles are based on differences in gender socialization in a particular (in this case Indonesian Muslim) society (2005: 40, 51). Other suggestions and generalizations seem less foreign to an American classroom such as the suggestion to disallow any kind of interruptions when someone is speaking, and even to prevent body language that is disruptive. This is because men are more likely to interrupt women than other men (2005: 50). Other suggestions included making sure that equal numbers of men and women have the opportunity to speak in class (p. 49). Forms of affirmative action *might* be needed, such as turn quotas (one man and then one woman speaks). One professor selects a woman to be the head of the class and because of that women are more likely to speak. A particularly interesting suggestion is to use gender neutral language when using Arabic and English. Such a suggestion is less important in Indonesian because other than loan words from Arabic and Sanskrit, Indonesian does not typically gender-mark words. Given this, one can see why faculty might need to be made aware of these issues in Arabic and English.

In a 2004 book titled, *Isu-Isu Gender dalam Kurrikulum Pendidkan Dasar dan Mengengah (Gender Issues in Elementary and Middle School Curriculum)*, the center addresses how gender differences are taught in the government-regulated religious school curriculum (madrasah). In the front matter, the book lays out some basic differences between men and women such as the minimum coverage of the body for modesty's sake, percentage of inheritance, position in the family, and even how they should be prepared for burial and how they should be buried. The editors suggest that many of the issues listed require critical examination. In the first chapter they address some broad approaches to this critical rereading including how to consider "misogynistic Hadith" (Ghafur and Isnanto 2004: 18ff).

Muhammad Sodiq explained the critical importance of addressing gender issues in the madrasah at the K-8 level as a matter of impacting the cultural perceptions of men and women at a very young age. It is very difficult to change the gender stereotypes held by university students; they have been fully enculturated in to what Sodiq calls a patriarchal society. He considers Indonesian, and especially Javanese, culture as patriarchal because of practical matters of daily life, like boys never learning to cook and placing that task exclusively on women, even though Javanese kinship is bilateral (interview, June 2012). In looking at the critiques of the elementary level education (*Ibtidaiyah*), the concern is the representations in the textbooks that might leave a wrong impression. Much of the concern is about pictures and diagrams used in school books such as one that shows a man reciting the call to prayer or only men witnessing a sacrifice, which suggests that only men can or should do these things. Another picture shows men and women seated separately at a fast-opening during Ramadan, the implication, according to the editors, is that this should always be the case. They recommend explaining when this would be so and when it would be acceptable for men and women to break the fast together (like in the family). In other pictures, such as for prayers (*salat*) and other rituals only men are shown performing, whereas the editors suggest that both men and women should be depicted. When the second-grade textbook says that only men can lead prayers, the editors suggest pointing out that this is an issue that is debated (2004: 31). Sodiq acknowledges that this is a particularly difficult adjustment to make in the curriculum and so they leave it alone for the most part, concentrating on the less-controversial dimensions (showing both men and women praying) and on administrative dimensions of the madrasah schools, especially in encouraging these schools to promote women to positions of authority and responsibility; even to the level of principal (*kepala sekolah*) (interview, June 2012).

Veiling

Although *jilbab* is required on all Perguruan Tinggi Agama Islam Negeri (PTAIN) campuses, one never sees the full head-to-toe garments including a face veil. In fact, outsiders sometimes criticize PTAIN for being too lax in their enforcement of authentic *jilbab* and that some students, and even some professors, allow some of their hair to show. Some of these professors will still be critical of blouses that are too short. On the campus of IAIN North Sumatra, one could clearly distinguish the Indonesian women from the Malaysian women because the Malaysian women wore "more authentic" attire although none of them wore the full black *abaya* with *jilbab* (head covering) and *niqab* (face veil). The Malaysian men on the IAIN North Sumatra campus also dressed more conservatively than their Indonesian counterparts. The only time I saw such full-black covering on women was on a flight from Medan to Kuala Lumpur. The *jilbab*-wearing Indonesian woman sitting next to me scoffed at the Malaysian woman who ran into a bulkhead while boarding the plane because her vision was so badly obscured by her face veil. The form and meaning of appropriate attire is not a settled issue. At UIN Jakarta, it seems like the nonreligious fakultas are setting a higher standard when it comes to appropriate attire, as seen in figure 5.1. Some instructors from the religious fakultas attribute this to a greater presence of Prosperous Justice Party (PKS; Muslim

Figure 5.1 Examples of wrong and right female attire

Brotherhood)–oriented instructors in the general knowledge fakultas. In other words, in matters of religion, general fakultas adhere to more conservative forms, or dialects.

What is striking is that the prescribed attire is more distinctive for women than it is for men. The men's attire would not mark them as unambiguously Muslim once outside of the campus, as seen in figure 5.2. It seems that an uneven burden is placed on women to be the banner bearers for Islam.

Conclusion

Gender debates reflect core issues in the discourse about what kind of Islam will come to dominate Indonesia. Groups like HTI and other Islamist groups reject not only Western style feminism and

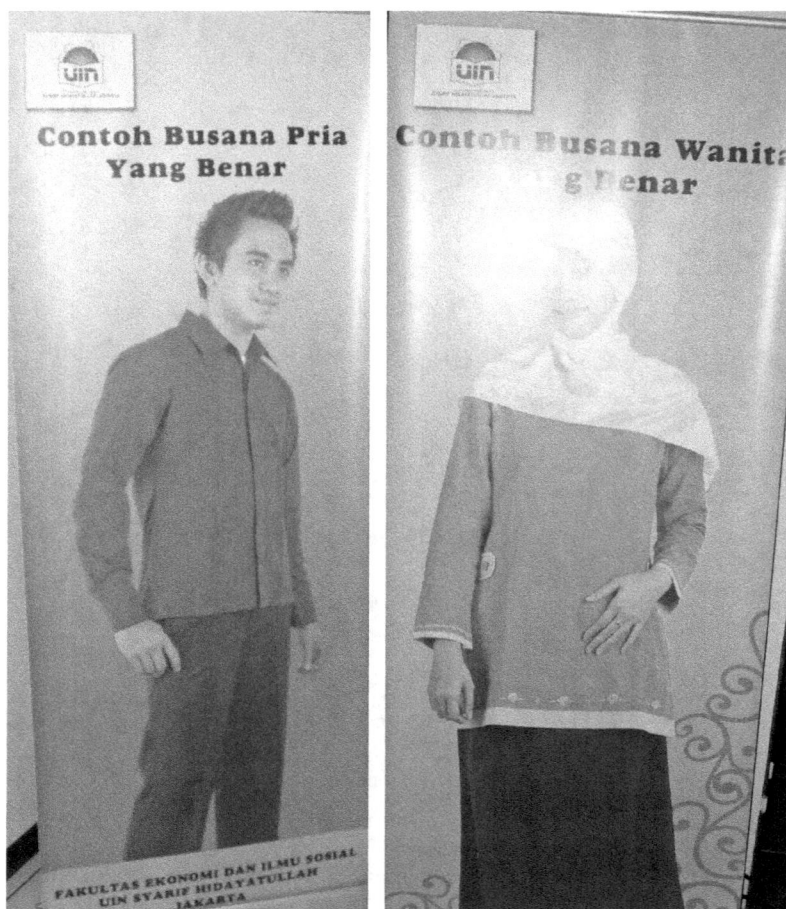

Figure 5.2 Economic faculty examples of correct male and female attire

gender equity, but even the relative gender parity that is often seen as characteristic of Southeast Asia, at least in the public sphere. For many, if not most, Indonesians, the Islamist vision for gender relationships, such as the government enforcing the use of male guardians when women leave their home, is downright foreign. The kinds of gender debates taking place in Indonesia are neither new nor unique in the Muslim world. Some of the basic concepts like rereading misogynistic texts come from scholars like Fatima

Mernissi, the Moroccan sociologist. What seem to be unique in the Indonesian case are two factors. The first is the active and enthusiastic involvement of men. The men involved in PSW and PSG are not trying to hijack the center and its efforts; they won't even take the director position. The second factor that seems unique to Indonesia is that these efforts are carried out by the faculty and staff of an Islamic university. Instead of being the efforts of people trained exclusively in the social sciences, like Mernissi, this work is being done by professors whose primary area of study is Islamic law (syari'ah) and the interpretations of sacred texts (Tafsir and Hadith).

Chapter 6

Where Is the Islam, and What Kind?

In 2008, it seemed that the Universitas Islam Negeri (UIN) conversion process was over. There had been a ministerial decree from the then minister of religious affairs, Maftuh Basyuni, that there were to be no more UIN, but it allowed for the possibility of a wider mandate for Institut Agama Islam Negeri (IAIN), a concept adopted by the Ministries of both Religious Affairs and Education as a way to bridge between being religion-only institutes and full universities (Azra 2011: 44). But as often seems the case in Indonesia, with a new change in minister, came a change in policy and some IAIN are now in the process of applying to become UIN. The debates (whether on or off campus) are far from over. Like many debates about education, these debates about Perguruan Tinggi Agama Islam Negeri (PTAIN) concern differences over the purpose of the institution and not only its future but also the future of society, in general.

For some, employability of graduates must be an essential part of the vision for PTAIN. Komaruddin Hidayat (rector at UIN Jakarta) said his vision for UIN Jakarta is for it to become a center of scholarship and civil society. For many at IAINs, the concern is not only about development but also making sure that the Muslim community, especially those from pesantren, share in future economic growth and not become further marginalized. He was also concerned about how to make it so that graduates care about society and have a strong character as well as strong academic records in keeping with the UIN Jakarta motto of "knowledge, piety, and integrity." Hidayat acknowledges that not all faculty are of the highest caliber and there are not enough PhDs in each field, but maintains that as a whole, UIN Jakarta is an excellent university. He argues that to improve the scholarship on campus and to become a world-class research university, they need professors who are the best in their field. He wants UIN Jakarta to create cadres of graduates who can build the future for Indonesian by imbuing them with optimism and enthusiasm (interview, February 2009).

Another important part of PTAIN developing into their full measure is for each campus to gain greater autonomy and to reduce the control Ministry of Religious Affairs (MORA) has over curricular design. However, Machasin when he was the director for Islamic higher education, was deeply concerned that not all campuses would be able to administer themselves effectively. There are also efforts for each campus to have greater fiscal control of their own budgets (interview, January 14, 2009).

Visions for the future of PTAIN are not limited to those on campus. Traditional leaders like kyai do not want PTAIN to be ideological neutral. The greatest concern of kyai and even society at large is that students are pious; many in society at large are less concerned about academic accomplishment. Many faculty members and administrators have identified an opportunity—to structure an environment so that the desired piety is delivered without committing to what many consider to be an outdated educational agenda. Yatsir Nasution, the rector of IAIN North Sumatra when I taught on his campus, argued that the traditional focus of PTAIN was on creating graduates who excelled in the Islamic sciences. In the past, what was called the Islamic sciences or Islamic Studies was limited to classical topics like fiqh, syari'ah, tafsir, and Sufism. Recently, they have sought to expand the meaning of Islamic Studies, so all the sciences that can be influenced by the Islamic-based philosophy of science are included. He wished to avoid controversies regarding a dichotomy between Islamic and non-Islamic studies by creating a wide range of academic fields influenced by Islam (interview, November 8, 2008).

Wider Mandate

Regardless of how the debate about IAINs becoming universities concludes, there is pressure to create a wider mandate; that all PTAIN would teach more than religion. Therefore some IAINs are adding programs like psychology, nursing, management, and public health under the existing fakultas. For example, IAIN Raden Saleh in Palembang was developing a psychology program within the Dakwah (missions) faculty. Since an Islamic version of pastoral counseling was already part of this program, it does not seem very odd. A bit stranger, at first glance, was the recommendation made at the IAIN North Sumatra campus to place a public health program in the *Fakultas Ushuluddin* (theology, or foundations of faith). On some campuses, public health is in the *Fakultas Dakwah*. On further examination is not as unusual as it seems. At most PTAINs, comparative religion is found in either *Ushuluddin* or *Dakwah*, depending on the educational paths of the faculty members. It is in comparative religion where one finds faculty members who have received graduate training in the social sciences. Since one dimension of public health is the application of social science theory and methods to community health issues, it makes sense to place public health in a faculty with the most social scientists, especially given the absence of a health or science faculty.

Hassan, the graduate director for IAIN North Sumatra in 2008, saw a "wider mandate" as the continuation of processes long in place. For example, the Fakultas Syari'ah includes the *Mualamah* program, which covers the classical fiqh on the legal means of buying and selling. It is more than just a theoretical interpretation of the Quran and Hadith. It speaks to practical application within a reality that does not allow for a strict adherence to fiqh. He said that there is therefore pressure to move out of classical fiqh and create a new "Islamic Economics" program. He went on to say that this is especially true given the job market and the desire for graduates to find employment. In some universities, Departments of Economics (even Islamic Economics) start from the social reality of the current economy. He argued that there is a need to bring them together and that is a reason for IAINs to become UINs (interview, January 2009).

"Where Is the Islam"

Many people both on and off of PTAIN campuses have asked that with the change of wider mandates, how will PTAIN remain distinctive. Muhammad Machasin suggests that I consider the question asked by many in wider Indonesian society, "Where is the Islam at PTAIN? (interview, January 14, 2009). Imam Suprayago, on the other hand, argued that to even ask the question "where is the Islam at PTAIN?" betrays a lack of sophistication in how one defines Islam. He suggests Indonesians of all religions need to move beyond an understanding of religion that limits it to rituals (interview, February 9, 2011). This book has reviewed a number of ways in which this question is addressed including the relationship between religion and the sciences, even the social sciences. If PTAIN is no longer exclusively religious in focus, how does it differ from other universities and if there is no difference, why have both? As we have seen, there are those who have argued that the PTAIN system remains different even when they offer nonreligious subjects. One major way in which the "where is the Islam?" question is addressed is through defining and redefining different approaches to the relationship between science and religion. As we saw in chapter 3, there have been a number of different approaches. A very popular one takes a proof-texting approach and tries to find Quranic verses and Hadith that support the findings and theory of science. This does not seem promising to me, such proof-texting of science leads to a crippled science because all findings must be verified in the holy text; science, by definition, must be open to discovery, verification, and falsification. It also leads to bad hermeneutics because it approaches the text with an intended outcome instead of reading the text and seeing where it leads.

Another approach has been to intensify religious education in certain areas, even as other fakultas take on a wider mandate. In 2001, in conjunction with the launch of the new nonreligious fakultas, UIN Jakarta started a new religious faculty called Dirasat Islamiyah. The effort to create this fakultas goes back to 1998 with Noer Samad who was the education and culture envoy at the Indonesian embassy in Cairo and other attachés who were Al-Azhar alumni (Kinoshita 2009: 9). The efforts came to fruition with 2002 Memorandum of Understanding (MOU) between Al-Azhar University and UIN Jakarta that allows graduates from the UIN Jakarta Fakultas Dirasat Islamiyah to earn two degrees: a Bachelor (*Sarjana*) of Islamic Studies from UIN and an LC (License) from Al-Azhar, provided they spend an additional year in Cairo. The MOU required the Indonesian partner to upgrade the quality of its instruction, so that it had the same academic standards as Al-Azhar. In this fakultas, the language of instruction is Arabic, unlike the older religious fakultas where Indonesian is the language of instruction. The stated aim is to graduate scholars with a "holistic and moderate understanding of Islam" (en.uinjkt.ac.id/index.php/dirasat-islamiya, accessed on December 12, 2012). Kinsoshita argues that by adopting Dirasat Islamiyah at the same time at becoming a full university, UIN Jakarta finally adopted the whole educational system of Al-Azhar (2009: 9), which had added nonreligious fakultas in 1961 before the PTAIN system was founded. It is interesting to note that while the Fakultas Dirasat Islamiyah in Jakarta is coed, for Indonesians at Al-Azhar, Dirasat Islamiyah attracts mostly women, while Indonesian men prefer the older religious fakultas, which unlike their Indonesian counterparts, use Arabic as the language of instruction.

The creation of this fakultas and its relationship with Al-Azhar is significant because it signals to the more conservative elements of UIN's constituency that while some of the older fakultas are expanding, there is one part of UIN Jakarta that is not only maintaining purely religious programs but is actually intensifying the students' experience with Arabic. Further, this new fakultas makes connections with one of the oldest and most respected institutions of Islamic higher education. Much like the change in the official madrasah education in the 1990s, this move allows most students to get a broader education while providing more intensive and expansive training in Islamic scholarship to a select number of students.

Bridges with Pesantren

One of the major answers to the question of "where is the Islam?" is to focus on emphasizing a specifically Islamic environment. Machasin asked the rhetorical question that since a general university can take on an Islamic environment, why should PTAINs become universities, what would be their unique contribution? On Java, at least, the answer is to emphasize the pesantren roots of the IAIN system.

In the midst of the controversy over PTAIN, some professors choose to emphasize their pesantren background over additional training and preparations. One professor confided to me that when speaking to the general public she starts by clearly identifying herself as coming from a family that has run a pesantren for generations. She also points out that she is from the most pesantren-like department at UIN, Fakultas Tafsir-Hadith. Nostalgic claims to an imagined pesantren tradition are not restricted to individuals but are part of the branding of many PTAIN. Different campuses define themselves differently vis-à-vis the pesantren tradition. Some campuses on Java, want to be seen as preserving the special character of pesantren. When those who advocate such preservation are asked how it might be achieved, they can only give vague ideas about how it might be done. The answer is basically to encourage those instructors and students who are from pesantren backgrounds to continue to carry out the values and practices of the pesantren. Other professors at the same campuses state that those who are promoting such ideas are just really frightened of the more conservative elements of society.

The pesantren community has long been concerned about IAIN education and perceived reduction in its quality. The pesantren community in East Java started reaching out to IAIN students in order to round out their education in the 1990s. One example of a pesantren established to address these issues was *Pesantren Mahasiswa An Nur* in Surabaya, run by an IAIN Surabaya professor, Imam Ghazali Said, who was the professor mentioned in chapter 5 who became an ally and advocate of the Women's Studies Center at UIN Yogya after a careful reexamination of the source texts. As a Middle East graduate, he is also an example of a traditional yet progressive Muslim leader in the manner of Abdurrahman Wahid. I attended the dedication of this pesantren in August 1995, at which time most of the 70 *santri* were IAIN students. In his speech for this event, Ghazali said that because these students will become members of Indonesia's religious bureaucracy, it was crucial that they have a firm grounding in classical Islam, as found in kitab kuning. However, the students at this pesantren generally did not have the skills for a traditional advanced pesantren pedagogy and curriculum so they used a combination of derivative texts and skills building so that they can access kitab kuning. Grounding in the traditional learning of pesantren is a way to stem fundamentalism and radicalism, according to Hasyim Muzadi, founder of *Pesantren Mahasiswa Al-Hikam* and former head of Nahdlatul Ulama (NU) (Lukens-Bull 2001: 362). Imam Ghazali Said asserted in a public meeting with an Australian diplomat that NU pesantren are not involved in radicalism (Julian 2011). In recent years, as liberalism became a named threat, kitab kuning were also seen as a prophylactic for that perceived ill as well.

While there is a deep historical connection between PTAIN and pesantren, Azra and Suwito, former rector and vice rector at UIN Jakarta observed a change in the pool of incoming students. This change has not been about where incoming students had been educated but the nature of that education. Almost all PTAIN students come from Islamic day schools called madrasah that follow a government-recognized curriculum, although many are operated out of pesantren. In the 1970s, madrasah curriculum was 70 percent religious subjects and 30 percent general subjects. In the 1990s, the percentages were reversed so that only 30 percent of the curriculum was focused on religion. One reason PTAIN must change, Azra and Suwito argue, is that most students do not have the capacity or the desire to train intensively to become ulama (interview, January 16, 2009). Regardless of how the discourse on the Islamization of all knowledge concludes, some argue that the best way for PTAIN to maintain a unique character as Islamic institutions is the creation of an Islamic environment.

Creating Pesantren Environments on Campus

An important way some PTAIN seek to maintain an Islamic environment has been to draw on aspects of the pesantren tradition. At UIN Malang there is an on-campus pesantren in which all freshmen are required to live. To an outsider, these might appear to be mere dormitories, however, the students are organized in ways similar to pesantren and special attention is paid to their spiritual, moral, and character development, exactly like a traditional pesantren.

Once when visiting UIN Malang, I was allowed to stay in a guest house inside the compound of the on-campus pesantren. As day gave way to evening, milling college students in shirts and trousers (sometimes even jeans and T-shirts) gave way to *santri* in sarongs, long sleeve shirts, and peci. But, it's the exact same young men. As is typical of pesantren for university students, the pesantren education takes place in the early morning before classes and in the evening after class (Lukens-Bull 2001). It is absolutely required for all first-year students, even those in a general fakultas, to stay in the pesantren. Second-year students may elect to continue to reside in the pesantren; upwards of 200 students do so each year. Although the facilities have capacity for 1,600 men and 2,000 women only a total of 1,600 students, men and women, currently live within the grounds. The stated goal is to create a pesantren in a university setting, to blend the two institutions to create intellectuals who are ulama, and ulama who are intellectuals.

A special feature of the pesantren at UIN Malang is the focus on learning Arabic. In addition to the normal schedule of introductory courses, and pesantren lessons, first-year students spend 5–6 hours daily studying Arabic to address some of the concerns about language ability that were debated in the mid-1990s. All graduates have more than rudimentary skill in Arabic, although, since they come in at different levels of competency, they leave with different levels of competency.

One Western-educated faculty member at UIN Malang, Basri, expressed concern about the Arabic-language program. Although, in their first year, the student's regular coursework is reduced somewhat, the Arabic program becomes burdensome in subsequent years with six hours of language study each day. He argued that the program is strongly supported by Middle East graduates and the PKS (Prosperous Justice Party) faction on campus. He suggested two reasons why this might be the case. The first is practical; graduates can find work as an Arabic teacher regardless of their actual degree program. The second is that it gives the campus a greater Middle East orientation. Basri is concerned about the growing influence of PKS on the campus because of the Arabic program. He argued that the NU faction on campus hold the vast majority of leadership positions now, however, the PKS faction is working hard to prepare future leaders and it is likely that in 5–10 years they will have more qualified personnel and will be able to take control of the campus leadership (interview, February 2009).

UIN Malang's on-campus pesantren is particularly interesting in the context of educational crisis faced by the pesantren community in the mid-1990s. The problem was that pesantren, like Tebu Ireng, who had added the government curricula were no longer able to produce graduates with the basic skills to be religious leaders. It was widely accepted that the training of leaders was going to be through the IAIN system but there was significant dissatisfaction with the system. IAIN graduates in the 1990s did not possess the basic competency in Arabic to read and understand the classical Islamic texts (kitab kuning), which was of high importance to the pesantren community. Jabar Adlan, then rector of IAIN Sunan Ampel in Surabaya tried to establish extracurricular sessions on kitab kuning (classical texts), but due to lack of interest he abandoned this effort. Mark Woodward reports that the Muhummadiyah University system faced and is facing similar difficulties in creating ulama and other religious leaders (personal communication, February 6, 2009).

Chamzawi, who runs the pesantren and is a professor of Arabic, compares the UIN Malang pesantren to the one at Universitas Islam Malang (UNISMA), where he was involved in the instruction in the early morning *pengajian* twice a week until a few years ago. The pesantren in UNISMA is small and is completely voluntary. In that way UIN Malang is very different because it really infuses the whole campus with a pesantren feel. There are certain symbols present that to the trained eye signal the connection with pesantren and with NU. Once such symbol is the large drum (*beduk*) in the new campus mosque. The drum is beaten in a distinctive pattern before the call to prayer is broadcasted. Before the invention of loud speakers, this was the only way for Muslims in rural setting to know it was time for prayer because the unaided human voice would not travel far enough in a setting with dense vegetation (see figure 6.1).

The idea and practice of on-campus pesantren was not original to IAIN. In the 1990s, UNISMA, which had several fakultas including Tarbiyah (Islamic education), law (secular), agronomy, animal husbandry, engineering, education (general), administration, syari'ah (Islamic law), and math and sciences, established an on-campus pesantren so that it would be more integrated into campus life and the two areas of knowledge (secular and religious) can be more easily integrated. The goal was not to create ulama, but people who have both academic potential and Islamic morality. The motivations for establishing this on-campus pesantren sound strikingly similar for the reasons given for the much later pesantren at the IAIN Surabaya and UIN Malang campuses.

Because of the successes at UIN Malang, other PTAIN campuses are encouraged to establish a campus pesantren. It remains to be seen if these will be optional and how successful this reproduction will be. It may be that it works in Malang because East Java is where the pesantren community is strongest. Whether or not this model is meaningful or would be successful in other provinces remains to be seen. For example, Medan has very few pesantren in the surrounding area (five total) as compared to the thousands found near Malang and Yogya.

Figure 6.1 The UIN Malang campus mosque beduk

In 2009, IAIN Sunan Ampel in Surabaya had a small pesantren, which had 160 women and 110 men, most of whom were in one of two scholarship programs from the MORA that targeted special needs in *Tafsir-Hadith* and Islamic family law. Living in the pesantren was a condition of the scholarship. During the day, they took the normal curriculum for IAIN students. The material in the pesantren is not very different from what they study in their regular courses, but it is all in Arabic. The vision for the pesantren is to be a center for language study and for some students to memorize the Quran. At the time, I was told that the women seem to be more serious students and have enough Arabic so that these women were already studying classical texts on mysticism once a week. The men were more attracted to seminars and attended as many as two a week.

UIN Yogya has taken another step to strengthen its pesantren roots and to build bridges to local pesantren by taking advantage of a new MORA program for students in Tafsir-Hadith to receive scholarships contingent on their living in a pesantren. Instead of creating an on-campus pesantren, UIN Yogya has taken advantage of the large number of pesantren in town by negotiating with a number of pesantren to place entire cohorts at a particular pesantren.

As of May 2009, UIN Jakarta had not established a pesantren on campus, but there was considerable concern about creating and maintaining a pesantren environment on the campus. In speaking about the special character of UIN Jakarta, Komaruddin Hidayat emphasized that with the urban nature of the campus it is essential that the atmosphere and values of the madrasah and pesantren are not lost. Hidayat added "not wanting to become a government employee" and "being close to the masses" to the standard list of pesantren values: sincerity (*ikhlas*), simplicity (*kesederhanan*), brotherhood, and self-sufficiency (*kemandiran*). He argued that it is essential that the kind of teacher-student relationship found in pesantren must be continued, so that the professors who come from pesantren can be role models. This includes deep respect for the teachers on the part of students and deep concern for the students on the part of teachers. To create the communal feeling common to pesantren, he wanted to follow Malang's example. It is the values and character building as well as the place of the kitab kuning and other religious symbols that are most important. Since not all students and teachers come from pesantren, he fears that UIN could lose the pesantren character. For those not from a pesantren, he felt it unwise to force too high a standard upon them but that by creating an Islamic atmosphere, they can be brought along. Hidayat said the community around UIN helps them enforce their values. Most, if not all, landlords enforce single gender roommates and restricted visiting hours for members of the opposite sex. Through a landlord association, they encourage landlords to report infractions of the campus morality standards and have even expelled students based on these reports. Further, he argued that in order to keep the pesantren values, the core community needs to come from a pesantren background and their values can be protected as they are modernized. Therefore, he wants to have excellence in the general fakultas so that pesantren graduates want to pursue their degrees there. He argued that it is the pesantren students who are most likely to return to their rural communities with their new knowledge (interview, February 2009).

Some senior professors argue, contrary to Hidayat's statements otherwise, that his desire to uphold and expand the pesantren atmosphere was based in fear and to his inability to confront community criticism or even radical elements (interview, January 2009). These senior professors argue that becoming a full university was a real boon in strengthening pesantren values. Following the fall of the Suharto, when all students were from pesantren and madrasah, they sometimes used the relative freedom of the IAIN campus to express ideas and behaviors that they could not express before coming to college. Students would routinely organize protests against campus policies, formed Marxist study groups, and did things that upset those on the religious right, like saying "Dog is Great (*Ajinghu Akbar*)" and "Welcome to a God-Free Zone." Once the institution became a university and the nonreligious fakultas enrolled students from nonreligious high schools, these behaviors lessened because the general school background students behaved more politely, more "Islamically," and studied hard—this embarrassed the students from pesantren background and brought them back in line.

Defining Islam Is Political

If how to remain Islamic and true to tradition is one aspect of the concerns and debates, then another major concern is defining what kind of Islam is to be followed in Indonesia and taught at PTAIN. What is considered to be properly Islamic is inherently political. The Dutch knew this when they sought to control and limit the impact of Islam. Sukarno knew this in 1926 when he envisioned a nation born of the combined efforts of Nationalism, Communism, and Islam. Suharto knew this when he neutered Muslim political parties by combining them into a single party and when he sought to create the PTAIN system as an institution that would be counter to an Islamist vision of the state.

First and foremost, the kind of Islam to be advocated by PTAIN is an intellectual Islam; a well thought out and reasoned faith. An intellectual Islam does not restrict what can be examined. The tradition established by Harun Nasution warmly embraces the idea that much can be learned from all expressions of Islam, even those that have historically been considered heretical. The possibility to examine forms of Islam other than the government endorsed form and the quality of Islamic education at PTAIN are key reasons why students come from Malaysia to study at PTAIN.

Chapter 4 examined at length the debate of whether to follow a Middle Eastern and theological intellectual tradition or a Western and social scientific one. However, it is not really a binary choice between Middle Eastern and Western intellectual traditions. To accept this binary is to accept the idea of civilizations ala Huntington and to perpetuate the idea of a clash of civilization.[1] There are a myriad of different intellectual traditions in both "civilizations." Even if someone takes a degree in anthropology, like Zamakhsyari Dhofier, the intellectual traditions within that discipline are sufficiently diverse that one cannot assume a homogenous point of view. Further, PTAIN academics are working to create an Indonesian tradition of Islamic Studies.

Secularism, Pluralism, and Liberalism

A significant part of Indonesian Muslim discourse over most of the last decade surrounds conservative concerns around secularism, pluralism, and liberalism, known collectively by the pun *sipilis* (syphilis), a concatenation of these three terms meant to suggest that they are a corrupting social disease. In a July 2005 edict (*fatwa*) from the Indonesian Ulama Council, or Majelis Ulama Indonesia (MUI) declared these three ideas to be deviant and should be repudiated by all good Muslims (MUI 2005). The edicts of MUI do not carry any official weight and are often ignored by the vast majority of Indonesian Muslims. The Islamist group *Dewan Dakwah Islam Indonesia* (DDII) endorsed this MUI edict and instructed DDII affiliated preachers to support it. Cholil Ridwan, who is both a DDII leader and a MUI executive said,

> People who are against the edicts are *munafikin* (hypocrites) and are more dangerous than *kafir*, since they attack from inside Islam (*Jakarta Post* 2005).

Although the edict addresses a trifecta of progressive ideas, the central concern in Indonesian discourse is secularism with liberalism and pluralism being symptomatic of the larger issue.

The issues of pluralism, tolerance, and religious freedom are central debates about the future of Islam in Indonesia and they found their way into the PTAIN campuses. In 1999, IAIN Syarif Hidyatullah in Jakarta took on the role of developing a civic education course (Jackson and Bahrissalim 2007). The design of the curriculum was based in part on a survey that was conducted across various IAIN campuses. During the Suharto regime, there was mandated training in the national ideology of *Pancasila* (Five Principles) at all levels of education. The goal of this education was focused on social integration and national unity (Kraince 2008: 347). It was a de facto peace and pluralism training program. When IAIN Jakarta recast this curriculum in the post-Suharto era, they first retrained the former instructors of the *Pancasila* curriculum. some of those trained not only taught the new curriculum on their own campuses but also trained other faculty at other public and private Islamic institutes. This new civic education program has not been mandated, so different campuses have adopted different aspects of the curriculum. For the instructor of this course at IAIN North Sumatra, collaborative learning is at the heart of civic education; not just a way to transmit the information but as a way to manifest the core lessons of cooperation, collaboration, and conflict resolution. In general, the civic education curriculum is considerably broader than the *Pancasila* education which it replaced, and includes an examination of theories about democracy, participation, and development.

Secularism and pluralism are closely related concepts. Secularism is about the place of religion in society. Since practically no one is arguing that religion has no place in Indonesian society, the real question is about the relationship between Islam and the state. Defined this way, secularists would include people like the late Muslim intellectual, Nurcholish Madjid, who advocated for an

Islamic society but not an Islamic state. Islamist groups like Islam Defender's Front (FPI), DDII, and Majelis Mujahiddin Indonesia (MMI) argue that syari'ah law should be enforced by the state. They oppose the very idea of a nonreligious government. As mentioned before, Hartono Ahmad Jaiz argues that supporting the existence of the Republic of Indonesia as a secular state is tantamount to apostasy. Islamists want to see Indonesia become an Islamic state. Therefore pluralism is a problem for them. The *Pancasila* ideology holds that all Indonesians must be monotheists but recognizes six religions: Islam, Protestantism (*Kristen*), Catholicism, Hinduism, Buddhism, and Confucianism. Further, the very definition of religion used by the Indonesian government also requires a Prophet and a Book. Clearly some of the officially recognized religions have been reimagined so that they fit an Islamic model. *Pancasila* recognizes all religions as equally valid for the purposes of the state. Islamists reject this claim and all forms of pluralism.

In Indonesian discourse, there are two distinct ways of thinking of pluralism. One is in regard to salvation and the other is in regard to life in Indonesia. Very few people are willing to say that all religions, as currently practiced, are equally good in matters of the eternal (i.e., getting into heaven). Some say that all religions were true and from God when they were first revealed, however, all except Islam have been corrupted. Therefore, Indonesian pluralists, for the most part, keep to the idea that all religions are equally valid for the creation of a just and moral society in Indonesia. Although there are some PTAIN faculty who see the possible for salvation for non-Muslims. Pluralists, like Sahiron at UIN Yogya, argue that pluralism was part of Islam from the very start. They point to the idea of the People of the Book (*ahli kitab*) and that Jews and Christians were parties to the Medina Charter, which established a pluralist society under the rule of the Prophet Muhammad. Jews and Christians were free to practice their own religion but still obligated to help defend the community as a whole. Those who are arguing against pluralism deliberately seek to confuse these two kinds of religious pluralism.

Most Indonesian Muslims could accept the idea that all religions are equally useful to the nation. Where there is much debate is what God thinks about other religions. Some would argue that it is a matter between God and the followers of each faith. Others are uncertain whether Christians will go to heaven, and still others are quite adamant that they will not. Most Indonesian Muslims hold that being a good Muslim is one's best chance for reward in heaven. Since the Prophet Muhammad is the last prophet, Islam is the last, and hence best, revelation. By confusing the social and theological meanings of religious pluralism, Islamists are starting to change the tone of religious discussion in Indonesia. Increasingly, ordinary Indonesian Muslims are suspicious about pluralism in any form and with it liberal and progressive forms of Islam.

Liberalism

The term liberal Islam does not originate in Islamic discourse but in Western scholarship about it. However, Bustamam-Ahmad associates liberal thinking with Sufism (2011: 100). He traces liberal Islam's growth in Southeast Asia to the influence of Harun Nasution and Nurcholish Madjid (2011: 102). Bustamam-Ahmad identifies several factors that might lead someone to be associated with "liberal" Islam. The first is having a pesantren education; their familiarity with the text and methods of this tradition allowed them to develop into critical scholars. Another educational commonality is time spent at Al-Azhar and the Islamic education model at IAIN, which allows students to examine a wide range of Islamic scholarship. Further, there are important "Western influences" including liberal "Middle Eastern" Muslims in the West (Fazlur Rahman, Muhammad Arkoun, and Fatima Mernissi) and the influence of Western Indonesianists who have had a role in their education. Other factors include being involved with international NGOs and the general influence of Abdurrahman Wahid on Indonesian discourse (Bustamam-Ahmad 2011: 105–106).

The apostasy accusations aimed at both individual professors and at UIN themselves are not taken seriously on campus, but the rhetoric is not unique. Hanging in front of FPI Headquarters is a sign that labels all forms of progressive Islam as apostasy. The main slogan says, "Eliminate Liberal(s), Dismantle Ahmadiyah," thereby linking liberal, progressive Muslims with minority religious group that self-identifies as Muslim but recognizes a prophet after Muhammad. Ahmadiyah has faced persecution and violence in Indonesia. By linking progressive Islam including all of the UIN with Ahmadiyah, this sign is a none too subtle call for violence against progressives. The checklist asserts that liberal, progressive

Muslims, and Ahmadiyah are lost (*sesat*), apostates *(murtad)*, unbelievers *(kafir)*, and not Islam *(bukan* Islam). The sign accuses all UIN, the Liberal Islamic Network or Jaringan Islam Liberal (JIL) (which it calls the God Damned Devil Network), and Paramadina (a progressive Muslim organization and university) of being non-Muslim. It also names specific persons including the rector of UIN Jakarta. These kinds of opinions may not have widespread support, but it is a mistake to dismiss them. Groups like FPI are playing an important role in Indonesia, many would say a disproportionately important role, in shaping public opinion (figure 6.2).

While off-campus groups and individuals will include democracy in their definition of liberalism and secular, those on campus who otherwise are part of the "conservative turn" (van Bruinessen 2013) would not. On-campus conservatives want to limit liberalism, in the sense of something Muslims should reject, to liberal hermeneutics of the sacred texts. They support freedom of thought and expression within limits, namely that a person should position themselves first and foremost as a Muslim. Yusron at UIN Yogya argued that faculty members who position themselves first as a social scientist and not as Muslim, should not remain as faculty members in the PTAIN system. This argument harkens back to

Figure 6.2 Sign in front of FPI HQ in Jakarta (photo: Mark Woodward)

the model of PTAIN as a big pesantren and PTAIN professors as a potential source of religious leadership. This is one model for how PTAIN should interact with society but it is by no means the most commonly accepted model.

Yusron argued that Islam is established rules. If a matter is not settled then people are free to be liberal. However, he argued that if religion is clear on a matter, if the Prophet set an example, there is no room for liberalism. He concluded by arguing that there is no such thing as Islamic liberalism; to be Muslim means being obedient toward the Quran and Hadith. A professor at UIN Malang, identified as PKS in orientation, argued that liberalism and in particular, the JIL is based on human desires (*hawa nafsu*) and self-promotion, not devotion to God.

Some UIN faculty members have criticized the FPI as thugs in religious garb (*preman bersorban*). Yusron thinks that this is a generalization and that as scholars, his colleagues should be more specific. He asserts that some of FPI's activities are legitimate. He even defends some of FPI's "sweeping" raids on certain businesses, especially bars and nightclubs. He claims that some of the affected businesses were conducting illegal activities and that FPI had reported them to the police, who did nothing.

Irshad Manji, a Canadian Muslim author, is a central figure in some Indonesian debates about the future of Islam. Although her most recent book (2011) praises Indonesia as "a place where pluralistic Islam could be upheld in the real world" (*Jakarta Post* 2012b), the Indonesian book tour launching the Indonesian translation was plagued by protests, cancellations, and even physical attacks by MMI (Majelis Mujahiddin Indonesia; Indonesian Jihadists Council). It is clear from the media coverage of these events that those protesting Manji never mention her books but rather stress the fact that she is lesbian as their justification for their actions (*Jakarta Post* 2012a; *OkeJakarta* 2012). Since the protests include groups like FPI and others critical of the PTAIN system today, these events illustrate just what is at stake in the debates about the future of Indonesia.

Professors accused of being liberal explained to me why they thought the label was applied to them, although none used it for themselves. One said it was because he is not content with the status quo with Muslim thinking and is critical of an MUI *fatwa* declaring smoking as *haram* (forbidden). His point is not to defend smoking or the tobacco industry but to question why the MUI isn't tackling more important issues like wealth inequity or corruption. Another says he is considered too liberal because his academic work examines the literary aspects of the Quran. For some, examining the Quran as literature denigrates it. Another told me that he is considered too liberal because he advocates for women's rights and human rights and argues that they are consistent with the spirit, if not the letter, of the Quran.

Quo Vadis Indonesia

I first went to Indonesia in 1987 and fell madly in love. Not with a person, but with the people and the places; I was intoxicated. I decided that I wanted a lifetime of traveling to Indonesia, of studying it, writing and teaching about it. In 1992, I went back for advanced Indonesian language classes. This time, I was in Muslim majority areas of the country; and I still loved it, maybe even more. The Indonesia that I first met was built on an ideal of Diverse but One (*Bhinneka Tunggal Ika*). The reality was never as beautiful as the ideal but it was still amazing. This multicultural, multireligious ideal was not just the product of state mandate; although it was illegal to talk about the sometimes dark reality. Nor was it just a product of the national ideology, *Pancasila,* which mandated one of five officially recognized religions (it became six in 2000); the reality being that traditional, or so called tribal, religions and Chinese religions (other than Buddhism) had no place at the table. At a deep level Indonesians held this ideal dear. The eruption of violence against the Chinese in 1997 and the communal violence of 2000 did not give lie to that ideal. In fact, to the contrary, if this ideal of Diverse but One did not have deep roots, these periods of violence could have balkanized the country. Without this ideal, this ideology, the various groups in Indonesia have less in common that the divisions in the former Yugoslavia. Where did this ideal of unity and pluralism come from?

Those of us with long personal histories with Indonesia (25 years, in my case), remember telling friends and family that Indonesians were Muslim but different. A reasonable argument is that some of this ideal came from the Muslims of Indonesia themselves. I have already mentioned the *walisongo* several times, but have not discussed that the primary way they taught about Islam was through local art and culture, specifically the *slametan* (ritual meal) and the *wayang* or shadow puppet theater. One way this was done was by reinterpreting the Hindu epics. For example, in the Mahabharata, Arjuna has a secret weapon called the *Kalimasada*, which Javanese Muslims say is short for *Kalimah Shahada*, or the Islamic Confession of Faith. Some have argued that the highly stylized human forms in the Javanese *wayang* puppets reflect the influence of Islam, which discourages the artistic representation of the human form. To this day there are pesantren that sponsor *wayang*, *gamelan* orchestras, and other cultural events. The *walisongo* are also known for incorporating the *gamelan* (percussion orchestra), the slit gong, and the *beduk* (large drum) into the call for prayer. The purported logic was that by using sounds that people already associated with large gatherings, people would be more interested in attending the prayers. One of the most famous episodes of this accommodation is the case of Sunan Kudus who built the *minaret* of his mosque so that it looked like a Hindu temple. It stands to this day and looks more like something that belongs as part of temple in Bali than as part of mosque in Java. He built it this way, legend says, so that the mosque fit into what was a Hindu landscape. Legend also holds that he taught his followers not to eat beef so as not to offend their Hindu neighbors. In Indonesia, towns are often known for a signature dish or two, and the town of Kudus is known for its buffalo soup, keeping with the legendary injunction.

The *walisongo* legends are not deep background to Indonesian Islam, they are one main blueprint for contemporary Indonesian Islam. Kyai, the headmasters of pesantren and leaders of the Classicalist Muslim community, adopt the style and methods of the *walisongo*. This means meeting people where they are; rather than preaching against popular practices like *slametan* and *ziarah* (pilgrimage to holy tombs), they accept that people want to do these things and strive to teach them a more orthodox way of conducting and understanding these rituals. This history also means that Indonesian Islam has a strong pietistic element, meaning that doing right is left to the individual's conscience. The place of preachers and teachers is to heighten awareness (*keyakinan*) so that people will be inspired to live as good Muslims. It is not just the Classicalists who take this approach, it is what Nurcholish Majid meant when he said, "Islam, Yes; Islamic Party, No." Frequently repeated is the Quranic injunction that there should "be no compulsion in religion" (Q.S. 2: 256). Therefore the establishment of syari'ah as a national law enforced by the state has long been rejected by most Indonesian Muslims. Further, when Mukti Ali started comparative religion at PTAIN, it was with the explicit purpose of expanding the intellectual basis for Muslim appreciation of other religions. These legends and historical moments are the basis for the trope that Indonesia was the smiling face of Islam.

The face of Islam in Indonesia still smiles most of the time, but the 1965 involvement of Muslim militias in the slaughter of hundreds of thousands of alleged communists, the 1997 anti-Chinese attacks, the 2000 Christian-Muslim violence in Indonesia, the 2002 and 2005 Bali Bombings, the violence against Ahmaddiyah and even against progressive Muslims like Irshad Manji means that it is not, nor ever was, all smiles and giggles. The tensions that gave rise to these conflagrations have some depth; the ideal of Diverse but One was never perfectly realized. Although this was not the focus of my 1994–1995 research, underlying tensions forced their way into my anthropological gaze on repeated occasions. There were a few key features of specifically religious tensions. There was general sense in which Muslims are better served by limiting their social interactions to those with other Muslims. There was also some discussions about the limits of peaceful coexistence. Finally there was the idea that Islam was politically and spiritually superior to other religions.

People discussed the limits of peaceful coexistence. One junior teacher at a pesantren in rural East Java described a relationship with a church across the street as example of limited pluralism and unity. He stated that they tolerated and respected each other but they neither helped nor hindered each other as well. However, he suggested that the very presence of Christians limited the freedoms of Muslims. He complained that while in his home village, they were able to play Quranic recitations over loudspeakers, that in more densely populated areas they were not allowed to do this because it would be an affront to the Christians. This suggests that some Muslims felt constrained by government policies and by the presence of religious minorities.

There was also the sense that almost by definition, Muslims were better Indonesians than non-Muslims; only they could truly fulfill the *Pancasila* requirement of "monotheism," which is associated with *tauhid*, the Islamic concept of a single, unitary God with no subparts or divisions. Gods with many faces (whether it be three or millions) just don't fit the concept. In a 1995 focus group of IAIN students, one participant expressed that *Pancasila* was a way of making Islamic principles part of the law without explicitly using syari'ah. Further, Muslims complained that Christians were not playing fair and used humanitarian aid to recruit converts. Hussein Umar of Dewan Dakwah Islam Indonesia explained that his organization was countering such Christian efforts (interview, May 2000).

Both Christians and Muslims expressed feeling marginalized during the New Order. These feelings contributed to the sectarian tension already present during that era.

Christians expressed concern about Muslim hegemony. This manifested in Christians telling me that they felt during Ramadan that they needed to avoid smoking or eating in view of people fasting. They suggested that this had less to do with good manners and more to do with the fact that there would be repercussions for not following this standard. Christians also felt that Indonesian politicians were often swayed by the desire to please the Muslim majority with little thought to minority religions.

The social playing field was certainly uneven. In February 1995, I did a survey of a major bookstore (*Gunung Agung*) in Surabaya and found in the Islam section 26 books that exposed the shortcomings of other religions. These included books exposing Christmas and Santa Claus as cultural constructions rather than religious features. Others had titles like "Islamic Answers to Christian Questions" and "Dialogue between Christianity and Islam" written by an Islamic scholar. On the other hand, only one book in the much smaller Christian section dealt with other religions and this book was about why Catholics should not marry Muslims; an argument that few Muslims would disagree with, even if they had their own reasons. Minority religious groups were, and are, aware of their vulnerability; such books about Islam would not be tolerated.

The smiling face of Islam and the ideal of unity was not smoke and mirrors. There is always some disconnect between the ideal and the real in any social system. What is disconcerting is that recently greater numbers of Indonesians are speaking out against that ideal. Without wanting to sound overly dramatic, Indonesia is at a crossroads. Will it continue to be the kind of place where people have religious freedom, not only to choose which religion to practice, but in how to practice it? At least as an ideal? Will it continue to be the kind of place where intellectual figures like the late Nurcholish Madjid and Abdurrahman Wahid, and contemporary figures like Amin Abdullah and Azyumardi Azra shape public opinion to create a rational, tolerant, and multireligious society? Or will increasingly narrow and intolerant forms of Islam dominate society? The intolerant groups that attack book launchings, commit violence against minority religious groups, and commit acts of terror are a small but significant part of the picture; the bit of *kangkung* (a spinachlike vegetable) in the smile of Indonesian Islam—a reminder that the picture is not perfect. There are multiple counter-radical elements in Indonesian Islam that are working to maintain the ideal of Diverse but One. This book has reviewed the efforts found in State Islamic Higher Education system. The vast majority of PTAIN faculty members are committed to a rational and intellectual approach to Islam, and because that approach leads most of them to broader understandings of what it means to be Muslim and to be Indonesian, there is hope for the Indonesia that I first met in 1987—one which had Diverse but One as an ideal, however imperfectly realized—will continue into the future.

Theoretical Epilogue: Linguistic Modeling of Variation in Islam*

This epilogue is by no means an afterthought. It explores in greater detail the theoretical underpinning of the book. In chapter 2, I laid out the barest minimum of the theoretical frame needed to understand the ethnographic material. An expanded version of this chapter was completed before I started the book and so the book was written with the fully developed theoretical frame in mind. The purpose of this chapter is to expand on the theory used in the book and to draw the connections more explicitly. A key reason for including this theoretical excursus is to address the lacuna in Islamic Studies highlighted by Aaron Hughes, when he posed the rhetorical question, "Why are experts in Islam so indifferent to issues of theory and method in the academic study of religion?" (2007: 6). Hughes may be correct in his assessment of Islamic Studies in general, but he clearly underestimates the level of concern about theory and method found in the anthropological study of Islam (Asad 1986; El-Zein 1974a; Lukens-Bull 1999; Marranci 2008; Varisco 2005, 2007).

More than a decade ago, I argued that the anthropological study of Islam was plagued by problems of definition (1999). In short, the problem concerned understanding the relationship between local practices and understandings, and universal Islam—whatever that might be. Although there have been recent and laudable attempts to address the anthropology of Islam (Marranci 2008; Varisco 2005), these efforts were not focused on how to approach the simultaneous continuity and diversity in Islam. How do we account for practices such as the Javanese Horse Trance ritual, in which dancers are placed into a trance by a shaman who gets his power from meditating at the grave of a medieval Islamic saint? In trance, they enact the events that befell those that fought the expansion of the Islamic kingdom of Mataram. They are said to have become possessed by the spirits of their own horses and ran around crazy. The trancers eat rose petals, tear open coconuts with their teeth, roll on glass, dance on fire, pierce their cheeks with pins and they do not get hurt. The message to the villagers is clear—embrace Islam and be protected; reject Islam and go insane (Hartley 1974). Although this particular example may be an outlier, there are many others to include such as *ziarah* or pilgrimage to saints' graves (Bhardwaj 1998; Chambert-Loir and Reid 2002; Subtelny 1989), the keeping of spirit familiars (Saniotis 2004) and the Mevlevi Order, better known as the Whirling Dervishes (Friedlander 1992). When we add the Nation of Islam with its unorthodox doctrine (Berg 1999; Lee 1996), and Al-Qaeda (Gunaratna 2002) we are faced with having to explain how a disparate set of practices and practitioners are related.

Not only must we consider what ties them together but also what distinguishes them from each other. As Roy avers:

> The notion of a single "Muslim culture" cannot survive analysis. If it refers to Islam as a religion it is redundant. The different Muslim populations have some element in common such as diet and holidays, which are nothing more than the basic tenets of the rituals and beliefs, but in themselves they do not constitute a culture. What is beyond the strict tenets of religious rituals and beliefs refers to specific national or ethnic cultures, or which Islam is just a component, even it is indistinguishable. (Roy 2004: 129)

This is not a particularly new observation, even scholars now denigrated by some as "Orientalists" observed that "Islam does not have the uniformity of a church" (Goldziher 1981: 4). Goldziher demonstrated the dynamics of diversity evident in Islam from early in its history to the time of his writing (ca. 1910). The worldwide Islamic community is typified by cultural diversity (Davies 1988: 63). Even the Islam found within a single village is not unified (Antoun 1989: 39; Loeffler 1988). Therefore, it is critical to consider the relationships between that which ties various Muslim communities together and what makes them distinct. This is what Talal Asad calls for when he suggests that the anthropology of Islam must devise a conceptual organization of the diversity in Islam (1986: 5). After reviewing the various ways anthropologists have proposed how to deal with the diversity in Islam, the chapter will expand on the model used in the book. A linguistic model that starts with the idea that variation in religious expression is analogous to dialects. Here, I will explore how the dialects analogy fits with the framework of Saussurian semiology to more fully develop the theory.

Earlier Approaches

An early approach to the diversity in world religions is Robert Redfield's notion of great and little traditions (1956), which came to be one way to solve the problem of understanding diversity in Islam (Asad 1986: 5). In its most developed form, the great and little traditions model was employed as a means of understanding the relationship between the traditions known via religious texts and the expression of those concepts within a folk or cultural context (Eickelman 1982: 59).

Although not what Redfield intended, the dichotomy allowed scholars to treat great and little traditions as isolates with anthropologists staying in their comfort zone in villages and allowing Orientalists to stay in their comfort zone of texts (Bowen 1993a: 185)—a tidy division of labor. This, however, leads to an overly narrow view of the tradition and a tendency to see the universal aspects of the tradition as the core of Islam. Further, this "lent a normative and cultural priority to the Middle East vis-à-vis the rest of the Muslim world" (Bowen 1993b: 6). Bowen states that anthropologists and other scholars concerned with local forms of culture looked for the rites, myths, or ideas that made the group they were studying distinctive rather than focusing on those they shared with other Muslims (1993b: 4).

El-Zein argues that the dichotomy of folk Islam (little tradition) versus elite Islam (great tradition) is infertile and fruitless primarily because it privileges elite Islam and regards local Islam as "less ordered, less objective, and somehow less complete versions of the religious experience" (1974a: 243). He argues that various theological and anthropological interpretations of the meaning of Islam are dependent upon assumptions that define and limit what can be properly considered "religious" and "Islamic." These assumptions distinguish a "folk from an elite, and a real from a false Islam" (El-Zein 1974a: 249). El-Zein suggests that it is ironic that anthropology studies folk Islam while using the principles of elite Islam (El-Zein 1974a: 246). Clearly, a rigid dichotomy is fruitless. This model moves beyond this dichotomy by acknowledging that both elite and nonelite Islam are forms of expressed Islam.

Redfield's approach has largely been rejected but it has not been entirely abandoned. There is still intense theoretical interest in the relationship between what people do and what some texts might be interpreted as saying what they should do. Talal Asad critiqued three scholarly approaches to diversity in Islam that move beyond great and little traditions. The first suggests that there is "no such theoretical object as Islam" and therefore there is no need to deal with the diversity between Muslim societies. This approach is currently expressed in the rejection of the term and the very concept of the "Muslim world," which is discussed more in news articles (Khanna 2009) and online conversations on mail lists (sociology_of_islam@lists.pdx.edu, October 2009), than in academic articles. The claim is that there is not sufficient similarity between various Muslim societies to categorize them vis-à-vis non-Muslim societies. Similarly, Marranci calls for anthropologists studying Islam to interrogate the very concept of a Muslim *umma*, or community (2008: 137–139). And yet Islamaphobes and Muslim preachers alike allude to a Muslim civilization or a brotherhood of Muslims. While we can discount hate-mongering views of a unified threat from one billion Muslims (and correctly so), we cannot dismiss the Muslim notion of *umma* and that at some level all believers are interconnected. Of course, the Muslim concept of *umma* is fluid and contested, but nonetheless it is an important component of Muslim identity.

The second approach identified by Asad uses Islam as a label for a "heterogeneous collection of items, each of which has been designated Islamic by informants" (1986: 2). Asad rejects what might be called a typical anthropological approach to Islam, by asserting that the idea

> that Islam is simply what Muslims everywhere say it is—will not do, if only because there are everywhere Muslims who say that what other people take to be Islam is not really Islam at all. (1986: 2)

Implicit in Asad's assertion is that these competing claims cannot all be true and therefore a "true" form of Islam must be identified by anthropologists to be used in their analyses. Recently, Gabriele Marranci argued that the core of an Islamic identity is neither tradition nor text but whether or not people "feel" themselves to be Muslims. He suggests "*emotions* and *feelings* should be at the centre of our studies of Islam" (2008: 6, emphasis added). Further he argues,

> Fieldwork...should incorporate an analysis of the emotional context within which we operate as anthropologists. This means refocusing my attention to how human beings make sense of the "map" that we call Islam. To do so we need to observe interpretations of Islam as part of networks of shared meanings...to observe concepts...as the result of interpretations affected by personal identity, emotions, feelings, and the environment. (2008: 6)

Marranci has a valid point, however, before someone can "feel" themselves to be Muslim, Scottish, a Boy Scout, a good father, or any other identity, they must have some idea what the relevant category means. Further, they must belong to a community that has a (differentially) shared conception of what constitutes those categories. In other words, they have to engage the universal aspect and create a local expression of it. Whether we use the terms great and little traditions, the universal and the local, the textual and the popular, the territory and the map, we are describing the same phenomena.

The third approach identified by Asad holds that Islam is a "distinctive historical totality which organizes various aspects of social life" (1986: 1). This approach can yield proto-theological[1] perspectives such as Asad's which privileges discourse about orthodoxy (Marranci 2008: 42). It is essential that anthropologists not favor elite, orthodox forms over local, popular forms. When they do, they distort their understanding. For example, Geertz's (1960) tripartite division of Javanese society into syncretic peasants (*abangan*), Hindu-Buddhist administrators (*priyayi*), and orthodox merchants (*santri*) suffered from this problem and has been thoroughly critiqued (Dhofier 1978; Hefner 1987; Koentjaraningrat 1963; Ricklefs 2006; Woodward 1988). The historian Merle Ricklefs observes that the categories emerged in the nineteenth century. He argues,

> It was only from about the middle of the nineteenth century that there emerged in Javanese society *a category of people who were defined by their*

failure—in the eyes of the more pious—to behave as proper Muslims. These were the *abangan,* the nominal or non-practising Muslims. (2006: 35, emphasis mine)

By using the categories of those who Ricklefs called "the more pious," Geertz was favoring their expression of Islam. Whether the essentializing definition of Islam we use is of our own design or borrowed from the religious elite, such approaches deny agency and the complexity born of it. I concur with Hughes that theoretical rigor is the path out of essentialism (2007: 1).[2]

These three basic approaches fail to examine how expressed forms of Islam are related to each other and to a culturally postulated universal or transcendent Islam. The most insightful contemporary theories regarding this relationship have attempted to explain variation within Islam by constructing linguistic analogies, including studying religion as discourse (Asad 1986; Bowen 1989). Mark Woodward's definitions of the components of Islamic discourse shed light on its nature. He argues that the universal Islam with which local islams interact is concerned with far more than the Quran and Hadith. It includes rituals such as the *hajj,* the *salāt, Id al-Adha, Id al-Fitr,* and the fast of *Ramadan* among others. However, local islams do not enter into discourse with the entire universalist corpus of Islam. Received Islam is what Woodward calls that portion of universal Islam present in specific local contexts; this hints at the idea of a postulated universal Islam. Local islams are those rituals and texts, both oral and written that are not known outside of a specific local context. These local rituals and texts arise from the interaction of local culture and received Islam (Woodward 1988: 87–88). Further, local islams can interact with each other (Woodward 1988: 65). While useful, Woodward's model does not examine exactly how the universal and local actually interact. I argue that a fuller linguistic analogy moves beyond the idea of a universal core Islam and allows us to examine the relationship between what any particular Muslims conceive of as universal Islam and what they do in their local setting.

Dialects and Variation in Islam

I have argued in this book that many of the debates in Indonesia today reflect differences in dialect. I diagrammed the differences using simplified diagrams that show what elements are present or absent in a particular dialect, or variation, of Islam. For example, in chapter 2, I showed how two dialects, namely cultural Islam, and *salafi* Islam define apostasy. The different elements used in defining apostasy are used to show the ways they differ (table 2.1). In chapter 5, dialect differences between the professors at the Women's Studies Center and women from Hizbut Tahrir Indonesia (HTI) were diagrammed (table 5.1) by examining the elements involved in their difference of opinion about women leading prayers.

When a religion expands into new areas, it gains new inflections; others will rise from historical developments in each local setting. Over time, local expressions would become completely unintelligible to one another, and as such, be "dialects" of the same religious language, or perhaps be regarded as separate entities all together. For example, *djinn*—beings created from fire that can be Muslim or non-Muslim—appear in the Quran, but the kinds of relationships Muslims have with them varies by culture. Arthur Saniotis, reports that an Indian Sufi of his acquaintance "captured" them and kept them as familiars (2004). I knew second generation Yemenis in Indonesia, who by reciting the correct Quranic verses invoked djinn to join them and together transformed into tigers and prowled the area. Indonesians will invoke djinn through the use of small scraps of paper on which they have written Quranic verses and tucked into door jambs and automobile bumpers to protect homes and cars. They will also exorcise non-Muslim djinn that are bothering believers and causing mental illness (Lukens-Bull 2005: 98). Religious concepts, like *djinn,* not only change meaning slightly as they develop in different dialects, they can be borrowed into completely different symbolic systems and utterly transformed. Just as certain French and Spanish words and phrases are common in American English, djinn are part of the American vocabulary of the fantastic. Much like how the French phrases "à la carte" and "entrez vous," and the Spanish word "armadillo" are rarely pronounced or used as they would be in their language of origin, djinn show up in the American imagination as belly-bared blond bombshells or blue-skinned comedians granting wishes rather than forms more familiar to Indonesian or other Muslims. Barbara Eden's Jeannie and Robin William's Genie of the Lamp, owe more to Richard Burton's rendering of *1001 Arabian Nights* than to the lived experiences of Muslims. Yet, these symbols have crossed over into a completely different context. Peter Lamborn Wilson (aka Hakim Bey) also describes how elements of Islamic symbols can be used in marginal ways including the Moorish Science Temple, Muslim Satanists, Rumi, and even by non-Muslims such as the Shriners (Wilson 1993). Another book project could be dedicated to the myriad of detailed examples that show the ways in which different local expressions develop. However, the variation is not completely free-floating; the *hajj* and the education of *ulama* (Islamic scholars) kept widely dispersed Muslims from becoming entirely isolated.

The simplified model used in the book seems to echo earlier approaches used in the study of Indonesian Islam. There is no benefit in imagining *abangan, santri,* and *priyayi* dialects following Geertz (1960). Nor does imagining Wahabi, Sufi, Muhammadiya, or Nahdlatul Ulama (NU) dialects help us if we use those labels to explain behavior. The labels may be useful in identifying major dialect families, but to really understand the dynamics involved in various expressions, we will need to understand the ways in which the variation in religious practice is affected by a number of factors and how expressions of religion can be diglossic, polysemic, and even idiosyncratic.

In speaking about what connects two different Muslim cultures, Clifford Geertz writes,

> The hope for general conclusions in this field lies not in some transcending similarity in the content of religious experience or in the form of religious behavior from one people to another, or one person to another. It lies in the fact, or what I take to be a fact, that the field over which that content and that behavior range is not a mere collection of unrelated ideas and emotions and acts, but an ordered universe. (1968: 54)

My goal here is to develop a way to model the "ordered universe" of Islam. Since this "ordered universe" is not the result of a religious polity or hierarchy, as may be the case in Catholicism or the Southern Baptist Convention and other traditions, the approach taken here is particularly useful. To understand the "ordered universe" of Islam, I apply Saussure's (1972) concepts of *langue* (language as a system) and *parole* (speech acts) to religion. The transcendent generative form of a religion, which is parallel to langue, is an imagined form in the minds and hearts of believers.

The expressed form, which is analogous to parole, includes interpretations, discourse, debates, rituals, and daily life of believers.

Islam and Its Expressions

What is the form of Islam that connects diverse localities? One approach would be to posit a translocal Islam that encompasses all possible concepts and ideas that can be drawn upon by a given Muslim community. Such a summative catch-all does not begin to approach the complexity of the Saussurean concept of langue. We are still left with the task of defining what is analogous to langue? Muslims often agree in principle that an universal, or core, Islam exists, even if they do not always agree what constitutes that core. Many Muslims would agree that the core of Islam is the Quran and the Sunna (Traditions), although between different groups one will find little agreement on which Hadith or Hadith collections best represent the Sunna or how best to interpret various passages of the Quran. This is to suggest that "Core Islam" is in the eyes of the beholder. As social scientists, we do not have the tools or the inclinations to determine a real form of Islam. To the extent that there is an universal or core Islam, it is imagined (cf. Hobsbawm and Ranger 1992). Unlike the form of Western imagined essence of Islam decried by Hughes (2007: 34), my approach, to the extent it calls on an essential Islam, uses an essential Islam imagined by Muslims[3]; there is no need to posit ontological reality to it. Nor is there any need for there to be any unity or agreement on how it is imagined.

If we add to the Saussurean idea of langue, the notion of generative grammar, we can talk about generative Islam, which is the understanding of Islam used to generate a particular expression. Generative Islam includes an imagined complete set of concepts of Islam, as well as "grammar" for compiling the concepts into meaning. Any given concept may or may not be used in a particular form of expressed Islam much like how any given speaker of a language may not know every single word in that language, but the ignorance of a particular speaker does not cause those words to cease to exist. Further, dialects will also have slightly different lexicons. In this way, the generative form of Islam contains all of the possible concepts and ideas that any given Muslim may or may not accept as part of their practice of Islam. The acceptance of a particular expression does not nullify the existence of those other concepts and ideas that are not present in a given practice. The generative form is an abstraction, something that even attempts to talk about it become an expressed interpretation. As such, anthropologists may not be able to fully describe or understand the generative due to this nature.

The term "expressed religion" encompasses much of what is sometimes called the little tradition or local tradition. However, whereas these terms marginalize nonelite practices, "expressed religion" does not because it also includes the elite forms typically associated with "great traditions." Also part of expressed Islam would be any particular interpretation of the Quran and the Hadith.

This model for understanding the dynamics between the generative and expressed forms of Islam expands from this linguistic analogy. Hence, religious concepts or ideas are the basic units of generative Islam. Like morphemes, they come into their full meaning when combined into larger units and become an expression in the practices of the Islamic community. Other anthropologists have argued for similar approaches in examining other dimensions of culture including archaeological artifacts (Deetz 1967), religion (Durbin 1970, 1972) as well as culture in general (Pike 1964). These approaches have been found wanting by some (Keesing 1972; Preucel and Bauer 2001), primarily because they rely on positing an underlying structure that generates the expressed form. We do not need such a crypto-theological term for this model. Because Muslims imagine an underlying form of Islam and attempt to express it, we can use this approach to model the variation found in Islam.

It is common to explain variation between two Muslim societies as cultural. Although expressing it in an elaborate and sophisticated manner, Clifford Geertz's groundbreaking comparison of Islam in Indonesia and Morocco states that because of the different cultural contexts, Islam is different in each place. How then do we explain variation within a culture? In *Religion of Java* (1960), Geertz maintains his culturist approach and explains variation as the result of different social and cultural strata in Javanese society. Very few anthropologists today use such monolithic and deterministic conceptions of culture. If we are to understand variation, we cannot just offhandedly refer to differences and be done with it. Such approaches are tautological at best: Moroccan Islam and Indonesian Islam are different because they are Moroccan and Indonesian. The method I propose allows us to look at different components of culture.

Linguistic Rules Modeling

Before examining linguistic models of variation in Islam and how such modeling can solve some of the problems caused by labeling different variations or dialects of Islam, the mechanics of such modeling must be reviewed. In linguistics, rule diagrams can show how such a relationship can exist between langue (within the mind) and parole (spoken language), and congruently for generative and expressed religious traditions. These diagrams also emphasize the importance of social context, an element missing in Saussure's model (Chandler n.d.: 14; Voloshinov 1973: 21). The basic approach taken here suggests that the generative takes the form of a particular expression in a particular context. A basic way to diagram this would be as follows (figure 7.1):

I borrow from linguistics certain conventions for diagraming the process suggested in figure 7.1. In order to gain a better understanding of the terminology and symbols used in the diagrams, we refer to the chart given in table 7.1).

Langue (becomes) *Parole* (in the context of) Context
Generative (becomes) Expression (in the context of) Context

Figure 7.1 Transformations of langue and the generative

Table 7.1 Reading rule diagrams

Symbol	Linguistic use	This model
{#}	Morpheme	Generative
	Langue	Gross constituent units
		Greatest level of abstraction
/#/	Allomorph	Mid-level
	Phoneme	
[#]	Allophone	Expressed
	Parole	Least abstract
/	"in the context of"	"in the context of"
+		Presence of an element
–		Absence of an element

{*Langue*} → [*Parole*] / Context
{Generative} → [Expressed] / Context

Figure 7.2 Linguistic diagramming

Therefore the basic ideas expressed in figure 7.1 can be better rendered using these conventions (see figure 7.2).

To demonstrate how such modeling might work and how it is an improvement on simply asserting differences in dialects, I consider the question of kiblat, or the direction of prayer. While all Muslims pray towards Mecca, there can be variation in how that direction is determined. In the Javanese tradition based on the legends of the *Walisongo* (or nine saints who brought Islam to Java), Sunan Kalidjaga determined the direction of prayer by placing one hand on the center pillar of the mosque he had just built and the other on the *kabah* in Mecca. The direction determined in that legend is said to be due West. This is the direction traditional Javanese mosques are oriented even when they are built in Suriname, South America (Suparlan 1995: 141). With rise of modernist movements in the early twentieth century, some mosques were built with a kiblat determined by map and compass. In the table 7.1, slashes /#/ are used to represent the first-level variations because they are still at an intermediate, conceptual level, that is, what the kiblat should be. Mosques built in a particular direction or arrows indicating the direction of prayer in a particular building would be concrete expressions.

In Muslim Java, a mosque defines a community because it is the center of prayer, and praying together defines a community, even at significant cost and inconvenience (Lukens-Bull 2003: 210). According to the Shafii madhhab (legal/ritual school) all men in a given geographical community are required to worship in the same mosque on Fridays except when it is physically impossible for all the inhabitants to meet in one building (Juynboll 1953: 93). This ethic stands even in the face of ritual differences. Woodward relates how in one Central Javanese community the mosque is divided into two, so that the Classicalists may pray due west, as has always been done in Java, and the Reformists may pray facing the direction determined by modern compasses (personal communication, February 1997). Using the approach described in chapter 2, we can understand the differences in practice as differences between the Classicalist and Reformist dialects. In this approach there is little room for agency and individual choice and there is no space for a third possibility. Unfortunately, a third possibility exists: building a mosque with both kiblats, presumably with two different spaces behind a single imam (Woodward, personal communication, February 1997).

Using the conventions described above, this situation can be diagrammed as given in figure 7.3.

When there is community consensus about the traditional direction, then the kiblat is due West. Consensus does not require complete agreement, only the absence of an organized and substantial public dissent. When there is disagreement, but the value of community cohesion holds sway, then there will two parts to the mosque, each with its own kiblat. In all other cases, the kiblat uses the calculated direction. This kind of modeling allows us to explore greater variation than the dialect analogy alone.

To further demonstrate the utility of the modeling it is useful to look at a similar Islamic concept in two different Muslim societies. For this, I turn to Geertz's (1968) analysis of Morocco and Java. Although they share religious concepts, the concepts are expressed differently. For example, saints (*wali, marabout*) exist in both societies. However the quietist Sunan Kalijaga would hardly be seen as worthy of the title in Morocco. Likewise, the Berber zealot Lyusi is far too coarse and unrefined to be considered a saint by the Javanese[4] (1968: 54). As Geertz says,

> On the Indonesian side, inwardness, imperturbability, patience, poise, sensibility, aestheticism, elitism, and an almost obsessive self-effacement, the radical dissolution of individuality; on the Moroccan side, activism, fervor, impetuosity, nerve, toughness, moralism, populism, and an almost obsessive self-assertion, the radical intensification of the individuality. (1968: 54)

```
{Kiblat}   →    [due West]   /   + Walisongo tradition
                                  + Community agreement
                [dual Kiblat] /   + Walisongo tradition
                                  − Community agreement
                [compass point] / + Community cohesion
                                  − Walisongo tradition
```

Figure 7.3 Javanese variation in direction of prayer

I use the term "quietist" as a gloss for the constellation of traits that Geertz attributes to Indonesia (properly Java) and "activist" as the umbrella term for the traits Geertz attributes to Morocco. We can then model the differences and similarities in Javanese and Moroccan Sufi saints (figure 7.4).

Here we can see the utility of this modeling technique. To stop here and declare that the difference is due to culture is unsatisfactory. Geography is not destiny; mere location did not make for the differences. Simply to call the difference cultural gives us no sense of the dynamics. More than that, there is no space for "agency"; membership in a culture determines practice. Although Saussurean semiology does not explicitly examine agency, there is a space for it: the movement from langue to parole takes place at the level of the speaker.

Not all differences between practices in different populations is due to cultural inflections. Madhhab (ritual/legal school) also influences ritual. We might expect to find greater similarities in ritual practice between Java and Somalia, both of which were historically Shafii in orientation, than say Java and Morocco, which historically was Maliki. Differences between Java and Somalia might be explained primarily in terms of cultural inflection, however, to do so for Java and Morocco, as Geertz did (1968) may be skipping the important step of understanding some of the conceptual differences between the Shafii and Maliki madhhabs. We need to examine the various ways in which Java and Morocco differ. There are four things we can examine: (1) differences in madhhab, (2) difference in Sufi practices and brotherhoods, (3) the pre-Islamic context, (4) and modal (most common) personalities. As for madhhab, Java is predominately Shafii, whereas Morocco is predominately Maliki. In this particular case, there is little to be found that can be traced to madhhab, but certainly in other areas of Muslim life, part or even most of the difference might be explained by which madhhab is followed in a particular region. There are some Sufi brotherhoods that are found in both Java and Morocco. Specifically, in Java there is a branch of the Shadhiliyah order (Dhofier 1982: 142), which also had branches in West Africa (Johns 1987: 348; Massignon 1953: 577).

{Wali} → /quietist/ /Java

/activist/ /Morocco

Figure 7.4 Saints in different Muslim societies

THEORETICAL EPILOGUE

Geertz attributes the forms of Javanese Islamic spirituality to syncretism with animist and Hindu pre-Islamic Javanese beliefs. Judith Becker argues that once Indian tantric mystical forms were firmly entrenched in the culture they continued to shape later religious expression (Becker 1993). Islam was brought to the region by merchants who were also Sufi mystics. They picked up on the strong interest in mysticism and emphasized that dimension of their faith. So successfully did they contextualize Islam with the existing tantric forms that Indonesians who still practice the Hindu-Buddhist forms use Arabic terms, *lahir* (external) and *batin* (internal) to describe them (Geertz 1960: 232).

This is at best a partial explanation. Modal personalities might need to be included to round out an explanation. Culturally, the Javanese value the traits attributed to Kalidjaga and attempt to cultivate them in themselves; this makes for a feedback loop between the ideals held for society and the characteristics of men considered saintly. The utility of this model is to indicate the various factors that should be included in my consideration (see figure 7.5).

The model includes two unknowns because it allows us to consider factors found in Java (+ X −Y) and not in Morocco (−X +Y), which we have not yet considered. In this way, the model allows us to identify areas for further investigation.

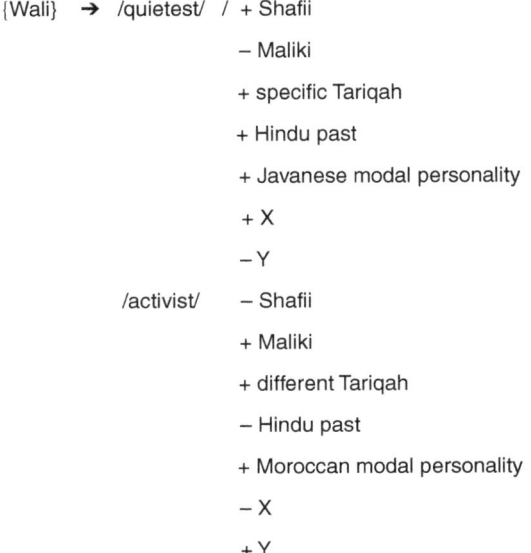

Figure 7.5 Diagramming factors in different expressions

Revisiting the question of how apostasy is defined by different people, the dialect model yielded the following diagram (see table 7.2).

This chart is useful for understanding the broad outlines of the debates. However, it does not accommodate other contextual factors. The linguistic rules modeling that I propose using allows us to consider greater variation. In figure 7.6 I have shown how endorsing secularism, pluralism, and secularism, known by the abbreviation *sipilis*, is differently interpreted as apostasy or not.

If anyone on Institut Agama Islam Negeri (IAIN) campuses might agree with accusations that some professors are apostates, it would those be those associated with Prosperous Justice Party (PKS), Dewan Dakwah Islam Indonesia (DDII), and other Islamist groups; they share a dialect. However, in fact, no Perguruan Tinggi Agama Islam Negeri (PTAIN) faculty members allow the possibility of apostates on other campuses but deny any on their campus and reject the label when asked about specific individuals on other campus, such as Asyurmadi Azra. I asked a PKS-affiliated faculty member, what makes someone an apostate. He said that it takes a clear statement of rejection or a lapse in *ibadah*. He makes a distinction between apostasy and liberalism and holds that being liberal on worldly issues does not make someone an apostate. Imam Suprayogo, the rector of UIN Malang, similarly limits apostasy to converting to another religion, "There are no IAIN professors

Table 7.2 What makes for an apostate

"Universal"	Expression	Dialect	Elements
Apostasy	Apostate/Murtad	Cultural Islam	+converting to another religion +denying Islam +forgoing Ibadah
Apostasy	Apostate/Murtad	Salafi	+gender parity +feminism +shia −polygamy −Syari'ah state +Pluralism +Hermeneutics +democracy +getting a liver transplant from Chinese person

Figure 7.6 Linguistic rules modeling of apostasy accusations

who have become Christian or Hindu" (February 2009). The variation in how the accusations of apostasy are applied as follows. The off-campus *salafist* accuses faculty members of apostasy if they advocate gender parity or believe in a form of pluralism that holds that all religions as equally valid for matters of eternity (salvation pluralism). The on-campus *salafist* would see these views as too liberal but would not call the person an apostate. For them, the key is whether or not the person keeps the ritual requirements of *ibadah*. For the off-campus *salafist*, the keeping of *ibadah* is irrelevant, the ideas are sufficient to condemn the person.

Conclusion

I have examined a particular approach to variation within Islam and other world traditions. There are three components to this approach. The first draws an analogy between Religion and Language[5] where "Southern Baptist" and "Anglican" are to Christianity and Christianity is to Religion as Parisian and French Creole are to French and French is to Language. Second, this model moves beyond a simple analogy between dialect and sect. This is done by drawing on Saussurean semiology and positing a difference between the form of a religion as it is conceived and the form of its expression.

This model about the relationship between the generative (langue) and the expressed (parole) in Islam is not wholly new, but rather builds upon the work of other anthropologists and seeks to refine the definitions of these two concepts by examining the mechanisms through which they interact. From this point, we can see that anthropologists studying Islam must shift or refocus their research questions to take into account the nature of what they are studying. In one sense, Islam cannot be found in the texts. In another sense, what makes Islam a world religion and not just a collection of local practices is found primarily in the texts. But the real task of the anthropologist of Islam is to describe the relationship between text and practice, or more correctly, the universal and the local.

The last part of my approach is to use rules modeling to examine variation in Islam. This technique helps to illustrate the theoretical approach to variation previously discussed in the chapter. In using models such as these a scholar can map out variation and look for all possible contributing factors. It also moves us beyond the limitations of the dialect model, which while useful, potentially returns us to a mode of explanation that arose from Geertz's tripartite division of Javanese religious practice, where categories of expression become explanatory. The dialect model is a useful heuristic, but the Sausserian theory coupled with linguistic rules modeling allows us to accommodate a much wider range of variation.

Notes

1 The Politicization of the "Apolitical": Islamic Higher Education in Indonesia

1. The history of Harvard is much more complex than it appears in Indonesian discourse in which it is simply a religious school that lost its way. Harvard has not functioned exclusively as a clergy-training institution since the seventeenth century. It is clear that the Harvard that exists in Indonesian discourse bears only a passing resemblance to the Harvard in Cambridge, Massachusetts.
2. I am using the Indonesian word *fakultas* instead of the English faculty because of the confusion it can cause North American readers who use the word faculty to mean academic staff. Fakultas are units of academic organization that comprise of several departments. They are roughly equivalent to colleges at American universities. The main difference is what would be arts and sciences at an American university would be multiple fakultas like social and behavior sciences, natural sciences, arts and music.
3. The rector was called away before I could ask him about his. All the rectors and faculty members that I asked about this exchange were quite certain that I had misunderstood. Misunderstood or not, this conversation highlights important aspects of the current discussions about the PTAIN system.
4. Readers familiar with other Muslim societies might find the Indonesian usage of this term a bit odd. The strict denotation of the Arabic word, *madrasa*, is school and can be applied to any school, religious or not. It is common in Western discourse to use the term madrasa a shorthand for madrasa Islamiya or Islamic school signifying a traditional sort of Islamic "seminary." The Indonesian pesantren fits in the translocal category of madrasa, whereas the Indonesian madrasah is a different institution entirely. To make a distinction in meaning based on one silent letter may frustrate some readers, but if we are to recognize the specific Indonesian usage, we have no choice.

5. After the end of the Suharto regime, the effort to convert madrasah to the lower percentage religious curriculum came to an end. Pesantren Tebu Ireng in Cukir also had some schools accredited in the government general school system which had a few required religion classes. However, this kind of school in pesantren is exceedingly rare, if not unique.
6. When IAIN Surakarta and IAIN Mataram were branch campuses, they were known by the name of the main campus. When they became independent, the name was dropped.
7. This is not as strange a suggestion as might first be assumed. Comparative religion often draws on social science as does public health. It is the social science components of both that suggest the appropriateness of that placement.

2 Religious "Dialects," Variation, and Accusations of the Worst Kind

1. For a more complete review of the academic debates about the variation in Islam, see Lukens-Bull 1999 and Marranci 2008.
2. For example, Straits Chinese call their dialect of Malay, *Babah-Nonya*, and deny any similarity with standard Malay in a national context in which "speaking Malay" would deny their own ethnic heritage.

3 Becoming Universities: Old Traditions, New Directions

1. By 2012, the moratorium had been lifted under a different minister and a number of campuses, including Surabaya and Medan, were in the process of applying to become UIN.
2. It was very difficult to figure out if he was talking about Hartford Seminary or Harvard Divinity School. Later in the interview, he told another story that was clearly about Harvard because he named the dean.
3. The connection between PKS and the Egyptian Muslim Brotherhood was made to me by Dr. Abdulmawgoud R. Dardery, one of the foremost spokesmen for the Brotherhood in May 2012, when I was in Luxor on a University of North Florida–funded faculty trip. Robert Hefner specifically connects PKS with a moderately conservative wing of the Muslim Brotherhood (Hefner 2009: 74).
4. IAIN and UIN have interpersonal conflicts and politics like any other organization. Any detailed analysis of such conflicts would not serve to illuminate anything new about the system but could create problems for people and be a clear breach of personal confidence.
5. Students must earn 400 on the TOEFL (Test of English as a Foreign Language) and a 500 on the TOAFL (Test of Arabic as a Foreign Language).

5 Women Pushing the Limits: Gender Debates in Islamic Higher Education

1. The term used in Indonesian discourse is *poligami* (polygamy), which is technically too broad a term that includes both polygyny (multiple wives) and multiple husbands (polyandry). Even though what is allowed by Islam is what anthropologists call polygyny, Indonesian discourse uses the term polygamy to mean having multiple wives and contrasts it with polyandry.

6 Where Is the Islam, and What Kind?

1. I have deliberately chosen not to capitalize the phrase "clash of civilizations" because I do not want to reify what has become a misguided way to understand the relationship between the West and the rest.

Theoretical Epilogue: Linguistic Modeling of Variation in Islam

*A much earlier version of this essay was coauthored with my undergraduate student, Kristen Angelucci. Although it has been countless versions and several years since she has contributed to this work, I still wish to acknowledge her contribution.

1. In an earlier article (Lukens-Bull 1999: 43–44), I argued that Asad's approach was theological. He now agrees with Gabrielle Marranci (2008: 42) that it is proto-theological.
2. Hughes includes self-reflexivity as another important component of the solution to essentialism. I concur and have engaged such work elsewhere (Lukens-Bull 2007). Here I am primarily focused on theoretical rigor.
3. To say that is imagined is not to dismiss it as imaginary but to assert agency; people use their minds to engage all they have heard, read, or experience to derive ideas of what they should do.
4. In *Islam Observed* (1968) Geertz conflates Indonesia with Java. In comparing Indonesia with Morocco, he was really comparing a Javanese saint with a Moroccan one. Here I correct Geertz's mistake and clearly identify Kalidjaga as Javanese.
5. Capitals here reflect common usage in linguistics and anthropology whereas Christianity is a religion and French is a language, the ability to speak French, or English, or anything is Language. Likewise, the ability to be Christian, or Muslim, or anything is Religion.

Glossary

Term	Definition
Adab	Civilization
Barakah	Literally, blessing. Has a substantial quality and can be absorbed into objects.
Classicalist	An expression of Islam that keeps to the classical Sufi practices of Islam, see Nahdlatul Ulama.
Dakwah	Preaching, proselytizing, and missions.
Dewan Dakwah Islam Indonesia (DDII)	Indonesian Islamic Proselytizing Committee. Founded in 1967.
Fakultas	Literally, faculty. A unit of academic organization comprising of several departments. Roughly equivalent to colleges within American universities.
Fakultas Adab	The Faculty of Islamic Civilization.
Fakultas Dakwah	The Faculty of Missions and Preaching.
Fakultas Syari'ah	The Faculty of Islamic Law.
Fakultas Tarbiyah	The Faculty of Islamic Teaching and Pedagogy.
Fakultas Ushuluddin	The Faculty of "Theology."
Fatwa	Considered legal opinion.
Fron Pembela Islam (FPI)	Islamic Defenders Front. Founded on August 17, 1998, the fifty-third anniversary of Indonesia's declaration of independence.

Hadith	Sayings and vignettes attributed to the Prophet Muhammad.
Hizbut Tahrir Indonesia (HTI)	The Indonesian chapter of the Hizbut ut-Tahrir, or Party of Liberation, an Islamist organization founded in Jerusalem in 1953.
IAIN	Insitut Agama Islam Negeri; State Islamic Institute. Has four or more religious faculties.
Ijtihad	Interpretation.
Islamist	Sometimes called political Islam; the use of Islam as a political ideology with a focus on establishing an Islamic State. Some Islamist groups are violent and others work entirely within the framework of democratic processes.
Jihad	Struggle in the cause of God. Two forms: (1) greater jihad against one's base desires; (2) the lesser jihad to create a society in which the greater jihad is easier. A subset of the lesser jihad is a defensive war.
Jihadi	Groups that use a narrow reading of jihad and use violence to achieve the goal of an Islamic State.
Kabah	Cube-like structure in Mecca, center of Hajj ritual.
Kodrat	God-given nature, especial in terms of gender.
Kyai	Religious leader; headmaster of a pesantren.
Laskar Jihad	Jihad Troops. Organized in Yogyakarta, Java. Under the leadership of Ustadz Umar Jaffar Thalib, went to the Moluccas to become involved in a local "interfaith" conflict in June 2000. Disbanded shortly thereafter.
Maddhab	Ritual-legal schools.
Madrasa	Islamic boarding schools found throughout the world. Pesantren fit in this category.
Madrasah	Islamic day schools in Indonesia. Most follow a government approved curriculum, but not all.

Modernist	See Reformist.
MORA	Ministry of Religious Affairs.
Muhammadiyah	Founded in 1912. The largest Reformist organization in Indonesia.
Murtad	Apostate.
Nahdlatul Ulama	The Renaissance of the Scholars. Founded in 1926, the largest Islamic organization in Indonesia. Classicalist in Orientation.
Pancasila	Indonesian National Ideology; Five Principles: (1) Monotheism, (2) Just and Civilized Humanity, (3) Indonesian Unity, (4) Democracy, and (5) Social Justice.
Pesantren	Traditional Islamic boarding school in Indonesia, also known as pondok and pondok pesantren. See, Madrasa.
PTAIN	Perguruan Tinggi Agama Islam Negeri; State Islamic Higher Teaching Institution. There are two ways in which this abbreviation is used: (1) an institution for training officials in the Islamic bureaucracy, which was subsumed into IAIN when it was created; (2) the official term used to refer to the IAIN system.
Rector	President of a university, college, or institution in Indonesia. Unlike a president in an American university, this is an elected position for five-year terms.
Reformist	A broad term used to describe those who wish to reform Islam so that it uses only the Quran and Hadith as sources for understanding Islam. Sometimes also called Scripturalist.
Salaf	A term used in the pesantren community to refer to very traditional, sufi-oriented pesantren.
Salafi	A form of Reformist Islam, often used by "Wahabis" as a term of self-identity.
Santri	Student at a pesantren; this term is used by some to identify orthodox Muslims.

STAIN	Sekolah Tinggi Agama Islam Negeri. A smaller, regional campus in the IAIN system that has only one or two religious Fakultas.
Sufi	The mystical expression of Islam.
Syari'ah	Islamic Law.
Tarbiyah	Pedagogy.
Traditionalist	See Classicalist.
UIN	Universitas Islam Negeri; State Islamic University. In addition to at least four religious faculties, has at least two nonreligious faculties. Part of the PTAIN system.
Ulum Uddin	The basics of the faith.
Usul Uddin	"Theology."
Walisongo	Nine saints who brought Islam to Java.
Wasilah	The use of intercessor, like dead saints.

Bibliography

Abuza, Zachary. 2004. "Muslims, Politics, and Violence in Indonesia: An Emerging Jihadist-Islamist Nexis." *NBR Analysis* 15(3): 1–55.

Adas, M. 1979. *Prophets of Rebellion: Millenarian Protest Movements against the European Colonial Order*. Cambridge: Cambridge University Press.

Ali, Muhamad. 2005. "The Rise of the Liberal Islam Network (JIL) in Contemporary Indonesia." *American Journal of Islamic Social Sciences* 22(1).

Allen, P. 2007. "Challenging Diversity?: Indonesia's Anti-Pornography Bill." *Asian Studies Review*. Available at: www.tandfonline.com/doi/abs/10.1080/10357820701373275 (accessed on February 27, 2013).

Antoun, Richard T. 1989. *Muslim Preacher in the Modern World*. Princeton, NJ: Princeton University Press.

Asad, Talal. 1986. "The Idea of an Anthropology of Islam." Occasional Papers Series. Center for Contemporary Arab Studies. Georgetown University.

Aspinall, Edward. 2013. "A Nation in Fragments: Patronage and Neo-Liberalism in Contemporary Indonesia." *Critical Asian Studies* 45(1): 27–54.

Azra, Azyumardi. 2005. "Salafisme." *Republika*. April 14.

———. 2011. "From IAIN to UIN: Islamic Studies in Indonesia." In Kamaruzzaman Bustamam-Ahmad and Patrick Jory, eds., *Islamic Studies and Islamic Education in Contemporary Southeast Asia*.Bustamam Kuala Lumpur: Yayasan Ilmuwan.

Badran, Margot. 2008. "Engaging Islamic Feminism." In Anitta Kynsilahto, ed., *Islamic Feminism: Current Perspectives*. Finland: Tampere Peace Research Institute.

Bagir, Zanal and Irwan Abdullah. 2011. "The Development and Role of Religious Studies: Some Indonesian Reflections." In Kamaruzzamin Bustamam-Ahmad and Patrick Jory, eds., *Islamic Studies and Islamic Education in Contemporary Southeast Asia*. Bustamam. Kuala Lumpur: Yayasan Ilmuwan.

Bailey, F. G. 1977. *Morality and Expediency: The Folklore of Academic Politics.* Chicago: Aldine Pub. Co.

Bakar, Osman. 2010a. "The Spiritual and Ethical Foundation of Science and Technology in Islamic Civilization." In Nur Syam, ed., *Integrated Twin Towers: Arah Pengembangan Islamic Studies Multidisipliner.* Surabaya: Sunan Ampel Press, pp. 34–63.

———. 2010b. "Traditional Muslim Classification of the Sciences: Comparative Notes on Qutb Al-Din Al-Shirazi and Ibn Khaldun." In Nur Syam, ed., *Integrated Twin Towers: Arah Pengembangan Islamic Studies Multidisipliner.* Surabaya: Sunan Ampel Press, pp. 65–78.

Bakhtiar, Laleh. 1996. *Encyclopedia of Islamic Law: A Compendium of the Major Schools.* Chicago, IL: ABC International Group, Inc.

Barlas, Asma. 2002. *"Believing Women" in Islam: Unreading Patriarchal Interpretations of the Qur'an.* Austin, TX: University of Texas Press.

———. 2004. "Amina Wadud's Hermeneutics of the Qur'an: Women Rereading Sacred Texts." In Suha Taji-Faruqi, ed., *Modern Muslim Intellectuals and the Qur'an.* Oxford: Oxford University Press.

———. 2008. "Engaging Islamic Feminism: Provincialing Feminism as a Master Narrative." In Anitta Kynsilehto, ed., Islamic Feminism: Current Perspectives. Finland: Tampere Peace Research Institute.

Barton, Greg. 2002. *Abdurrahman Wahid: Muslim Democrat, Indonesian President.* Sydney: University of New South Wales Press.

Becker, Judith. 1993. *Gamelan Stories: Tantrism, Islam, and Aesthetics in Central Java.* Tempe, AZ: Program for Southeast Asian Studies, Arizona State University.

Berg, Herbert. 1999. "Elijah Muhammad and the Qur'an: The Evolution of His Tafsir." *Muslim World* 89(1): 42–55.

Berlitz, Charles. 1987. *The Lost Ship of Noah: In Search of the Ark at Ararat.* New York: Putnam.

Bhardwaj, Surinder. 1998. "Non-Hajj Pilgrimage: A Neglected Dimension of Religious Circulation." *Journal of Cultural Geography* 17(2): 69–87.

Bowen, J. R. 1989. "Salat in Indonesia: The Social Meanings of an Islamic Ritual." *Man* 24(4): 600–619.

———. 1993a. "Discursive Monotheisms." *American Ethnologist* 20(1): 185–90.

———. 1993b. *Muslims through Discourse: Religion and Ritual in Gayo Society.* Princeton, NJ: Princeton University Press.

Brenner, S. 1995. "Why Women Rule the Roost: Rethinking Javanese Ideologies of Gender and Self-Control." In Aihwa Ong and Michael Peletz, eds., *Bewitching Women, Pious Men: Gender and Body Politics in Southeast Asia.* Berkeley: University of California Press.

———. 1996. "Reconstructing Self and Society: Javanese Muslim Women and 'the Veil.'" *American Ethnologist* 23(4): 673–697.

———. 2011. "Private Moralities in the Public Sphere: Democratization, Islam, and Gender in Indonesia." *American Anthropologist* 113(3): 478–490.

Bruinessen, Martin van. 1990. "Kitab Kuning: Books in Arabic Script Used in the Pesantren Milieu." *Bijdragen to en taal* 146(2/3): 226–269.

———. 2002. "Genealogies of Islamic Radicalism in Post-Suharto Indonesia." *South East Asia Research* 10(2): 117–154.

———. 2006. "Divergent Paths from Gontor: Muslim Educational Reform and the Travails of Pluralism in Indonesia." Available at: www .hum.uu.nl (accessed on March 20, 2013).

———. 2009. "Traditionalist and Islamist Pesantren in Contemporary Indonesia." In Farish Noor, Yoginder Sikand, and Martin van Bruinessen, eds., *The Madrasa in Asia*. Amsterdam: Amsterdam University Press, pp. 217–245.

Bruinessen, Martin van (ed.). 2013. *Contemporary Developments in Indonesian Islam: Explaining the Conservative Turn*. Singapore: ISEAS Publishing.

Burhanudin, Yusuf. 2008. "Napak Tilas Universitas Al-Azhar." *Islamia* III (3): 13–22.

Bush, Robin. 2009. *Nahdlatul Ulama and the Struggle for Power within Islam and Politics in Indonesia*. Singapore: ISEAS Publishing.

Bustamam-Ahmad, Kamaruzzaman. 2011. "Contemporary Islamic Thought in Indonesian and Malay World: Islam Liberal, Islam Hadhari, and Islam Progressive." *Journal of Indonesian Islam* 5(1): 91–129.

Chambert-Loir, Henri and Anthony Reid (eds.). 2002. *The Potent Dead: Ancestors, Saints, and Heroes in Contemporary Indonesia*. Honolulu: University of Hawai'i Press.

Chandler, Daniel (n.d.). "Semiotics for Beginners." PDF version. Available at: j314intromediastudies.files.wordpress.com/.../semiotics _for_beginners.pdf (accessed on August 26, 2011).

Cheneb, Mohammed ben. 1974. "'Ibn Taimiya.'" In H. A. R. Gibb and J. H. Kramers, eds., *Shorter Encyclopedia of Islam*. Leiden, Netherlands: E. J. Brill, pp. 151–152.

Chernov-Hwang, J. 2009. *Peaceful Islamist mobilization in the Muslim World: What Went Right*. New York: Palgrave Macmillan.

Chomsky, Noam. 2002. *Language and the Brain*. Cambridge: Cambridge University Press.

Cohen, Abner. 1979. "Political Symbolism." *Annual Review of Anthropology* 8: 87–113.

Cone, Malcom. 2002. "Neo-Modern Islam in Suharto's Indonesia." *New Zealand Journal of Asian Studies* 4(2): 52–67.

Dark, Alx. 1999. "The Makah Whale Hunt." *Native Americans and the Environment*. Available at: www.cnie.org/nae/cases/makah/index.html (accessed on March 5, 2013).

Davies, Merryl Wyn. 1988. *Knowing One Another: Shaping an Islamic Anthropology*. New York: Mansell Pub.

Dawkins, Richard. 1976. *The Selfish Gene*. Oxford: Oxford University Press.

Deetz, James. 1967. *Invitation to Archaeology*. Garden City, NY: The Natural History Press.

Dhofier, Zamakhsyari. 1978a. "Santri-Abangan dalam Kehidupan Orang Jawa: Teropond dari Pesantren." *Prisma* 7(5): 48–63.

———. 1978b. *Tradisi Pesantren: Studi tentang Pandangan Hidup Kyai*. Jakarta: LP3ES.

———. 1985. "Transformation of Islamic Education in Indonesia." *Prisma* 38: 21–27.

———. 1991. "Beri Saya Tiga Ratus Juta." *Kiblat* (July 15, 1991): 32–34.

———. 1999. *The Pesantren Tradition: The Role of the Kyai in the Maintenance of Traditional Islam in Java*. Arizona State University Program for Southeast Asian Studies.

———. 2000. "History of Islamic Studies in Indonesia." In Isma-ae Aleo et al., eds., *Islamic Studies in ASEAN: Presentations of an International Seminar*. Thailand: College of Islamic Studies, Prince of Songkala University.

Doorn-Harder, Pieternella van. 2006. *Women Shaping Islam: Reading the Qur'an in Indonesia*. Chicago: University of Illinois Press.

———. 2008. "Controlling the Body: Muslim Feminists Debating Women's Rights in Indonesia." *Religion Compass* 2(6): 1021–1043.

Durbin, Mridula Adenwala. 1970. "The Transformational Model of Linguistics and Its Implications for an Ethnology of Religion: A Case Study of Jainism." *American Anthropologist New Series* 72(2): 334–342.

———. 1972. "Linguistic Models in Anthropology." *Annual Review of Anthropology* 1: 383–410.

Dzuhayatin, Sita Ruhaini. 2006. "Islamic Family Law in Indonesia." In Rachmad Hidayat, Scot Scholssberg, and Alex H. Rambadeta, eds., *Islam, Women, and the New World Order*. Yogyakarta: Women's Studies Center UIN Sunan Kalijaga, pp. 95–109.

Effendi, Djohan. 2008. *A Renewal with Breaking Tradition: The Emergence of a New Discourse in Indonesia's Nahdlatul Ulama During the Abdurrahman Wahid*. Yogyakarta: Interfidei.

Eickleman, Dale F. 1976. *Moroccan Islam: Tradition and Society in a Pilgrimage Center*. Austin, TX: University of Texas Press.

———. 1982. "The Study of Islam in Local Contexts." *Contributions to Asian Studies* 17: 1–18.

Elson, R. E. 2009. "Another Look at the Jakarta Charter Controversy of 1945." *Indonesia* 88: 105–130.

El-Zein, Abdul Hamid M. 1974a. "Beyond Ideology and Theology: The Search for the Anthropology of Islam." *Annual Review of Anthropology* 6: 227–254.

———. 1974b. *The Sacred Meadows: A Structural Analysis of Religious Symbolism in an East African Town.* Evanston, IL: Northwestern University Press.

Fairclough, Norman. 1989. *Language and Power.* Sydney: Longman Group.

Federspiel, Howard. 1996. "The Endurance of Muslim Traditionalist Scholarship: An Analysis of the Writings of the Indonesian Scholar Siradjuddin Abbas." In Mark Woodward, ed., *Toward a New Paradigm: Recent Developments in Indonesian Islamic Thought.* Tempe: Arizona State University Program for Southeast Asian Studies.

Feener, Michael. 2007. *Muslim Legal Thought in Modern Indonesia.* Cambridge: Cambridge University Press.

Feillard, Andree, and Lies Marcoes. 1998. "Female Circumcision in Indonesia: To 'Islamize' in Celebration or Secret." *Archipel* 56: 337–367.

Florida, Nancy. 1995. *Writing the Past, Inscribing the Future: History as Prophecy in Colonial Java.* Durham, NC: Duke University Press.

Friedlander, Shems. 1992. *The Whirling Dervishes.* Albany, NY: SUNY Press.

Foucault, Michel. 1980. *Power/Knowledge: Selected Interviews and Other Writings, 1972–1977.* Ed. Colin Gordon. New York: Pantheon Books.

Furqan, Arief. n.d. "Potret Penelitian di PTAI: Harapan dan Kenyataan." *Artikel Pilihan: Direktorat Perguruan Tinggi Agama Islam, Deparmen Agama RI.* Available at: www.ditpertais.net/artikel/arief01.asp (accessed on October 26, 2008).

Gal, S. 1989. "Language and Political Economy." *Annual Review of Anthropology* 18: 345–67.

Geertz, Clifford. 1957. "Ritual and Social Change: A Javanese Example." *American Anthropologist* 59(1): 32–54.

———. 1960. *The Religion of Java.* New York: The Free Press of Glencoe.

———. 1968. *Islam Observed: Religious Development in Morocco and Indonesia.* Chicago: University of Chicago Press.

———. 1973. *The Interpretation of Cultures.* New York: Basic Books.

Ghafur, Waryono Abdul and Muammad Isnanto (eds.). 2004. *Isu-Isu Gender Dalam Kurikulum Pendidkan Dasar dan Mengenah.* Yogyakarta: Women's Studies Center (PSW) UIN Sunan Kalijaga.

Gilsenen, Michael. 1982. *Recognizing Islam: Religion and Society in the Modern Middle East.* New York: Croon Helm.
Goldziher, Ignaz. 1981 [1910]. *Introduction of Islamic Theology and Law.* Princeton, NJ: Princeton University Press.
Gould, Steven J. 1997. "Non-overlapping Magisteria." *Skeptical Inquirer* 23: 55–61.
Gunaratna, Rohan. 2002. *Inside Al-Qaeda.* New York: Columbia University Press.
Hafidz, Tatik S. 2003. "Assessing Indonesia's Vulnerability in the Wake of the American-Led Attack on Iraq." In Kumar Ramakrishna and See Seng Tan, eds., *After Bali: The Threat of Terrorism in Southeast Asia.* Singapore: Institute of Defence and Strategic Studies, Nanyang Technological University.
Hakimi, M., E. Nur Hayati, M. Ellsberg, and A. Winkvist. 2001. *Silence for the Sake of Harmony: Domestic Violence and Health in Central Java, Indonesia.* Yogyakarta: CHN-RL GMU.
Hamdi, S., and B. J. Smith. 2012. "Sisters, Militias and Islam in Conflict: Questioning 'Reconciliation' in Nahdlatul Wathan, Lombok, Indonesia." *Contemporary Islam* 6(1), 29–43.
Hartley, Edna. 1974. *Sacred Trances of Java and Bali.* Hartley Foundation. Available at: http://hartleyfoundation.org/en/sacred-trances-bali-and-java (February 26, 2013).
Hasan, Noorhaidi. 2006. *Laskar Jihad: Islam, Militancy, and the Quest for Identity in Post-New Order Indonesia.* Ithaca, NY: Cornell University Southeast Asia Program.
———. 2011. "Salafi Madrasa and Islamic Radicalism in Post-New Order Indonesia." In Kamaruzzaman Bustamam-Ahmad and Patrick Jory, eds., *Islamic Studies and Islamic Education.* Kuala Lumpur: Yayasan Ilmuwan, pp. 93–112.
Hefner, Robert. 1987. "Islamizing Java? Religion and Politics in Rural East Java." *Journal of Asian Studies* 46: 533–554.
———. 2009. "Islamic Schools, Social Movements, and Democracy in Indonesia." In Robert Hefner, ed., *Making Modern Muslims: The Politics of Islamic Education in Southeast Asia.* University of Hawaii Press, pp. 55–105.
Hidayat, Komaruddin. 1991. "'Dogmatissasi Ilmu Agama." *Kiblat* (15 July): 37–38.
———. 2003. *Wahyu di Langit Wahyu di Bumi.* Jakarta: Paramadina.
———. 2005. *Psikologi Kematian.* Jakarta: Mizan.
———. 2008. "Saya Ingin Hidupkan Tradisi Pesantren." *Dinamika:* 9–11.
Hidayat, Rachmad (ed.). 2005. *Gender Best Practice: Pengarusutamakan Gender dalam Universitas Islam Negeri Sunan Kalijaga.* Yogyakarta: Women's Studies Center (PSW) UIN Sunan Kalijaga.

Hobsbawm, Eric and Terrance Ranger (eds.). 1992. *The Invention of Tradition*. Cambridge: Cambridge University Press.
Hodgson, Marshall. 1974. *The Venture of Islam*. 3 vols. Chicago: University of Chicago Press
Hoesterey, James. 2008. "Marketing Morality: The Rise, Fall and Rebranding of AA Gym." In Greg Fealy and Sally White, eds., *Expressing Islam*. ISEAS: Singapore, pp. 90–107.
Hughes, Aaron. 2007. *Situating Islam: The Pat and the Future of an Academic Discipline*. London: Equinox.
Husaini, Adian. 2006. *Hegemoni Kristen-Barat dalam studi Islam di perguruan tinggi*. Jakarta: Gema Insani.
———. 2008. "IAIN Dulu dan Sekarang." *Islamia* III(3): 54–64.
IAIN (Institut Agama Islam Negeri) Sunan Ampel Research Team. 1992. *Sistem Pendidikan Pesantren Kecil and Pengaruhnya Terhadap Perkembangan Kepribadian Anak (Educational System of Child Pesantren and the Influence on the Development of the Childrens' Sense of Personhood)*. Surabaya: IAIN (Institut Agama Islam Negeri) Sunan Ampel.
Ingersoll, Julie. 2003. *Evangelical Christian Women: War Stories in the Gender Battles*. New York: New York University Press.
International Crisis Group (ICG). 2004. *Indonesia Backgrounder: Why Salafism and Terrorism Don't Mix*. Asia Report No. 83.
———. 2005. *Understanding Islamism*. Middle East/North Africa Report No. 3.
Ilyas, Hamim and Rachmad Hidayat. 2006. *Membina Keluarga Barokah*. Yogyakarta: Women's Studies Center (PSW) UIN Sunan Kalijaga.
Ilyas, Hamim, Sekar Ayu Ariyani, and Rachmad Hidyat. 2006. *Men's Involvement in Reproductive Health: In Islamic Perspective*. Yogyakarta: Women's Studies Center (PSW) UIN Sunan Kalijaga.
Jackson, Elisabeth and Bahrissalim. 2007. "Crafting a New Democracy: Civic Education in Indonesian Islamic Universities." *Asia Pacific Journal of Education* 27(1): 41–54.
Jacobson, Shari. 2006. "Modernity, Conservative Religious Movements, and the Female Subject: Newly Ultraorthodox Sephardi Women in Buenos Aires." *American Anthropologist* 108(2): 336–346.
Jakarta Post. 2005. "Preachers Told to Support Controversial MUI Edicts." Available at: www.thejakartapost.com/news/2005/08/08/preachers-told-support-controversial-mui-edicts.html (accessed on April 8, 2013).
———. 2012a. "Hardline Group Raids Manji's Book Discussion in Yogyakarta." May 9. Available at: www.thejakartapost.com/news/2012/05/09/mmi-disrupt-irshads-book-discussion-yogyakarta.html (accessed on March 17, 2013).

———. 2012b. "Irshad Manji Is Having Second Thoughts on Indonesia." May 10. Available at: www.thejakartapost.com/news/2012/05/09/irshad-manji-having-second-thoughts-indonesia.html (accessed on March 17, 2013).
Jaiz, Hartono Ahmad. 2005. *Ada Pemurtadan di IAIN*. Jakarta: Pustaka al-Kautsar.
Johns, A. H. 1987. "Tariqah." In Mircea Eliade, ed., *The Encyclopaedia of Religion. Encyclopedia of Islam* Vol. 14: 342–352.
Julian, Rony. 2011. "Between PP Al-Mukmin, Gontor, and Said Ghazali." *My Way: Information, Education, and Inspiration* (blog). Available at: Rony-julian.blogspot.com/2011/08/between-pp-al-mukmin-gontor-and-said.html (accessed on March 17, 2013).
Juynboll. Th. W. 1953. "Djum'a." In H. A. R. Gibb and J. H. Kramers, eds., *Shorter Encyclopedia of Islam*. pp. 92–93.
Kartanegara, Mulyadhi. 2010. "Islamization of Knowledge and Its Implementation: A Case Study of CIPSI." In Nur Syam, ed., *Integrated Twin Towers: Arah Pengembangan Islamic Studies Multidisipliner*. Surabaya: Sunan Ampel Press, pp. 104–115.
Kartodirdjo, Sartono. 1966 *The Peasants' Revolt of Banten in 1888*. The Hague: Martinus Nijhoff.
Kasdi, Abdurrahman. 2003. "Munawir Sjadzali dan International Studies; Menembus Kekekuan Pendidikan Islam." *Perta: Journal Inovasi Pendidikan Agama Islam* 6(2). Available at: www.dipertais.net/journal/vol62003lo.asp (accessed on October 26, 2008).
Keesing, Roger M. 1972. "Paradigms Lost: The New Ethnography and the New Linguistics." *Southwestern Journal of Anthropology*. 299–332.
Kersten, Carool. 2009. "Islam, Cultural Hybridity and Cosmopolitanism: New Muslim Intellectuals on Globalization." *Journal of International and Global Studies* 1(1): 89–113.
Khanna, Parag. 2009. "Why We Should Get Rid of the Term 'Muslim World.'" *The Washington Post*. April 19, 2009. Available at: http://articles.washingtonpost.com/2009-04-19/opinions/36871784_1_osama-bin-laden-islamic-president-obama (accessed on March 16, 2013).
Kinoshita, Hiroko. 2009. "Islamic Higher Education in Contemporary Indonesia: Through the Islamic Intellectuals of al-Azharite Alumni." Kyoto Working Papers on Area Studies (79).
Klinken, Gerry van. 2001. "The Maluku Wars: Bringing Society Back In." 2001. *Indonesia* 71: 1–26.
Koentjaraningrat, R. M. 1963. "Review of *The Religion of Java*." *Majalah Ilmu-Ilmu Sastra Indonesia* 2: 188–91.
Kraince, Richard G. 2000. "The Modernization of the National Institute for Islamic Studies (IAIN) and the Advancement of Muslim

Intellectualism in Indonesia." *Islamic Studies in ASEAN*. Pattani, Thailand: Prince of Songhla University.

———. 2008. "Islamic higher education and social cohesion in Indonesia." *Prospects* 37(3): 345–356.

Kusama (ed.). 2006. *Integrasi Keilmuan: UIN Syarif Hidayatullah Jakarta Menuju Universitas Riset*. Jakarta: UIN Jakarta Press.

Kynsilehto, Anitta. 2008. "Islamic Feminism: Current Prespectives. Introductory Notes." In Anitta Kynsilehto, ed., *Islamic Feminism: Current Prespectives*. Finland: Tampere Peace Research Institute.

Labov, William. 1972. *Language in the Inner City: Studies in Black English Vernacular*. Philadelphia: University of Pennsylvania Press.

Lee, Martha Frances. 1996. *The Nation of Islam: An American Millenarian Movement*. New York: Syracuse University Press.

Lévi-Strauss, Claude. 1963. *Structural Anthropology*. New York: Basic Books.

———. 1998. "The Meaning and Use of the Notion of Model." In Hans Penner, ed., *Teaching Lévi-Strauss*. Atlanta: Scholars Press.

Liddle, William. 1996. "Media Dakwah Scripturalism: One Form of Political Though and Action in New Order Indonesia." *Towards a New Paradigm: Recent Developments in Indonesian Islamic Thought*. Tempe: Program for Southeast Asia Studies Arizona State University.

Loeffler, Reinhold. 1988. *Islam in Practice: Religious Beliefs in a Persian Village* (Google eBook). Albany, NY: SUNY Press.

Lukens-Bull, Ronald. 1997. "A Peaceful Jihad: Javanese Islamic Education and Religious Identity Construction." Doctoral Dissertation. Arizona State University.

———. 1999. "Between Text and Practice: Considerations in the Anthropological Study of Islam." *Marburg Journal of Religion* 4 (2): 10–20.

———. 2000. "Teaching Morality: Javanese Islamic Education in a Globalizing Era." *Journal of Arabic and Islamic Studies*.

———. 2001. "Two Sides of the Same Coin: Modernity and Tradition in Islamic Education in Indonesia." *Anthropology & Education Quarterly*.

———. 2003a. "An Accidental Imago Mundi: Spatializing Religious and Social Change in Islamic Java." *Sacred Places and Modern Landscapes: Sacred Geography and Social-Religious Transformations in Asia*. Tempe: Arizona State University Program for Southeast Asian Studies, pp. 203–226.

———. 2003b. "Ronald McDonald as a Javanese Saint and Indonesian Freedom Fighter: Reflections of the Global and the Local." *Crossroads: An Interdisciplinary Journal of Southeast Asian Studies*: 108–128.

———. 2005. *A Peaceful Jihad: Negotiating Identity and Modernity in Muslim Java*. New York: Palgrave Macmillan.

———. 2007. "Lost in a Sea of Subjectivity: The Subject Position of the Researcher in the Anthropology of Islam." *Contemporary Islam* 1(2): 173–192.

———. 2008. "The Traditions of Pluralism, Accommodation, and Anti-Radicalism in the Pesantren Community." *Journal of Indonesian Islam* 2(1): 196–211.

———. 2010. ""Madrasa by Any Other Name: Pondok, Pesantren, and Islamic Schools in Southeast Asia" *Journal of Indonesian Islam* 4(1).

Lukens-Bull, Ronald and Mark Fafard. 2007. "Next Year in Orlando." *Journal of Religion & Society.* Vol. 9.

Lukens-Bull, Ronald, and Mark R. Woodward. 2010. "Goliath and David in Gaza: Indonesian Myth-Building and Conflict as a Cultural System." *Contemporary Islam* 5(1): 1–17.

Mahmood, Saba. 2005. *Politics of Piety: The Islamic Revival and the Feminist Subject.* Princeton, NJ: Princeton University Press.

Malinowski, Bronislaw. 1948. *Magic, Science and Religion and Other Essays.* Glencoe, IL: The Free Press.

Manji, Irsahd. 2011. *Allah, Liberty, and Love: The Courage to Reconcile Faith and Freedom.* Glencoe, IL: Free Press.

Marhuma. 2009. "Poligami dalam Pandangan Dosen UIN Sunan Kalijaga, Yogyakarta." In Inayah Rohmaniya and Mohammad Sodik, eds., *Monyoal Keadilan dalam Poligami.* Yogyakarta: PSW UIN Sunan Kalijaga.

Marhuma and Alfatih Suryadilaga (eds.). 2006. *Membina Keluarga Barokah.* Yogyakarta: Women's Studies Center (PSW) UIN Sunan Kalijaga.

Marranci, Gabriele. 2008. *The Anthropology of Islam.* New York: Berg, p. 224.

Martin, R. C., M. R. Woodward, and D. S. Atmaja. 1997. "Defenders of Reason in Islam: Mu'tazilism from Medieval School to Modern Symbol." Oxford, UK: One World Publishers.

Massignon, L. 1953. "Tarika." In H. A. R. Gibb and J. H. Kramers, eds., *Shorter Encyclopaedia of Islam.* Leiden, The Netherlands: E. J. Brill, pp. 573–578.

McGibbon, R. 2006. "Indonesian Politics in 2006: Stability, Compromise and Shifting Contests Over Ideology." *Bulletin of Indonesian Economic Studies.*

McGregor, E. Katharine. 2009. "Confronting the Past in Contemporary Indonesia: The Anticommunist Killings of 1965–6 and the Role of the Nahdlatul Ulama." *Critical Asian Studies* 41(2): 195–224.

Meuleman, Johan. 2000. "Tradition and Renewal within Islamic Studies in South-East Asia: The Case of the Indonesia IAIN." In Isma-ae Aleo et al. eds., *Islamic Studies in ASEAN: Presentations of an International*

Seminar. Thailand: College of Islamic Studies. Prince of Songkala University, pp. 283–299.

———. 2002. "The Institute Agama Islam Negeri at a Crossroads: Some Notes on the Indonesian State Institutes for Islamic Studies." In Johan Meuleman, ed., *Islam in the Era of Globalization: Muslim Attitudes toward Modernity and Identity*. Vol. 6. London: Routledge.

Mir-Hosseini, Ziba 2006. "Gender Rights and Islamic Law: New Horizons." Yogyakarta: Center for Women's Studies (PSW) UIN Sunan Kalijaga, pp. 81–94.

MUI. 2005. "Keputusan Fatwa Majelis Ulama Indonesia Nomor: 7 /Munas VII/MUI/11/2005 tentang Pluralisme, Liberalism, dan SekulerismeAgama."Availableat:www.eramuslim.com/berita/tahukah-anda/fatwa-mui-tentang-pluralisme-dan-sekulerisme-agama.htm (accessed on March 14, 2013).

Nasution, Harun. 1977. *Islam Ditinjau dari Berbagai Aspek (Islam from Different Perspectives)*. Jakarta: University of Indonesia Press.

Noer, Deliar. 1978. *Administration of Islam in Indonesia*. Ithaca, NY: Cornell University, p. 82.

OkeJakarta. 2012. "Alasan FPI Minta Bubarkan Diskusi Irshad Manji." May 5. Available at: Jakarta.okezone.com/read/2012/05/05/500/624463/alasan-fpi-minta-bubarkan-diskusi-irshad-manji (accessed on March 17, 2013).

Osman, Nurfika. 2010. "Indonesian History Professor Honored by British Queen." *Jakarta Globe* September 28, 2010. Available at: www.thejakartaglobe.com/home/indonesian-history-professor-honored-by-british-queen/398465 (accessed on March 20, 2013).

Peacock, J. L. 1978. *Muslims Puritans: Reformist Psychology in Southeast Asia Islam*. Berkeley and Los Angeles: University of California Press.

Pemberton, John. 1994. *On the Subject of "Java."* Ithaca, NY: Cornell University Press.

Pike, Kenneth. 1964. "Toward a Theory of the Structure of Human Behavior." In Dell Hymes, ed., *Language in Culture and Society*. New York: Harper & Row.

Pringle, Robert. 2010. *Understanding Islam in Indonesia: Politics and Diversity*. Honolulu: University of Hawaii Press.

Preucel, Robert and Alexander Bauer. 2001. "Archaeological Pragmatics." *Norwegian Archaeological Review* 34(2): 85–96.

Qamar, Muhammad Fiaz and Ifrah Raza (n.d.). "Scientific Evidences That Pig Meat (Pork) Is Prohibited for Human Health." *Scientific Papers, Animal Science, Series D*. Available at: animalsciencejournal.usamv.ro (accessed on March 21, 2013).

Qibtiyah, Alimatul. 2010. "Self-identified Feminists Among Gender Activists and Scholars at Indonesian Universities." *ASEAS-Austrian Journal of South-East Asian Studies* 3(2): 151–174.

Qur'anic Path (n.d). "Circumcision—Does the Qur'an Approve It?" Available at: www.Qur'anicpath.com/misconceptions/circumcision.html (accessed on February 9, 2011).
Rahardjo, M. D. 1985. *Pergulatan Dunia Pesantren: Membangun Dari Bawah*. Jakarta: Perhimpunan Pengembangan Pesantren dan Masyarakat.
Rahman, Fazlur. 1984. *Islam and Modernity: Transformation of an Intellectual Tradition* (Publications of the Center for Middle Eastern Studies). Chicago: University of Chicago Press.
Raza, Moulana. 1997. "Tassawul Wasila." Islamic Study Circle: Education Department of the Islamic Center Leceister. Available at: www.islamiccentre.org/presentations/wasilah.pdf (accessed on May 8, 2013).
Redfield, Robert. 1956. *Peasant Society and Culture*. Chicago: University of Chicago Press.
Rickelfs, Merle. 2006. "The Birth of Abangan." *Bijdragen tot de Taal-, Land- en Volkenkunde* 162(1): 35–55.
Rickford, John and William Labov. 1999. *African American Vernacular English: Features, Evolution, Educational Implications*. Oxford: Blackwell.
Rinaldo, R. 2008. "Envisioning the Nation: Women Activists, Religion and the Public Sphere in Indonesia." *Social Forces* 86(4): 1781–1804.
———. 2010. "The Islamic Revival and Women's Political Subjectivity in Indonesia." *Women's Studies International Forum* 33(4): 422–431.
Robinson, K. 2008. "Islamic Cosmopolities, Human Rights, and Anti-Violence Strategies in Indonesia." In P. Werbner, ed., *Anthropology and the New Cosmopolitianism*. New York: Berg.
Rohmaniya, Inayah. 2009. "Poligami dalam Perundang-undangan di Indonesia." In Inayah Rohmaniya and Mohammad Sodiq, eds., *Menyoal Keadilan dalam Poligami*. Yogyakarta: PSW UIN Sunan Kalijaga.
Roy, Olivier. 1996. *The Failure of Poltical Islam*. Cambridge, MA: Harvard University Press.
———. 2004. *Globalized Islam: The Search for the New Ummah*. CERI Series in Comparative Politics and International Studies, Columbia University Press.
Rumadi. 2008. *Post Tradisionalisme Islam: Wacana Intelektualisme Dalam Komunitas NU*. Cirebon, West Java: Fahmina Institute.
Ruse, Michael. 1982. "Creation Science Is Not Science." *Science, Technology, & Human Values* 7(40): 72–78.
Saeed, Abdullah. 1999. "Toward Religious Tolerance through Reform in Islamic Education: The Case of the State Institute of Islamic Studies of Indonesia." *Indonesia and the Malay World* 27(79): 177–190.
Saleh, Fauzan. 2001. *Modern Trends in Islamic Theological Discourse in 20th Century Indonesia: A Critical Survey*. Leiden, The Netherlands: Brill.

Samuel, Henry. 2003. "Grand Mufti Condones French Headscarf Ban." *The Telegraph*. Available at: www.telegraph.co.uk/news/worldnews/europe/france/1450642/Grand-Mufti-condones-French-headscarf-ban.html (accessed on October 11, 2012).

Saniotis, Arthur. 2004. "Tales of Mastery: Spirit Familiar in Sufis' Religious Imagination." *Ethos* 32(3): 397–411.

Saussure, Ferdinand. 1972. *Course in General Linguistics*. Trans. Roy Harris. La Salle, IL: Open Court.

Schimmel, Annemarie. 1991. "Sacred Geography in Islam." In Jamie Scott and Paul Simpson-Housely, eds., *Sacred Places and Profane Spaces: Essays in the Sacred Places and Profane Spaces: Essays in the Sacred Places and Profane Spaces: Essays in the Geographics of Judaism, Christianity, and Islam*. New York: Greenwood Press.

Scott, Eugenie C. and Henry P. Cole. 1985. "The Elusive Scientific Basis of Creation 'Science.'" *Quarterly Review of Biology*: 21–30.

Scott, James C. 1972. "Patron-Client Relations and Political Change in Southeast Asia." *The American Political Science Review* 66(1): 91–113.

———. 1990. *Domination and the Arts of Resistance: Hidden Transcripts*. New Haven, CT: Yale University Press.

Sebastian, Leonard C. 2003. "The Indonesian Dilemma: How to Participate in the War of Terror without Becoming a National Security State." In Kumar Ramakrishna and See Seng Ta, eds., *After Bali: The Threat of Terrorism in Southeast Asia*. Singapore: Institute of Defence and Strategic Studies, Nanyang Technological University.

Sederberg, Peter C. 1984. *The Politics of Meanings: Power and Explanation in the Construction of Social Reality*. Tucson: University of Arizona Press.

Setiawati. "Bali to Fight Porn Law to the End." *The Jakarta Post*. December 22, 2008.

Siar News Service 2000. PBNU Akan Kirim Banser ke Maluku. June 27. Available at: www.minihub.org/siarlist/msg04872.html (accessed on March 20, 2013).

Sirry, Mun'im. 2010. "The Public Expression of Traditional Islam: the Pesantren and Civil Society in Post-Suharto Indonesia." *The Muslim World* 100(1): 60–77.

Smith-Hefner, N. J. 2007. "Javanese Women and the Veil in Post-Soeharto Indonesia." *Journal of Asian Studies*.

Snouck Hurgronje, Christiaan. 1906. *The Achenese*, translated from the Dutch by R. J. Wilkinson. Leiden: E. J. Brill.

Steenbrink, Karel. 1974. *Pesantren, Madrasah, Sekolah: Pendidikan Islam dalam Kurun Modern*. Jakarta: LP3ES.

———. 1999. "The Pancasila Ideology and an Indonesian Muslim Theology of Religions." In Waardenburg, Jacques, ed., *Perceptions of Other Religions*. New York: Oxford University Press, pp. 280–296.

Subhan, Zaitunah. 2006. "The State Ministry for Women's Empowerment." In Rachmad Hidayat, Scot Schlossberg, and Alex H. Rambadeta, eds., *Islam, Women, and the New World Order*. Yogyakarta: PSW UIN Sunan Kalijaga, pp. xix–xxiii.
Subtelny, M. E. 1989. "The Cult of Holy Places: Religious Practices among Soviet Muslims." *Middle East Journal* 43(4): 593–604.
Sukma, Rizal. 2003. "Indonesia and the Challenge of Radical Islam after October 12." In Kumar Ramakrishna and See Seng Ta, eds., *After Bali: The Threat of Terrorism in Southeast Asia*. Singapore: Institute of Defence and Strategic Studies, Nanyang Technological University.
Suparlan, Parsudi. 1995. *The Javanese in Suriname: Ethnicity in an Ethnically Plural Society*. Tempe, AZ: Arizona State University, Program for Southeast Asian Studies.
Syam, Nur (ed.) 2010a. *Integrated Twin Towers: Arah Pengembangan Islamic Studies Multidisipliner*. Surabya: Sunan Ampel Press.
———. 2010b. "Membangun Keilmuan Islam Multidisipliner: Memahami Proses Saling Menyapa Ilmu Agama dan Umum." In Nur Syam, ed., *Integrated Twin Towers: Arah Pengembangan Islamic Studies Multidisipiliner*. Surabya: Sunan Ampel Press, pp. 2–15.
———. 2010c. "Relasi Islam dan Sains: Membangun Kembali Ilmu KeIslaman Multidispliner." pp. 18–31.Tomsa, Dirk. 2010. "The Indonesian Party System after the 2009 Elections: Towards Stability?". In Edward Aspinall and Marcus Mietzner, eds., *Problems of Democratisation in Indonesia: Elections, Institutions and Society*. Singapore: Institute of Southeast Asian Studies, pp 141–159.
UIN Sunan Gunung Jati. 2008. *Transformasi IAIN Menjadi UIN: Menuju Research University*. Bandjung: Gunung Jati Press.
United States Department of State. 2001. *Indonesia: Report on Female Genital Mutilation (FGM) or Female Genital Cutting (FGC)*. Available at: www.unhcr.org/refworld/docid/46d57879c.html (accessed on January 20, 2013).
Urban, Greg. 1991. *A Discourse-Centered Approach to Culture: Native South American Myths and Rituals*. Austin: University of Texas Press.
Varisco, Daniel. 2005. *Islam Obscured*. New York: Palgrave McMillan.
———. 2007. *Reading Orientalism: Said and the Unsaid*. Seattle: University of Washington Press.
Vikør, Knut S. 1995. "The Development of Ijtihad and Islamic Reform, 1750–1850." Paper Presented at the Third Nordic Conference on Middle Eastern Studies: Ethnic Encounter and Culture Change, Joensuu, Finland. June 19–22, 1995. Available at: www.hf-fak.uib.no/smi/paj/Vikor.html (accessed on May 1997).
Voloshinov, Valentin. 1973. *Marxism and the Philosophy of Language*. Ed. and trans. Ladislav Matejka and I. R. Titunia. New York: Seminar Press.

Wahid, Abdurrahman (ed.). 2008. *Ilusi Negara Islam: Ekspansi Gerakan Islam Transnasional di Indonesia*. Jakarta: LibForAll Foundation.

Wahid, Marzuki. 2003. "PTAI Perkembanag Pemikiran Islam: Mempertanyakan Kontribusi." *Perta: Journal Inovasi Pendidikan Tinggi Agama Islam* 6(2). Available at: www.dipertais.net/jurnal/vol62003e.asp (accessed on October 26, 2008).

Webster, D. 2009. *Fire and the Full Moon: Canada and Indonesia in a Decolonizing World*. Vancouver: The University of British Columbia Press.

Weck, Winifried, Noorhaidi Hasan, and Irfan Abubakar (eds.). 2011. *Islam in the Public Sphere: The Politics of Identity and the Future of Democracy in Indonesia*. Jakarta: Center for the Study of Religion and Culture UIN Syarif Hidayatullah.

Van Wichelen, S. 2010. *Religion, Politics and Gender in Indonesia: Disputing the Muslim Body*. Taylor & Francis.

Wallerstein, Immanuel. 1974. *The Modern World-System I: Capitalist Agriculture and the Origins of the European World-Economy in the Sixteenth Century*. Vol. 1. California: University of California Press.

Wilson, Peter Lamborn.1993. *Sacred Drift: Essays on the Margins of Islam*. San Francisco, CA: City Lights Books.

Wilson, Ian Douglas. 2008. "'As Long as it's Halal': Islamic Preman in Jakarta." In Greg Fealy and Sally White, eds., *Expressing Islam: Religious Life and Politics in Indonesia*. Singapore: Institute of Southeast Asian Studies, pp. 192–210.

Wiseman, Boris and Judy Groves. 1997. *Introducing Lévi-Strauss*. New York: Totem Books.

Woodward, Mark. 1988. "'The 'Slametan': Textual Knowledge and Ritual Performance in Central Javanese Islam." *History of Religions* 28(1): 54–89.

———. 1989. *Islam in Java: Normative Piety and Mysticism in the Sultanate of Yogyakarta*. Association for Asian Studies. Tucson: The University of Arizona Press.

———. 2001. "A Theology of Terror." *Anthropology Newsletter*. December 6.

———. 2008. "Resisting Wahhabi Colonialism in Yogyakarta." COMOPS Journal. Available at: http://csc.asu.edu/2008/11/06/resisting-wahhabi-colonialism-in-yogyakarta/ / (accessed on July 19, 2011).

———. 2010. "Tropes of the Crusades in Indonesian Muslim Discourse." *Contemporary Islam* 4(3): 311–330.

———. 2011. *Java, Indonesia and Islam*. Muslims in Global Societies Series. Dordrecht: Springer Netherlands. Available at: www.springerlink.com/content/978-94-007-0055-0/ (accessed on July 20, 2011).

Woodward, Mark, Ali Amin, Inayah Rohmaniyah, and Chris Lundry. 2012. "Getting Culture: A New Path for Indonesia's Islamist Justice and Prosperity Party?" *Contemporary Islam* 7(2): 173–189.

Woodward, Mark, Inayah Rohmaniyah, Ali Amin, and Diana Coleman. 2010. "Muslim Education, Celebrating Islam and Having Fun as Counter-Radicalization Strategies in Indonesia." *Perspectives on Terrorism* 4(4): 28–50.

Zainuddin, M., Roibin, and Muhammad In'am Esha, (eds.). 2004. *Memadu Sains dan Agama: Menuju Universitas Islam Masa Depan*. Surabaya: Universitas Islam Negeri Malang.

Zarkasyi, Hamid Fahmy. 2008. "Peran Sentral Universitas Islam." *Islamia* III(3): 5–12.

Zeghal, Malika. 2007. "The 'Recentering' of Religious Knowledge and Discourse: The Case of al-Azhar in Twentieth Century Egypt." In Robert Hefner and Muhammad Qasim Zaman, eds., *Schooling Islam: The Culture and Politics of Modern Muslim Education*. Princeton, NJ: Princeton University Press, pp. 107–130.

Index

Abdul Mukti Ali, 45–7, 49, 61, 82, 131
Abdurrahman Wahid, 24, 33, 78, 89, 116, 126, 133
Adian Husaini, 45, 47, 48, 82
Al-Azhar, 16, 43–7, 70, 114–15, 126
Amin Abdullah, 15–16, 50, 81–5, 99, 133
Annual Conference on Islamic Studies (ACIS), 1, 43, 71, 78
apostasy, 17, 34–6, 38–40, 70, 74, 78, 127, 141, 150–1
apostasy accusations, 1, 4, 17–18, 21, 34, 88, 125–6,
Azyumardi Azra, 5, 12, 21, 35, 50, 77, 133

civics education, 82, 124
Classicalist, 18, 23–4, 33, 56, 13, 146

Dewan Dakwah Islam Indonesia (DDII), 27, 37, 39, 69, 123–5, 150, 157
dialects, 18, 19, 23, 34–41, 55–6, 72, 82, 91–4, 107, 137, 140–52

fakultas Adab, 2, 44, 51–2, 113
fakultas Dakwah, 2, 10, 44, 51, 71, 119
fakultas Syari'ah, 2, 12, 44, 51–2, 57, 113, 119
fakultas Tarbiyah, 2, 5, 12, 44, 51, 71, 119
fakultas Ushuluddin, 2, 10, 40, 44, 51–2, 57, 113
fatwa, 93, 123, 128
Fazlur Rahman, 45–6, 69, 126
feminism, 35–6, 74, 85, 91–2, 95, 107, 150
Fron Pembela Islam (FPI), 30–1, 125–8

gender, 9, 36, 62, 87, 89, 91–2, 95–9, 105, 107
gender activism, 90–4, 100
gender parity, 19, 35–6, 85, 88, 91, 93, 98, 103–4, 108, 150–1
gender studies, 74, 85, 88, 90

Hartono Ahmad Jaiz, 17, 21, 34–40, 88, 125
Harun Nasution, 15, 35, 45–9, 61, 123, 126
Harvard, 1, 75, 15, 154
Hasyim Muzadi, 30–1, 33, 116
History of IAIN, 12–18, 45–52, 80
Hizbut Tahrir Indonesia (HTI), 30, 55, 56, 91–7, 107, 141

IAIN North Sumatra, 6, 13, 14, 16, 39, 49, 83–4, 100, 112–13, 124
IAIN Surabaya, 2, 17–18, 55, 58, 60, 73, 82, 89, 91, 116

ijtihad, 23–5
Imam Suprayogo, 38, 77, 150
Inayah Rohmaniyah, 67, 74
Irshad Manji, 128, 131
Islamic Studies, 1, 15, 17, 18, 43, 46–52, 55, 57, 61, 64, 67–8, 71–85, 112, 114, 123, 135
Islamism, 26–7, 34
Islamists, 13, 18, 25, 27, 29–33, 37, 45, 55–6, 69, 92, 95, 107–8, 123–6, 150

Jakarta Charter, 12, 26, 30, 32–3, 45
Jihad, 27, 28, 33
Jihadi/Jihadists, 18, 27, 85, 128

kiblat, 70, 146–7
kitab kuning, 7, 17, 81, 116, 118–19, 121
kodrat, 92, 96–7
Komaruddin Hidayat, 4, 53, 76, 79, 111, 121
kyai, 6, 10–1, 24, 47, 53–4, 72, 100, 112, 130

Laskar Jihad, 26, 29–33
linguistic analogy, 19, 22–3, 34–5, 137, 140
linguistic rules modeling, 145–6, 150–2

maddhab, 24, 38, 49, 96
madrasah, 3, 9–10, 12, 27–8, 40, 53–4, 64, 80, 105–6, 115, 117, 121–2
Modernist(s), 23–6, 33, 70, 146, *see also* Reformist(s)
MORA, 3, 12, 48–9, 51–2, 61, 68, 71–2, 74, 84, 87, 112, 120–1
Muhammadiyah, 9, 24–6, 29, 31–4, 38, 56, 91
Muhammad Machasin, 78, 112–13, 115

Muhammad Rasjidi, 47–9
Munawir Sjadzali, 15, 49, 61

Nahdlatul Ulama, 24, 32, 56, 91, 116, 142
Nurcholish Madjid, 5, 31, 33–4, 61, 68, 74, 124, 126, 133

Orientalism, 19, 46, 67, 71
Orientalist(s), 40, 70, 83, 136–7

Pancasila, 3, 5–13, 17, 20, 26, 29, 40, 44, 46–8, 53–4, 124–5, 131–2
pesantren, 56, 58, 60, 64, 70–1, 73, 80–1, 85, 89, 111, 115–22, 126, 128, 130–1, 153, 154
PKS, 27, 2, 37, 55–6, 62, 106, 118, 128, 150, 154

Reformist(s), 18, 25, 56, 146, *see also* Modernist(s)

salafi, 25–28, 35–6, 141, 150–1
science, 47, 50, 54, 58, 60–1, 119
science and religion, 19, 59, 64–5, 85, 112
social sciences, 16, 18, 39–40, 45, 57, 59, 62, 70, 74–82, 102, 109, 113–14
Sufi, 6, 7, 24, 29, 40, 48–9, 60, 73, 112, 126, 141–2, 148–9
Suharto, 9, 12–13, 17, 26–9, 33, 50–1, 88, 122–4, 154
Sukarno, 45, 122
Syari'ah, 12, 25–6, 30, 32–4, 36–7, 45, 52, 94, 97–9, 125, 131–2, 150

traditionalist, *see* Classicalist

UIN Jakarta, 4, 12, 16, 21, 30, 35, 38–40, 50–1, 53, 59, 70, 79–80, 106, 111–2, 114, 115, 117, 121, 127

UIN Malang, 2, 38, 54–5, 58, 61–2, 77, 117–20, 128, 150–1
UIN Yogya, 14–15, 19, 50, 52–3, 59, 67, 74, 77, 79, 81, 87, 89–90, 93, 99, 116, 121, 125, 127

Wahid Hasyim, 9
walisongo, 6, 70, 129–30, 146–7
wasilah, 24

Zamaksyari Dhofier, 4, 10, 24, 48, 76, 123

GPSR Compliance
The European Union's (EU) General Product Safety Regulation (GPSR) is a set of rules that requires consumer products to be safe and our obligations to ensure this.

If you have any concerns about our products, you can contact us on

ProductSafety@springernature.com

In case Publisher is established outside the EU, the EU authorized representative is:

Springer Nature Customer Service Center GmbH
Europaplatz 3
69115 Heidelberg, Germany

www.ingramcontent.com/pod-product-compliance
Lightning Source LLC
LaVergne TN
LVHW051912060526
838200LV00004B/107